AUSTRALIAN MIGRANT SHIPS 1946 - 1977

Peter Plowman

Johan van Oldenbarnevelt in Sydney on 16 December 1956.

ROSENBERG

First published in Australia in 2006
by Rosenberg Publishing Pty Ltd
PO Box 6125, Dural Delivery Centre NSW 2158
Phone: 612 9654 1502 Fax: 612 9654 1338
Email: rosenbergpub@smartchat.net.au
Web: www.rosenbergpub.com.au

Reprinted in 2007 and 2008

The National Library of Australia Cataloguing-in-Publication

Plowman, Peter.
Australian migrant ships 1946 - 1977.

Includes index.
ISBN 9781877058400.

1. Passenger ships - Australia - History. 2. Shipping - Australia - History. 3. Immigrants - Australia - History - 20th century. 4. Australia - Emigration and immigration - 20th century. I. Title.

387.20994

Cover design by Highway 51 using the author's photograph of *New Australia* on the front and a photograph of *Fairstar* with author in foreground on the back

Set in 11 on 13 pt Warnock Pro
Printed in China through Colorcraft Ltd, Hong Kong

Contents

Introduction	4
Volendam	6
Hwa Lien	7
Johan de Witt	8
Misr and *Al Sudan*	9
The "Generals"	10
Radnik	14
Partizanka	15
Tidewater - Continental	16
Strathmore and *Stratheden*	17
Orion	19
Ormonde	20
Strathnaver and *Strathaird*	21
The "Bays"	23
Sitmar "Victory" Ships	24
Toscana	27
Komninos	28
Skaugum	29
Dominion Monarch	30
Orcades	31
Mooltan and *Maloja*	32
Napoli	33
Ranchi	34
Svalbard	35
Goya	36
Derna - Assimina	37
Charlton Sovereign	38
Luciano Manara	39
Protea - Arosa Kulm	40
Cameronia	42
Rena	43
Somersetshire and *Dorsetshire*	44
Chitral	46
Nea Hellas	47
The "Navigators"	48
Georgic	50
Oxfordshire	52
Dundalk Bay	53
Cyrenia	54
Indian Pilgrim Ships	55
Surriento	56
Anna Salen - Tasmania	58
Cheshire	60
Haven	61
Canberra (1912)	62
Columbia	63
Hellenic Prince	64
Kanimbla	66
Otranto and *Orontes*	67
Asturias	68
Nelly - Seven Seas	69
Himalaya	71
Empire Brent	72
Fairsea	73
Groote Beer, Zuiderkruis and *Watermark*	75
Johan van Oldenbarnevelt	77
Australia, Neptunia and *Oceania*	79
Sontay	81
New Australia - Arkadia	82
Amarapoora	85
Brasil	86
Sibajak	87
Roma (1914)	88
Ravello	90
Liguria - Corsica	91
Florentia	92
Jenny	93
San Giorgio	94
Skaubryn	95
Arosa Star	96
Roma (1942) and *Sydney*	97
Oronsay	99
Castel Felice	100
Flaminia	102
Arcadia	103
Orsova	104
Aurelia	105
Southern Cross	107
Iberia	109
Oranje	110
Angelina Lauro	111
Fairsky	112
Willem Ruys	114
Achille Lauro	115
Gumhuryat Misr	116
Queen Frederica	117
Oriana	119
Patris	121
Conte Grande	123
Monte Udala	124
Canberra (1960)	125
Northern Star	127
Galileo Galilei and *Guglielmo Marconi*	128
Flavia	130
Chusan	131
Bretagne - Brittany	132
Ellinis	133
Fairstar	135
Australis	137
Ocean Monarch	140
Britanis	141
Le Havre Abeto	143
Index	144

Introduction

In 1992 my book, *Emigrant Ships to Luxury Liners*, was published. It contained information on passenger vessels to have come to Australia from overseas between 1946 and 1990. A large number of these ships had been used to transport new settlers to Australia, be they displaced persons, assisted migrants or self-funded migrants. The vessels these new settlers travelled on were generally known as migrant ships, and they varied considerably in age, background, size and comfort. My book brought all these ships together under a single title for the first time, along with many other liners that had come to Australia on regular services or cruises

Over the years *Emigrant Ships to Luxury Liners* continued to sell very well, but by the end of 2004 all available stocks had been exhausted. The question was raised, should there be another reprint of the original book, or was it time to produce something new and different. Since the book was published, there had been considerable changes affecting all of the ships that were still in service in 1992, while I had also come up with a large amount of new material on many other ships. I therefore decided it would be worth while producing a book that concentrated solely on the migrant ships that served Australia, as they were still a source of great interest to many people, especially those who travelled on them, and their families. It is with this in mind that I have put together this book, which includes many new pictures as well as extra information and some corrections.

It seems amazing now, but Australia did not even have a Minister for Immigration until Arthur Calwell was appointed to the position in 1945, and he immediately began drafting a new Immigration policy. On 2 August 1945, Calwell launched the new policy in the first speech he made to Parliament as Minister for Immigration, in which he emphasised the security aspect of immigration rather than the economic advantages.

"If Australians have learned one lesson from the Pacific war now moving to a successful conclusion," Calwell began, "it is surely that we cannot continue to hold our island continent for ourselves and our descendants unless we greatly increase our numbers. We are but seven million people and we hold three million square miles of this earth's surface ... Our first requirement is additional population. We need it for reasons of defence and for the fullest expansion of our economy."

What the Government wanted was an influx of 70,000 migrants a year, and it was hoped that all of them would come from Britain. In March 1946, an agreement was signed with the British Government, under which the Ministry of Transport would supply a number of older passenger liners to transport Britons wishing to migrate to Australia. The first departure under this arrangement was made on 10 October 1947 by *Ormonde* from Tilbury, carrying 1,052 new settlers.

It was only when an insufficient number of Britons applied to migrate that the Government decided to start looking elsewhere, primarily seeking people from Greece and Italy, and then suitable refugees who thronged the displaced persons camps in Europe. On 21 July 1947, the Australian Government signed an agreement with the International Refugee Organisation (IRO) in Geneva to accept 12,000 displaced persons per year, though this number would greatly increase over subsequent years.

Immigration officials were sent from Australia to go to these camps and interview persons wishing to migrate. However, before being accepted, they were put through a gruelling examination. Immigration officers were told to choose attractive, preferably fair types, who would fit into white Australia. Good health essential. If one family member was ill, including the blind and deaf, the rest could travel, but the infirm one would have to stay behind. This was unacceptable to most families in that situation, who declined to go. Once people were accepted, arrangements would be made for them to be transported to Australia by ship.

In order to move these people, a large number of ships would be required, but there were insufficient numbers of suitable passenger vessels available for such a task. The IRO began offering contracts to owners prepared to utilize ships in this role, and many vessels never designed to carry passengers, or travel vast distances, were quickly refitted with extremely austere accommodation before being sent to ports in Germany and Italy to load up huge numbers of passengers and carry them half way around the world to a new life.

The agreement with the IRO was terminated in 1952, and a new contract signed with the Intergovernmental Committee for European Migration (ICEM), whose ships were of a better calibre than the IRO vessels had been, but the number of Europeans seeking to migrate to Australia was declining. The only countries to supply migrants to Australia in large numbers were Italy and Greece, and they mostly travelled out on the liners of such companies as Lloyd Triestino, Flotta Lauro and Chandris Line.

Assisted migrants from Britain continued to be transported in old Ministry of Transport vessels until 1957, after which they were carried in the tourist class accommodation of British liners on a regular service to Australia, while contracts were also signed with foreign flag companies as well. From 1955 to 1970, the vessels of the Sitmar Line carried thousands of British migrants to Australia, but then the contract was transferred to the Greek owned Chandris Line.

During the 1950s, British migrants had also been arriving in Australia on planes, and the use of aircraft increased in the 1960s. By the mid-1970s, the majority of British migrants were being transported by air, and the number of ships needed had declined, until only *Australis* was carrying migrants. On 19 December 1977, *Australis* arrived in Sydney carrying 650 assisted migrants, this being the last migrant voyage to Australia from Britain and Europe.

Acknowledgments

While some of the written material in this book also appeared in my previous book, *Emigrant Ships to Luxury Liners*, published in 1992, I have endeavoured to add as much new material as possible, and also correct any mistakes. When researching this material, I have relied heavily on newspapers of the day, particularly the *Daily Commercial News* and *Sydney Morning Herald*, as well as information included in such publications as *The Log, Marine News, Steamboat Bill* and the newsletters produced by several branches of the World Ship Society around Australia.

I have included as many new pictures as possible in this book, including an increase in the colour content. I have had most of these pictures in my collection for many years, having obtained them from various sources, including the collections of the late Peter Britz, the late Fred Roderick, and the late Vic Scrivens. I have also been able to obtain over the years some excellent colour pictures taken by Stephen Berry, Ian Edwards, Alan Travers, Dennis Brook, Ken Lunney, and Jim Freeman, while Ross Gillett and the Victoria Branch of the World Ship Society have kindly supplied excellent material from their collections.

The largest number of pictures in this book have been supplied to me by Robert Tompkins, who has always been most generous in his assistance with photographs from his extensive collection for my various books over the years, and I am most grateful to him for this.

VOLENDAM

BUILT: 1922 by Harland & Wolff Ltd, Belfast
TONNAGE: 15,434 gross
DIMENSIONS: 472 x 67 ft (175.6 x 20.5 m)
SERVICE SPEED: 15 knots
PROPULSION: Geared turbines/twin screws

The vessels of Holland-America Line are not usually associated with the Australian trade, but *Volendam* made several voyages here in the post-war years.

Volendam was launched on 6 July 1922, and four months later left Rotterdam on its maiden voyage to New York, being joined six months later by a sister ship, Veendam. Initially they carried 263 first class, 436 second class and 1,200 third class passengers, but the latter was changed to 484 tourist class in 1928. Through the thirties, *Volendam* often cruised from New York.

Volendam was on a regular voyage from New York to Rotterdam when Holland was invaded in May 1940, and instead went to Britain. Taken over by the British Government, and under Cunard Line management, though retaining a Dutch crew, the vessel was first used to evacuate British children to Canada.

On 30 August 1940, with 335 children and 271 adult passengers on board, *Volendam* was torpedoed off the Irish coast. All aboard were put into lifeboats and rescued, while *Volendam*, heavily down at the bow, was towed to the Isle of Bute and beached. Later it was taken to the Mersey for repairs at the Cammell Laird shipyard, refitted to carry 3,000 troops, and returned to service as a troopship in July 1941.

In July 1945 *Volendam* was returned to Holland-America Line. The British Ministry of Transport then chartered the vessel for further service as a troopship, returning it to Holland-America Line in mid-1946. The Dutch Government then chartered the vessel, to make some trooping voyages to the Dutch East Indies, and also migrant voyages to Australia, the accommodation being refitted to carry 1,682 persons in a single class.

The first voyage by *Volendam* to Australia was really an extension of its first trooping trip to Batavia, leaving there in July 1946 and going first to Brisbane, then arriving in Sydney on 14 August for a 10-day stay. The vessel then visited Melbourne and Fremantle before returning to Rotterdam.

During 1947, *Volendam* returned to the North Atlantic trade again, though offering very basic accommodation. It usually also made one voyage each year to Australia, departing Rotterdam in December, and visiting Fremantle, Melbourne and Sydney. On its 1949 voyage, the liner left Sydney on 1 February 1950, bound for Noumea and then Jakarta on the return trip.

On 17 October 1950, *Volendam* left Rotterdam on its final Australian voyage, being in Fremantle on 20 November and Melbourne six days later. Leaving Sydney on 2 December, it went to Jakarta again before returning to Rotterdam on 12 November. *Volendam* was then withdrawn from service, and laid up until sold to Dutch shipbreakers in February 1952.

HWA LIEN

BUILT: 1907 by Wm Denny & Bros, Dumbarton
TONNAGE: 3,399 gross
DIMENSIONS: 350 x 47 ft (106.7 x 14.3 m)
SERVICE SPEED: 17 knots
PROPULSION: Geared turbines/triple screws

In January 1947, a small vessel named *Hwa Lien* arrived in Sydney at the end of a harrowing voyage from Shanghai. Although unfamiliar to Australians, this vessel was well known to New Zealanders as *Maori*, which operated on the Union Steam Ship Company express ferry service between Wellington and Lyttelton for almost 40 years.

When *Maori* was launched on 11 November 1906, it crashed into the opposite bank of the river, and on trials ran aground, having to go into drydock for repairs. On the second trial runs, it collided with and sank a small coaster, and *Maori* went back into drydock for more repairs. At the start of the delivery voyage, the vessel ran aground again, this time without suffering damage, and by the time *Maori* arrived in New Zealand during November 1907, the Union Steam Ship Company must have been wondering what sort of a jinx ship they had acquired.

With accommodation for 630 passengers in two classes, *Maori* gave its owner many years of excellent service on the overnight ferry service between the islands, and during a refit in 1923 was converted to oil firing. In 1931 *Maori* became relief ship when *Rangatira* entered service, then returned to full-time service during the war years. On 6 January 1944, *Maori* was laid up again in Wellington, and after two and a half years idle, was sold in June 1946 to the United Corporation of China Ltd, based in Shanghai. Renamed *Hwa Lien*, it left Wellington on 22 August, going first to Sydney, then to Shanghai.

It was intended to operate *Hwa Lien* on the China coast, and the local populace considered the vessel the last word in luxury. However, its first voyage was from Shanghai to Sydney, carrying 474 refugees, including 303 European Jews who had escaped as far as Shanghai, and been given permission to enter Australia.

Leaving Shanghai on 29 December 1946, *Hwa Lien* tried to make a direct voyage to Sydney, but on 10 January 1947, the ship radioed that it was running short of food and water. It had to divert to Darwin, arriving on 14 January, being the first passenger vessel to call there since the end of the war. Restocked and replenished, the voyage continued, reaching Brisbane on 26 January, and finally berthing in Sydney on 28 January, where the passengers disembarked.

Hwa Lien then returned to Shanghai, but the advance of communist forces on Shanghai brought its coastal service to an end in 1948. The vessel ferried Nationalist troops to Formosa, then in 1950 was laid up in Keelung Harbour.

On 13 January 1951 *Hwa Lien* sank at its moorings during a storm, being raised four months later and sold to shipbreakers. However, a section of the hull was converted into a barge and had a crane fitted, serving in Keelung Harbour for many more years.

JOHAN DE WITT

BUILT: 1920 by Netherland Shipbuilding Co, Amsterdam
TONNAGE: 10,474 gross
DIMENSIONS: 523 x 59 ft (159.4 x 18.1 m)
SERVICE SPEED: 16 knots
PROPULSION: Triple expansion/twin screw

This vessel had a long and varied career, mostly under the Dutch flag for the Nederland Line, which included one voyage to Australia with migrants. Launched on 2 May 1919, *Johann de Witt* entered service in July 1920 from Amsterdam to the Dutch East Indies, carrying 197 first class, 120 second class and 36 third class passengers. After a mere 10 years in service, *Johann de Witt* was laid up in December 1930, having been replaced by newer vessels.

In November 1932, one of these new vessels, *Pieter Corneliszoon Hooft*, was destroyed by fire in Amsterdam, and *Johann de Witt* was reactivated as a replacement. The vessel began a refit in April 1933, during which it was given a new Maierform bow, increasing its length by 24 ft/6.2 m. In October 1933 *Johann de Witt* returned to service again, and was in the Dutch East Indies when Germany invaded Holland in May 1940.

After a period laid up at Sourabaya, *Johann de Witt* was taken over by the British Government, and on 20 August 1941 arrived in Sydney, where it was fitted out as a troopship. In October 1940, *Johann de Witt* boarded Australian troops in Melbourne, and carried them to Egypt in convoy US5B. For five years the vessel served the Allies, manned by a Dutch crew and managed by the Orient Line.

In 1945, *Johann de Witt* was handed back to the Nederland Line, who decided against refitting the vessel for commercial service, as it was twenty-five years old, and the political situation in the Dutch East Indies had changed. *Johann de Witt* was fitted out with austere accommodation, for the carriage of migrants and displaced persons.

On 4 February 1947, the vessel left Ijmuiden on a voyage to Australia, calling at Batavia en route to Cairns, where it arrived on 13 March. *Johann de Witt* then proceeded to Sydney, berthing on 20 March, leaving three days later for Melbourne, and then Fremantle. The vessel went back to Batavia before returning to Holland. This was the only visit made by this vessel to Australia in peacetime.

On 15 December 1948, *Johann de Witt* was sold to the Goulandris Group, better known as the Greek Line, though registered in Panama under the ownership of Cia Maritime del Este. During an extensive refit, one funnel was removed, and accommodation installed for 39 first class and 748 tourist class passengers.

The vessel was renamed *Neptunia*, and in April 1951 entered service between Bremerhaven and New York. Four years later it began operating from Europe to Canada, partnered by two other vessels that had made one migrant voyage each to Australia, *Columbia* and *Canberra*.

On 2 November 1957, *Neptunia* was entering Cobh when it struck Daunt's Rock, and had to be run ashore with serious bottom damage. Abandoned as a total loss, the wreck was refloated four months later, and towed to Holland to be broken up.

MISR and AL SUDAN

BUILT: 1943/1944 by Consolidated Steel Corp, Wilmington, California
TONNAGE: 7,372 gross
DIMENSIONS: 417 x 60 ft (127.1 x 18.2 m)
SERVICE SPEED: 14 knots
PROPULSION: Geared turbines/single screw

This pair of Egyptian vessels was originally designed as standard C1 type cargo ships, *Misr* being launched on 8 September 1943, as *Cape St Roque*, while *Al Sudan* was named *Cape St Vincent* when launched on 16 November 1943. Both were completed as Landing Ships Infantry (Large), being fitted out with extensive accommodation for troops, and were handed over to the British Government under the lend-lease scheme.

Initially controlled by the Ministry of War Transport, they were renamed *Empire Mace* and *Empire Arquebus* respectively, then were transferred to the Royal Navy and became HMS *Galteemore* and HMS *Cicero*. They took part in the Normandy landings, and later served in the Pacific. During 1946 both ships were handed back to the Ministry of Transport, regaining their "Empire" names briefly before being handed back to the Americans, resuming their original "Cape" names.

The Americans had no use for the pair, and in 1947 they were sold to Soc *Misr* de Nav Maritime SAE, of Alexandria, who renamed them *Misr* and *Al Sudan*. The Egyptians retained the troop accommodation, and placed the vessels on the pilgrim trade to Jeddah for part of each year, offering them for charter at other times. They could carry about 770 persons, so were ideal for transporting migrants, or displaced persons on behalf of the IRO.

On 10 March 1947, *Misr* departed Haifa, called at Mombasa on 24 March, then voyaged to Fremantle, arriving on 14 April, and Melbourne on 20 April. Leaving on 6 May, it again stopped at Fremantle before crossing to Durban, and back to Egypt. On 1 December 1947, *Misr* departed Alexandria on its second voyage to Australia, calling at Fremantle before arriving in Melbourne on 31 December.

Al Sudan left Alexandria on 20 December 1947 for the same two ports, being in Fremantle on 27 February and Melbourne from 3 March for nine days loading cargo before returning to Egypt via Singapore. *Misr* returned to Genoa, departing there on 15 March 1948 on another voyage to Melbourne, arriving on 28 April, and departing on 12 May for Genoa and Marseilles. *Misr* made a further four voyages to Australia at irregular intervals up to 1951, but *Al Sudan* made only the one trip.

Subsequently the accommodation on these ships was altered to 54 first and 117 second class, but on pilgrim voyages they would carry up to 1,143 persons, using temporary quarters installed in the cargo holds.

In the late 1950s, Soc Misr de Nav Maritime amalgamated with the Alexandria Nav Co to form Soc Generale Pour la Navigation Maritime SAE, but in the early 1960s all Egyptian shipping companies were nationalised as the United Arab Maritime Co. Through all these changes, *Misr* and *Al Sudan* remained on their usual trades.

In 1980 both ships were laid up, and offered for sale. *Al Sudan* was sold to shipbreakers in Suez, where it arrived on 20 October 1980, but work did not start on the vessel until July 1984. *Misr* was sold to Millwala Sons Ltd of Pakistan, and arrived at their shipbreaking location on Gadani Beach on 30 January 1982.

Al Sudan

THE "GENERALS"

BUILT: 1944-45 by Kaiser Co., Richmond, California
TONNAGE: 10,645 gross
DIMENSIONS: 523 x 71 ft (159.3 x 21.7 m)
SERVICE SPEED: 17 knots
PROPULSION: Geared turbines/single screw

The Americans built many troopships during the Second World War, including a group of thirty vessels classified as Class C4-S-A1, all named after American generals from World War One. The first, *General G O Squier*, was launched on 11 November 1942, and the rest were launched at almost monthly intervals up to April 1945, when *General Stuart Heintzelmann* was the final ship.

They could carry up to 3,000 troops, with a crew numbering 256. *General Squier* entered service in October 1943, with a further 16 being completed during 1944, and the last entering service in October 1945.

All 30 ships served primarily in the Pacific, and all survived the war. During 1946, five of the vessels were laid up in the US Reserve Fleet, while the other 25 were transferred to the US Army. For some time these ships were kept busy carrying troops for the occupation force being established in Japan, and repatriating American soldiers from the various areas of the Pacific war.

A few of the class visited Australia in these years, the first being *General J H. McRae* in January 1945, followed by *General A W Greely, General C G Morten, General Le Roy Eltinge, General R E Callan,* and *General W F Hase*.

At the end of 1947, some of these ships were placed at the disposal of the International Refugee Organisation to assist in the transportation of displaced persons, with separate quarters for males and females being provided.

During September and October 1947, authorities from the Australian Government visited camps in Germany housing displaced persons from the Baltic States. 843 single adults, 726 men and 114 women comprising 440 Lithuanians, 262 Latvians and 138 Estonians, were selected to go to Australia as migrants, leaving Bremerhaven on 29 October 1947 aboard *General Stuart Heintzelmann*, which arrived in Fremantle on 28 November. The migrants all disembarked there, and were transferred to *Kanimbla* to complete their journey to Melbourne.

A further thirteen vessels of this class also made voyages to Australia with migrants. Initially the number of persons carried was between 800 and 900, but as the program of voyages progressed the number carried was increased to 1,300 or more.

In November 1949 *General Greely* made a special voyage from Samar in the Philippines to Sydney, while in February 1950, *General Langfitt* brought Polish refugees from Mombasa in Kenya.

With the outbreak of war in Korea in 1950, several of these ships were used to transport troops to the Korean Peninsula until that conflict ended in 1953. Other ships were transferred to the Military Sea Transport service. Most of the "Generals" were progressively laid up through the 1950s, but kept in mothballs so they could be reactivated at short notice.

Between 1967 and 1970 most of the "Generals", were sold, and many were converted into either dry cargo ships or container carriers. By the late 1970s they were being replaced by new, purpose-built ships, and gradually the former "Generals" began to disappear from the seas. A handful survived a few years longer, but today there are no former "Generals" in active commercial service, though a couple that were retained by the military are understood to be still afloat in the reserve fleet.

General Omar Bundy

The Voyages

Voyages made to Australia by the Generals are listed below in chronological order. The voyages between November 1947 and November 1950 were all made under the auspices of the International Refugee Organisation.

Ship	From	Date	Arrival port	Date	Passengers
General Stuart Heintzelmann	Bremerhaven	29/10/47	Fremantle	28/11/ 4	843
General M B Stewart	Bremerhaven	13/01/48	Fremantle	12/02/48	856
General William M Black	Bremerhaven	24/03/48	Melbourne	27/04/48	860
General Samuel D Sturgis	Venice	16/04/48	Sydney	14/05/48	860
General Omar Bundy	Naples	20/02/49	Sydney	20/03/49	842
General M B Stewart	Naples	12/03/49	Melbourne	13/04/49	816
General Stuart Heintzelmann	Naples	01/04/49	Melbourne	20/04/49	822
General C C Ballou	Naples	01/04/49	Sydney	27/04/49	876
General Samuel D Sturgis	Naples	24/04/49	Sydney	21/05/4	843
General W C Langfitt	Naples	23/05/49	Melbourne	17/06/49	826
General William M Black	Naples	25/05/49	Melbourne	24/06/49	826
General Omar Bundy	Naples	09/06/49	Sydney	08/07/49	842
General M B Stewart	Naples	30/06/49	Adelaide	20/07/49	816
General Harry Taylor	Naples	23/06/49	Sydney	21/07/49	864
General W C Langfitt	Naples	29/08/49	Melbourne	22/09/49	826
General A W Greely	Naples	13/09/49	Newcastle	12/10/49	1,281
General A W Greely	Samar	30/10/49	Sydney	09/11/49	576
General R M Blatchford	Naples	16/10/49	Sydney	11/11/49	1,219
General W G Haan	Naples	20/10/49	Melbourne	15/11/49	1,303
General Stuart Heintzelmann	Naples	29/10/49	Sydney	24/11/49	1,301
General Mark L Hersey	Naples	12/11/49	Melbourne	06/12/49	1,319
General William M Black	Naples	16/11/49	Sydney	13/12/49	1,302
General Robert L Howze	Naples	21/11/49	Melbourne	18/12/49	1,105
General W C Langfitt	Naples	20/12/49	Melbourne	14/01/50	1,232
General M B Stewart	Naples	03/01/50	Melbourne	31/01/50	1,262
General Harry Taylor	Naples	05/01/50	Newcastle	03/02/50	1,265
General W C Langfitt	Mombasa	03/02/50	Fremantle	15/02/50	1,118
General R M Blatchford	Naples	19/01/50	Sydney	18/02/50	1,222
General W G Haan	Naples	25/01/50	Melbourne	19/02/50	1,301
General Stuart Heintzelmann	Bremerhaven	??/02/50	Melbourne	04/03/50	1,302
General C H Muir	Naples	??/02/50	Sydney	16/03/50	1,278
General C C Ballou	Naples	23/02/50	Sydney	23/03/50	1,266
General Robert L Howze	Naples	28/02/50	Melbourne	28/03/50	1,316
General William M Black	Naples	11/03/50	Melbourne	13/04/50	1,316
General M B Stewart	Naples	22/03/50	Sydney	17/04/50	1,300
General Samuel D Sturgis	Naples	21/03/50	Sydney	17/04/50	1,309
General Mark L Hersey	Naples	??/03/50	Melbourne	27/04/50	1,336
General A W Greely	Naples	18/04/50	Melbourne	12/05/50	1,271
General C H Muir	Bremerhaven	25/09/50	Melbourne	27/10/50	1,280
General Mark L Hersey	Bremerhaven	??/10/50	Fremantle	02/11/50	1,370
General C C Ballou	Naples	??/11/50	Newcastle	16/12/50	1,300

Two voyages in 1957 were under the auspices of the Inter-Governmental Committee for European Migration.

| *General W C Langfitt* | Genoa | 17/05/57 | Melb/Syd | 13/06/57 | |
| *General Harry Taylor* | Marseilles | 28/05/57 | Sydney | 25/06/57 | |

General W C Haan

11

The Careers of the "Generals"

The following is a brief history of the career of each of the fourteen "Generals" that transported displaced persons and refugees to Australia between 1947 and 1957.

General C C Ballou

Yard No 28. Launched 7 March 1945. Commissioned 30 June 1945. Maiden voyage 29 July 1945 from San Diego to Marseilles. Transferred to US Army May 1946. Transferred to MSTS 1 March 1950. Laid up at Beaumont, Texas, 1 June 1960. Sold 1968 to Sea Land Services Inc, rebuilt as a container ship by Alabama Shipbuilding and Drydock Co. Renamed *Brooklyn*. Sold 1975 to Puerto Rico Shipping Authority, San Juan, renamed *Humacao*. Renamed *Eastern Light* 1981. Broken up 1981.

General William M Black

Yard No 6. Launched 23 July 1943. Commissioned 24 February 1944. Maiden voyage 26 March 1944 San Francisco to Pearl Harbor. Transferred to US Army 28 February 1946. Transferred to MSTS 1 March 1950. Laid up at Suisun Bay, California 1955. Sold 1967 to Central Gulf Steam Ship Co, rebuilt as cargo ship, renamed *Green Forest*. Entered service June 1968. Sold to Taiwanese shipbreakers 1979, arrived Kaohsiung 3 January 1980.

General R M Blatchford

Yard No 19. Launched 27 August 1944. Commissioned 26 January 1945. Maiden voyage 12 March 1945 San Francisco to Manila. Transferred to US Army June 1946. Transferred to MSTS 1950. Laid up 17 September 1968. Sold January 1969 to Waterman Carriers Inc, rebuilt as a container ship, renamed *Stonewall Jackson*. Renamed *Alex Stephens* 1973. Sold to Taiwanese shipbreakers 1980, arrived Kaohsiung April 1980.

General Omar Bundy

Yard No 18. Launched 5 August 1944. Commissioned 6 January 1945. Maiden voyage 10 March 1945 San Francisco to Pacific Islands. Transferred to US Army 30 August 1946. Transferred to Department of Commerce 12 December 1949 and laid up in reserve fleet in James River. Sold 10 April 1964 to Calmar Steam Ship Co, rebuilt as cargo ship, renamed *Portmar*. Renamed *Port* August 1976. Sold 1979 to Hawaiian Eugenia Corp, renamed *Poet*. Left Philadelphia on 24 October 1980 for Port Said with a cargo of corn and disappeared without trace.

General A W Greely

Yard No 22. Launched 5 November 1944. Commissioned 22 March 1945. Maiden voyage 16 April 1945 Los Angeles to Australia. Transferred to US Army 20 March 1946. Transferred to MSTS 1950. Transferred to Maritime Administration 29 August 1959 and laid up in reserve fleet at Olympia, Washington. Sold 1968 to Pacific Far East Line, rebuilt as a container vessel, renamed *Hawaii Bear*. Sold 1975 to Farrell Lines Inc, renamed *Austral Glade*. Laid up 13 March 1976 at San Francisco. Sold 1979 to American Pacific Container Line Inc, renamed *Pacific Enterprise*. Laid up again on 2 October 1980 in San Francisco. Sold 21 July 1981 by US Marshalls Office, at the direction of the US Court, renamed *Caribe Enterprise*. Laid up 1983 in New York with machinery damage. Sold 1986 to Taiwanese shipbreakers, left New York under tow 24 May 1986. Left Los Angeles under tow 25 July then sank in the Pacific.

General W G Haan

Yard No 29. Launched 20 March 1945. Commissioned 2 August 1945. Maiden voyage 4 September 1945 San Diego to Asia. Transferred to US Army June 1946. Transferred to MSTS 1 March 1950. Laid up 22 October 1958 at Beaumont, Texas. Sold 1968 to Hudson Waterways Corp, rebuilt as container vessel, renamed *Transoregon*. Sold 1975 to Puerto Rico Maritime Shipping Authority, renamed *Mayaguez*. Sold 1982, renamed *Amco Trader*. Sold to shipbreakers 1987, renamed *Trader* for final voyage to breakers' yard.

General Stuart Heintzelmann

Yard No 30. Launched 21 April 1945. Commissioned 12 September 1945. Maiden voyage 9 October 1945 San Diego to Yokohama. Transferred to US Army June 1946. Transferred to MSTS 1950. Laid up 1954 in Navy Reserve. Laid up June 1960 in reserve fleet at Beaumont, Texas. Sold 1968 to Sea Land Services Inc, rebuilt as a container vessel, renamed *Mobile*. Sold to shipbreakers 1984.

General Mark L Hersey

Yard No 13. Launched 1 April 1944. Commissioned 29 July 1944. Maiden voyage 5 September 1944 San Francisco to New Guinea. Transferred to US Army June 1946. Transferred to MSTS 1950. On 4 November 1951, collided with the Argentinian passenger vessel *Maipu* in the mouth of the Elbe River, West Germany, causing the *Maipu* to sink. Laid up 1954 in Navy Reserve. Laid up 3 September 1959 in Suisun Bay, California. Sold 1968 to Sea Land Services Inc, rebuilt as container vessel. The ship was cut in two, with a 513 foot prefabricated forward section being joined to the original 145 foot long after section. Length now 695 feet/211.8 m. Renamed *St Louis*. The original forepart of the ship was sold to Taiwanese shipbreakers, but sank in the Pacific on 5 January 1971 while being towed to Kaohsiung. *St Louis* was sold in 1988 to shipbreakers in Taiwan.

General Robert L Howze

Yard No 5. Launched 23 May 1943. Commissioned 7 February 1944. Maiden voyage 20 March 1944 San Francisco to New Guinea. Transferred to US Army June 1946, and laid up until 1948. Transferred to MSTS 1 March 1950. Laid up 17 July 1958 at Astoria, Oregon. Sold 1968 to Pacific Far East Line, rebuilt as container ship, renamed *Guam Bear*. 1975 renamed *New Zealand Bear*.

Sold 1976 to Farrell Lines, renamed *Austral Glen*, but laid up at San Francisco on 7 August 1976. Sold August 1979 to American Pacific Container Line Inc, renamed *Pacific Endeavour*. Sold to Pakistani shipbreakers 1980, arrived in Karachi 27 October 1980.

General W C Langfitt
Yard No 17. Launched 17 July 1944. Commissioned 30 September 1944. Maiden voyage 10 November 1944 San Diego to Eniwetok. Transferred to US Army June 1946. Transferred to MSTS 1950. Laid up 13 May 1958 in reserve fleet in James River. Sold 1968 to Hudson Waterways Corp, rebuilt as container ship, cut in two and 110 foot long midsection added, renamed *Transindiana*. Sold to shipbreakers 1983.

General C H Muir
Yard No 23. Launched 24 November 1944. Commissioned 12 April 1945. Maiden voyage 13 May 1945 San Francisco to Pearl Harbor. Transferred to US Army 18 June 1946. Transferred to MSTS 1950. Laid up 30 June 1960 in reserve fleet in Suisun Bay, California. Sold 1968 to Sea Land Services Inc, rebuilt as a container vessel. The ship was cut in two, with a 513 foot prefabricated forward section being joined to the original 145 foot long after section containing the superstructure and engines. Renamed *Chicago*. Sold 1975 to Puerto Rico Maritime Authority, renamed *San Juan*. Known to be still in existence in 1987, but no definite information available as to final fate.

General M B Stewart
Yard No 21. Launched 15 October 1944. Commissioned 3 March 1945. Maiden voyage 2 April 1945 San Francisco to Pearl Harbor. Transferred to US Army May 1946. Transferred to MSTS 1950. Laid up 1958 in reserve fleet in the Hudson River, New York. Sold 1967 to Albany River Transport Inc, rebuilt as a cargo ship, including 70-ton heavy lift crane. Renamed *Albany*. Sold 1974 to Avondale Shipyards Inc, converted to a drilling ship, renamed *Mission Viking*. Sold to shipbreakers 1987.

General Samuel D Sturgis
Yard No 9. Launched 12 November 1943. Commissioned 10 July 1944. Maiden voyage 18 August 1944 Seattle to Honolulu. Transferred to US Army 24 June 1946. Transferred to MSTS 1950. Laid up 22 August 1958 in reserve fleet at Beaumont, Texas. Sold 1967 to Central Gulf Steam Ship Corp, rebuilt as cargo ship, renamed *Green Port*. Arrived at Kaohsiung on 26 January 1980 to be broken up.

General Harry Taylor
Yard No 8. Launched 10 October 1943. Commissioned 8 May 1944. Maiden voyage 23 June 1944 San Diego to Milne Bay. Transferred to US Army June 1946. Transferred to MSTS 1 March 1950. Laid up 10 July 1958 in reserve fleet at Beaumont, Texas. Transferred in January 1963 to US Army Air Force, rebuilt as a missile tracking ship, renamed *General Hoyt S Vandenberg*. Used for monitoring of missile launchings at US Air Force ocean test ranges. In 1997 used as a Soviet spy ship in the making of the movie *Virus*. Placed in US Reserve Fleet. Believed to be still afloat.

General Harry Taylor

RADNIK

BUILT: 1908 by Newport News Shipbuilding & Drydock Co,
   Newport News
TONNAGE: 6,665 gross
DIMENSIONS: 437 x 53 ft (133.3 x 16.1 m)
SERVICE SPEED: 11 knots
PROPULSION: Triple expansion/single screw

One of the more unusual looking migrant ships to visit Australia was *Radnik*, owned by the Yugoslav shipping company Jugoslavenska Linijska Plovidba. It was a vessel with a most interesting history, having been launched on 11 January 1908 as *Lurline* for the Matson Line, being the first vessel built to the order of that company, which at the time had a large fleet of sailing ships, and only a few steamers. *Lurline* was fitted out with accommodation for 64 passengers, and also had a large cargo capacity.

On 8 June 1908 *Lurline* departed San Francisco on its maiden voyage to Hawaii, serving on this route until 29 October 1917, when it was taken over by the US Shipping Board. After nine trips to Honolulu and three to Manila it was returned to Matson Line on 31 January 1919.

Lurline spent the next nine years plying to Hawaii again, and had completed 218 voyages for Matson by the time it was sold to the Alaska Packers Association. Renamed *Chirikof*, it operated as a cargo ship, bringing Alaskan salmon to ports on the west coast of America.

In July 1940, *Chirikof* was bareboat chartered to the US Government, for a cargo service from Seattle to Alaskan ports, being handed back in April 1941.

In June 1942 the ship was again taken over by the US Government, and accommodation for 1,290 troops installed, as well as heavy lift gear, and for the first time the bridge was enclosed. The vessel mainly operated to Alaska in this role, but also made a voyage to Honolulu. When handed back to Alaska Packers on 6 February 1946, they had no use for the ship, which was offered for sale.

After a period laid up, *Chirikof* was purchased by the Yugoslavs, and renamed *Radnik*. It was their intention to operate the vessel on the migrant trade, using the former troop spaces, though a reduced number of passengers would be carried.

The first voyage by *Radnik* to Australia was from Malta on 4 December 1947. It was a slow passage, as the ship did not reach Fremantle until 25 January 1948, and Melbourne on 2 February. *Radnik* then crossed the Tasman to Auckland, arriving on 7 February and staying in port for a week. On 20 February *Radnik* arrived in Sydney, where cargo was loaded, and it then departed for the Middle East, with another call at Fremantle on 2 March.

Over the next three years *Radnik* was used on a variety of services, making several more voyages to Australia at varying intervals. On 15 January 1951, *Radnik* departed Rijeka on its final voyage to Australia, calling at Fremantle on 26 February, Melbourne on 7 March, and terminating in Sydney on 11 March. Several days later the vessel departed for Adelaide, where it berthed on 24 March, and after loading of cargo departed for Rijeka.

In June 1952 *Radnik* was laid up in Split, and sold to a local shipbreaking firm in August 1953.

PARTIZANKA

BUILT: 1927 by Newport News Shipbuilding & Drydock Co,
  Newport News
TONNAGE: 6,267 gross
DIMENSIONS: 395 x 62 ft (120.4 x 18.9 m)
SERVICE SPEED: 17 knots
PROPULSION: Geared turbines/twin screws

Partizanka, which made two trips to Australia, was a former American ship, having been built for the Clyde Line to operate along the east coast of America from New York to Miami. Launched on 18 April 1927, it was named *Shawnee*, and provided comfortable accommodation for 600 passengers. Clyde Line later merged with the Mallory SS Co to form Clyde-Mallory Lines, and in 1934 they amalgamated with the New York and Porto Rico SS Co to form the Atlantic, Gulf & West Indies SS Co, known as AGWI Lines.

Shawnee operated to Miami most of the year with a sister ship, *Iroquois*, but both ships were also used for occasional cruises during the 1930s from New York to either Bermuda or Havana. When war broke out in Europe in September 1939, *Shawnee* was chartered by the US Government, and on 13 September 1939 left New York on a trans-Atlantic voyage to Bordeaux, where it collected American citizens who had been stranded in France, and carried them home.

The vessel then returned to the coastal trade until December 1941, when it was taken over by the US Government for conversion into a troopship. At the Todd-Johnson shipyard in New Orleans, the interior of the ship was gutted and accommodation for 1,589 troops installed.

For some time *Shawnee* operated out of New York to the Caribbean, or Chile and Peru, then in January 1943 it crossed the Atlantic again, taking troops to North Africa.

Shawnee spent the remainder of that year on the Atlantic ferry to both British and African ports.

Early in 1944 *Shawnee* passed through the Panama Canal, and began operating from San Francisco to the South Pacific, making several visits to Brisbane and Townsville, as well as ports in New Guinea. In January 1946 *Shawnee* returned to New York, and on 4 March 1946 was handed back to AGWI Lines.

Shawnee was laid up in Norfolk, and purchased in October 1946 by Iberian Star Line, registered in Panama but owned in Portugal. Refitted and renamed *City of Lisbon,* the vessel was damaged in a collision with the cargo ship *Virgolin* on 28 May 1947, when some 150 miles from Lisbon.

The owners decided to sell the ship for scrap, but instead it was purchased in July 1947 by Jugoslavenska Linijska Plovidba, and renamed *Partizanka.* During a refit at Rijeka, accommodation for about 800 persons was installed, but externally the ship was not altered.

On 15 December 1947, *Partizanka* left Malta on a voyage to Australia, arriving in Fremantle on 9 January 1948, then went to Sydney, berthing on 15 January, and disembarking 808 migrants, including three babies born on the trip. *Partizanka* left four days later bound for the Middle East, with another call at Fremantle. For most of 1948 *Partizanka* operated from Rijeka to South America.

In March 1949, *Partizanka* left Trieste on its second voyage to Australia, arriving in Sydney on 6 April, when the picture below was taken as it came in to berth at No 2 Circular Quay. 298 migrants representing eighteen nationalities disembarked, and the vessel left on 7 April bound for Split.

On 12 August 1949, while the ship was in drydock, a fire broke out, leaving it 70 per cent destroyed. *Partizanka* was declared a total loss on 13 September, and the hulk was sold to local shipbreakers in 1950. However, the lower part of the hull was rebuilt as a barge, and used in the Split area for several years.

TIDEWATER - CONTINENTAL

BUILT: 1902 by Maryland Steel Corp, Sparrows' Point
TONNAGE: 10,005 gross
DIMENSIONS: 489 x 58 ft (149.1 x 17.7 m)
SERVICE SPEED: 13 knots
PROPULSION: Triple expansion/twin screws

Some migrant ships had unexpected claims to fame, and this vessel made the first official transit of the Panama Canal. Built as a large freighter for the Boston Steamship Co, it was launched on 19 December 1901 as *Shawmut*, having a sister named *Tremont*, and operated from California to Japan. In 1908, both ships were sold to the Panama Railroad Steamship Co, *Shawmut* being renamed *Ancon*, while *Tremont* became *Cristobal*. They were used to carry building materials to the canal construction areas.

On 3 August 1914, *Cristobal* became the first ship to traverse the entire canal, with a trip from the Pacific to the Atlantic. However, *Ancon* was selected to carry 300 guests for the first official transit, on 15 August, from Cristobal to Balboa.

Ancon continued to operate to the canal until 1917, then was used to transport nitrates, and later became a supply ship for the US Army. At the end of the war, *Ancon* made two trips from Europe to America, carrying 6,112 American soldiers home.

Returned to its owners, *Ancon* again became a cargo ship, then in 1924 was rebuilt, along with *Cristobal,* with accommodation for 200 passengers being installed. *Ancon* and *Cristobal* operated from New York to Haiti and the Panama Canal Zone until 1939, then were withdrawn.

Ancon was renamed *Exancon*, and laid up pending disposal. However, it was reactivated on 15 August 1939 to make a passage through the Panama Canal to mark the twenty-fifth anniversary of the first transit.

The vessel was sold in October 1940 to the Permanente Steamship Co, of San Francisco, and renamed *Permanente*, being used to carry cement. It later served as a supply ship in the Pacific, and in 1946 carried war brides from Australia to America. Later that year the vessel was sold to Tidewater Commercial Co, and renamed *Tidewater* under Panamanian registry.

Refitted at Genoa with accommodation for about 350 persons, on 9 September 1947 *Tidewater* left Marseilles with 353 migrants and a cargo of phosphate, arriving in Fremantle on 5 November, Melbourne on 13 November, and Sydney on 18 November, then crossing to Auckland to berth on 26 November, where the phosphate was unloaded. It then went to Cairns and Melbourne to load cargo for the return trip.

Shortly after, *Tidewater* was chartered to Arnold Bernstein Shipping Co, and renamed *Continental*. It left New York on 3 June 1948 for the first of four voyages to Plymouth, Antwerp and Rotterdam, the last departing New York on 13 September, following which the ship was returned to its owners.

The name *Continental* was retained, and on 12 January 1949 it left Genoa bound for Australia again. The vessel made two further voyages to Australia from Genoa during 1949, departing on 2 June and 15 September, each time calling at Fremantle, Melbourne and Sydney. On 20 January 1950, *Continental* left Genoa on its final voyage to Australia, but after leaving Melbourne on 5 March, bound for Alexandria, was in Fremantle from 13 March until 10 April with engine problems.

On 26 October 1950 *Continental* arrived at a Savona shipbreaking yard.

STRATHMORE and STRATHEDEN

Built: 1935–1937 by Vickers-Armstrong Ltd, Barrow
Tonnage: 23,580/23,732 gross
Dimensions: 665 x 82 ft (202.7 x 25 m)
Service Speed: 20 knots
Propulsion: Geared turbines/twin screws

Strathmore and *Stratheden* were the third and fourth units of the famous "Strath" liners built for P & O during the 1930s. The first pair, *Strathnaver* and *Strathaird,* had entered service in 1931 and 1932, having three funnels and turbo-electric machinery. When P & O ordered a third similar ship, it was slightly larger, but had only one funnel, geared turbines, and carried fewer passengers.

Strathmore was launched on 4 April 1935, being completed five months later. The liner was given accommodation for 445 first class and 665 tourist class passengers. Its first commercial voyage was a cruise from London on 27 September to the Canary Islands, then on 26 October the liner departed Tilbury on its maiden voyage to Bombay and Australia.

Despite the worsening depression, P & O ordered a further two liners similar to *Strathmore,* the first being named *Stratheden* when launched on 10 June 1937. There were minor differences to *Strathmore,* in particular the accommodation, which was divided between 448 first class and 563 tourist class. This was to make *Stratheden* more suitable for cruising, though its maiden voyage was on the regular trade to Australia, departing Tilbury on 24 December 1937.

The fifth and final "Strath" liner was launched on 23 September 1937 as *Strathallan,* commencing its maiden voyage from Tilbury on 18 March 1938. All three ships spent a considerable time cruising, and were so engaged when war broke out in September 1939.

Stratheden and *Strathmore,* on cruises out of Tilbury, were immediately requisitioned as troopships. *Strathallan* was cruising out of Sydney, and was taken over when it returned to Britain.

The three liners saw service in many parts of the world, and on 28 November 1940, *Strathmore* and *Stratheden,* along with *Orion* and the Polish liner *Batory,* left Fremantle in convoy bound for Colombo and Egypt. This was their last visit to Australia for several years.

In November 1942, all five "Straths" were among the vessels involved in the North African landings, *Strathnaver* in the first assault, the others in follow-up convoys. *Strathallan* was on its second voyage to North Africa, carrying 4,000 British and American troops and 250 nurses, when it was torpedoed in the Mediterranean early in the morning of 21 December. The troops and nurses were all taken off the heavily listing ship before it suddenly caught fire, and sank the next day off Oran.

Strathmore and *Stratheden* survived the war, and were then used to repatriate troops. *Strathmore* boarded New Zealand troops in Egypt and carried them to Wellington, arriving on 5 October 1945. From there it went to Melbourne, boarding several thousand Tasmanian troops disembarked from other troopships, and took them to Burnie.

In 1946 *Stratheden* was the first vessel to be returned to P & O after the war ended. Following an extensive refit at its builder's yard, the vessel left Tilbury in June 1947 on a voyage to Australia again, now having accommodation for 527 first class and 453 tourist class passengers.

Strathmore was retained by the government until 1948, then went to the Vickers-Armstrong yard in Newcastle for a refit, being given accommodation for 497 first class and 487 tourist class.

The work should have been completed in June 1949, but it was 8 October before it left the shipyard. *Strathmore* left Tilbury on 26 October for Australia.

The two ships were used only occasionally for cruises in the post-war years, spending almost all their time on the mail service from Britain. An unusual diversion for *Stratheden* was a charter to Cunard Line in 1950 to make four round trips across the Atlantic between Southampton and New York.

In 1954, *Strathnaver* and *Strathaird* had been converted into one-class liners, and when they were withdrawn in 1961, *Strathmore* and *Stratheden* were similarly converted, being given tourist class accommodation for 1,200 passengers. However, the demand for assisted migrant passages was declining, and within two years both ships were withdrawn.

On 20 June 1963 *Strathmore* left Tilbury on its final voyage to Australia, departing Sydney on 29 July and Fremantle on 7 August, then being laid up on its return to Britain. It was normal P & O policy to sell their old liners to shipbreakers, so it was a surprise when *Strathmore* was sold to Greek shipowner, John S Latsis, being delivered to him on 11 November 1963 at Piraeus.

Stratheden made its final departure from Tilbury on 7 August, leaving Sydney on 15 September and Fremantle on 23 September to return to Tilbury on 23 October. After a brief period laid up off Portland, *Stratheden* was chartered by the Travel Savings Association to make four cruises from Britain. After a further brief lay up, *Stratheden* was also sold to John S Latsis.

Under the Greek flag, *Strathmore* was renamed *Marianna Latsi*, while *Stratheden* became *Henrietta Latsi*. They were used to transport pilgrims from Asiatic countries to Jeddah for part of each year, and at other times were either laid up, or acted as floating hotels off Jeddah. In a most confusing move, the names of the two ships were swapped in 1966, so *Strathmore* became *Henrietta Latsi* and *Stratheden* was renamed *Marianna Latsi*.

In 1969, both ships were sold to shipbreakers at La Spezia in Italy, the former *Stratheden* arriving there on 19 May, *Strathmore* on 27 May.

Strathmore

18

ORION

BUILT: 1935 by Vickers-Armstrong Ltd, Barrow
TONNAGE: 23,696 gross
DIMENSIONS: 665 x 82 ft (202.7 x 25 m)
SERVICE SPEED: 20 knots
PROPULSION: Geared turbines/twin screws

Orion was built to the same hull design as *Strathmore*, and at the same time, but *Orion* was given a different superstructure, one mast, and a new colour scheme, introducing the corn hull and buff funnel. Launched on 7 December 1934, and completed in August 1935, *Orion* was the first British ship to have air-conditioning, though it was confined to the dining rooms only. Accommodation was provided for 486 first class and 653 tourist class passengers, but for cruises 600 passengers could be carried in a single class.

Its first voyage was a cruise from Southampton on 14 August to Norway, followed by a cruise to the Mediterranean. On 29 September 1935, *Orion* left Tilbury on its maiden voyage to Australia. The only problem encountered was smuts falling on the after decks, and the funnel was heightened in October 1936. *Orion* alternated line voyages with cruises out of Britain and Australia, and in 1937 was joined by a sister ship, *Orcades*.

Both liners were requisitioned within weeks of war breaking out in September 1939, and became troopships, making several voyages carrying Australian and New Zealand troops.

Both *Orion* and *Orcades* were selected to take part in the first convoy in January 1940, with *Orcades* boarding Australian troops in Sydney, while *Orion* embarked New Zealand troops in Wellington. *Orcades* later carried New Zealand troops in August 1940 in convoy US4, while *Orion* carried Australian

troops in convoy US7 in November 1940. Both liners were also selected to carry troops during the landings in North Africa in November 1942.

Orcades had to return to Britain from Egypt around South Africa, with 1,000 troops aboard, but on 10 October 1942 was torpedoed 300 miles west of the Cape of Good Hope, and sank. *Orion* played its part in the North African landings, making two trips with 5,000 troops each time.

Orion had voyaged over 380,000 miles and carried over 175,000 persons by the time it was released from government service in April 1946. *Orion* arrived back at its builder's yard for refitting on 1 May 1946.

With accommodation for 546 first class and 706 tourist class passengers, the vessel left Tilbury on 25 February 1947, being the first Orient Line vessel to resume the service to Australia. Over the next few years the liner made occasional cruises from Southampton and Sydney, but was mainly employed on line voyages.

During a refit in 1958, the accommodation of *Orion* was altered to 342 cabin class and 722 tourist class, and it began operating an independent schedule to the mail steamers. Most of the outbound passengers were assisted migrants, and in 1960 *Orion* became a one-class ship carrying 1,691 passengers.

On 28 February 1963, *Orion* left Tilbury on its final voyage to Australia, leaving Sydney on 8 April, Melbourne three days later, and Fremantle on 15 April, returning to Tilbury on 15 May.

Orion was then chartered for service as a floating hotel in Hamburg for the International Gardening Exhibition from 23 May to 30 September 1963.

On 1 October, *Orion* left Hamburg bound for Antwerp, where it was handed over to shipbreakers.

ORMONDE

BUILT: 1918 by John Brown & Co, Clydebank
TONNAGE: 15,047 gross
DIMENSIONS: 600 x 66 ft (182.9 x 20.3 m)
SERVICE SPEED: 18 knots
PROPULSION: Geared turbines/twin screws

During the war, the Orient Line lost their newest ship, *Orcades,* when it was less than five years old, yet their oldest liner, *Ormonde,* survived its second global conflict. Laid down in May 1913, construction was halted when war broke out in 1914. Late in 1916 work recommenced, and *Ormonde* was launched without ceremony in February 1917, being completed in June 1918 as a troopship.

Before the war ended *Ormonde* made a voyage to China via South Africa, then was handed over to the Orient Line, and fitted out with accommodation for 278 first class, 195 second class and 1,000 third class passengers.

On 15 November 1919, *Ormonde* left London on its maiden voyage to Australia, being the first new liner to enter the trade after the war, and the first vessel with geared turbines to operate to Australia. It was also the first Orient liner to have a cruiser stern, but was coal fired until July 1923, when converted to oil firing. In 1933 the accommodation was remodelled to carry 777 tourist class passengers only, and *Ormonde* joined the veteran *Orsova* on a secondary service to Australia.

In September 1939, *Ormonde* was requisitioned for its second war, again being used as a troopship, though in April 1940 it was returned to Orient Line to make one round trip to Australia. *Ormonde* later made numerous voyages across the Atlantic, and five trips to North Africa following the landings there. It spent the latter part of the war on voyages to and around Africa, then went to Madras late in 1945 to collect troops for the Pacific war, but the Japanese surrendered before they arrived.

In 1946 *Ormonde* was released from government service, having steamed over 300,000 miles and carried more than 120.000 troops. The Orient Line did not wish to refit the vessel for regular service again. Instead it was chartered by the British Ministry of Transport, and arrived at the Birkenhead shipyard of Cammell Laird in April 1947 to be refitted to carry 1,070 persons.

On 10 October 1947 *Ormonde* left London with 1,052 migrants on board, becoming the first vessel to make a voyage under the joint agreement between the British and Australian governments to transport British migrants on chartered ships.

On the return trips, *Ormonde* carried a limited number of fare-paying passengers on its owner's account. Over a five-year period, *Ormonde* made 17 voyages, bringing some 17,500 British migrants to Australia. Its final voyage departed London on 21 August 1952, and on returning to Britain, the old vessel was sold to shipbreakers.

On 1 December 1952, *Ormonde* left London bound for the breaker's yard at Dalmuir. During its entire peacetime career, *Ormonde* completed 75 round trips between Britain and Australia.

STRATHNAVER and STRATHAIRD

BUILT: 1931–32 by Vickers-Armstrong Ltd, Barrow
TONNAGE: 22,568 gross
DIMENSIONS: 664 x 80 ft (202.4 x 24.4 m)
SERVICE SPEED: 20 knots
PROPULSION: Turbo-electric/twin screws

This pair was built with three funnels, but after the war they returned to the Australian trade with only a single funnel. *Strathnaver* was launched on 5 February 1931, handed over to P & O on 2 September, and left Tilbury on its maiden voyage on 2 October 1931. This vessel was named in honour of Lord Inchcape of Strathnaver, who had been chairman of P & O for many years. *Strathaird* was launched on 18 July 1931, being delivered *to* P & O on 10 January 1932, and made its maiden departure on 12 February.

The ships were given a new colour scheme, white hull and yellow funnels, which was applied to all future P & O liners. The first and third funnels were dummies, but the paint on the middle funnel used to peel and darken at the top. Each ship provided excellent accommodation for 498 first class and 668 tourist class. They were also much higher powered than previous liners, to enable them to operate a combined mail schedule from London to Bombay and Australia.

Both vessels made occasional cruises from Britain, and on 23 December 1932, *Strathaird* became the first P & O liner to operate a cruise from Australia, departing Sydney on a five-day jaunt to Norfolk Island. However, their main employment was on the mail service from Britain to Australia, on which they were joined over the years by *Strathmore, Stratheden* and *Strathallan.* When war broke out in September 1939, *Strathaird* and *Strathnaver* were requisitioned as troopships.

No sooner had they been converted for their new role, and painted all black, than they returned to familiar waters, *Strathnaver* arriving in Sydney while *Strathaird* went to Wellington. They both carried troops in the first convoy to depart for the Middle East, in January 1940, with *Strathaird* returning to Melbourne in April to take part in the second convoy as well.

Strathaird then went to Liverpool for a refit, but this was interrupted when the vessel was sent to Brest to evacuate British troops. Having boarded 6,000 persons, both military and civilian, and carried them to safety in Plymouth, the ship resumed its refit.

All five "Straths" were included in the largest troop convoy to depart Britain during the war, some 23 vessels leaving Liverpool and Glasgow on 24 March 1941, to link up and proceed to Cape Town.

Both *Strathaird* and *Strathnaver* carried troops to the North African landings in November 1942, with *Strathnaver* being in the first convoy, and surviving several attacks by German bombers. *Strathaird* was in the second convoy. *Strathnaver* then spent some time in the Red Sea as a training ship for the invasion of Italy, in which it later took part. Both vessels completed the war doing general trooping duties.

Strathaird was handed back to P & O at the end of 1946, having carried 128,961 persons and covered 387,745 miles during the war. The vessel went back to the yard where it was built for refitting, which was completed in January 1948. *Strathaird* emerged with only a single, taller funnel, and accommodation for 573 first class and 496 tourist class passengers. On 22 January 1948, *Strathaird* left Tilbury bound for Bombay and Australia once again.

Strathaird in the pre-war years

Strathnaver was retained by the British Government until October 1948, by which time it had carried 128,792 persons while travelling 352,443 miles since 1939. On 5 November 1948 *Strathnaver* arrived at the Harland & Wolff shipyard in Belfast to be refitted in an identical way to its sister. *Strathnaver* was the last of the P & O liners that survived the war to return to service, making its first departure for Australia from Tilbury on 5 January 1950.

Both liners were mainly involved in the mail service from Britain to Australia, but also made occasional cruises. In June 1953, *Strathnaver* was selected to carry official guests to the Coronation Naval Review off Spithead.

In 1954, *Arcadia* and *Iberia* were delivered, so *Strathnaver* and *Strathaird* were refitted to carry 1,252 passengers in tourist class only. *Strathaird* left Tilbury in this guise for the first time on 8 April 1954, followed by *Strathnaver* on 29 July, and they operated to an independent schedule.

They were now the oldest units in the P & O fleet, not air-conditioned or fitted with stabilisers, and the bulk of their passengers from Britain were assisted migrants. *Strathaird* also began suffering engine problems, having to return to Fremantle in December 1955, being delayed in Port Said in August 1957, and delayed again in Sydney in September 1959.

In 1957 plans were drawn up for the construction of a giant new liner that would replace both *Strathaird* and *Strathnaver*, which entered service in 1961 as *Canberra*. *Strathaird* left Tilbury on its final voyage on 28 March 1961, leaving Sydney on 9 May for the homeward journey. Having been sold to shipbreakers in Hong Kong, it left Tilbury on 17 June, and on arrival in Hong Kong on 24 July was delivered for demolition.

This left *Strathnaver* to make its final voyage from Tilbury on 7 December 1961, departing Sydney on 17 January 1962 and arriving back in Tilbury on 23 February. Also sold to shipbreakers in Hong Kong, it then made the long voyage east, arriving there in April 1962.

Strathnaver departing Sydney for the last time

THE "BAYS"

MORETON BAY and ESPERANCE BAY

BUILT: 1921–22 by Vickers Ltd, Barrow
TONNAGE: 14,343 gross
DIMENSIONS: 549 x 68 ft (167.2 x 20.8 m)
SERVICE SPEED: 15 knots
PROPULSION: Geared turbines/twin screws

LARGS BAY

BUILT: 1921 by Wm Beardmore & Co. Ltd, Glasgow
TONNAGE: 14,362 gross
DIMENSIONS: 552 x 68 ft (168.3 x 20.8 m)
SERVICE SPEED: 15 knots
PROPULSION: Geared turbines/twin screws

When the Australian Government decided to become directly involved in the emigrant trade, five vessels were ordered on behalf of the Commonwealth Government Line of Steamers, from two British yards. Three came from Vickers Ltd, *Moreton Bay*, *Hobsons Bay* and *Jervis Bay*, while *Largs Bay* and *Esperance Bay* were built by Beardmores at Dalmuir. All five entered service between December 1921 and September 1922, offering rather basic accommodation for 723 passengers in one class.

In 1928 the five "Bay" vessels were sold to British shipowner, Lord Kylsant, and run as the Aberdeen & Commonwealth Line, with deep green hulls. Apart from reducing their passenger capacity to 635, the ships were not altered.

In 1931 the Kylsant empire collapsed, and in April 1933 the Aberdeen & Commonwealth Line was jointly purchased by P & O and Shaw Savill. Still maintaining their former colours, the "Bays" remained on the Australian emigrant trade. During 1936, *Esperance Bay* was transferred to Shaw Savill and renamed *Arawa*, and soon after the name of

Hobsons Bay was changed to *Esperance Bay*. The four remaining ships maintained a six-weekly schedule until September 1939, when *Jervis Bay*, *Moreton Bay*, and *Esperance Bay* were taken over and converted into armed merchant cruisers.

On 5 November 1940, *Jervis Bay* was escorting a convoy in the North Atlantic, when the German pocket battleship *Admiral Scheer* was sighted. *Jervis Bay* turned toward the enemy while the convoy scattered, but within an hour the gallant vessel had been battered to a hulk and sunk.

Largs Bay continued to operate to Australia until August 1941, then was converted into a troopship. Also during 1941, both *Moreton Bay* and *Esperance Bay* were converted into troopships, and all three served the remainder of the war in this capacity. On 2 January 1944, *Largs Bay* was damaged by a mine off Naples, and out of action for several months. All three "Bays" were released from government service during 1947, and refitted with accommodation for 514 tourist class passengers. By the end of 1948, the trio was back in service for the Aberdeen & Commonwealth Line on a two-monthly schedule.

In April 1955, *Esperance Bay* left London on its final voyage to Australia. Sold to Shipbreaking Industries, it arrived at their Faslane yard on 6 July 1955. The service continued with two ships for 18 months, then on 30 November 1956, *Moreton Bay* left London on its final voyage. Returning to Britain three months later, *Moreton Bay* was sold to T W Ward of Barrow, arriving there on 13 April 1957.

At that time *Largs Bay* was on its final voyage, having left London on 11 January 1957. Departing Sydney on 27 April and Melbourne three days later, *Largs Bay* was also sold to T W Ward on its arrival back in Britain, and arrived at their Barrow scrap-yard on 22 August 1957.

Esperance Bay

SITMAR VICTORY SHIPS

BUILT: Castelbianco 1945 by Bethlehem Fairfield Shipyard,
  Baltimore.
  Castelverde 1945 by California SB Corp,
  Los Angeles
TONNAGE: 7,604 gross
DIMENSIONS: 455 x 62 ft (138.7 x 18.9 m)
SERVICE SPEED: 15 knots
PROPULSION: Geared turbines / single screw

These two ships had been built as *Wooster Victory* and *Vassar Victory,* and both were among the 97 "Victory" ships completed as troopships, with multi-tiered bunks for 1,597 men.

Construction of *Wooster Victory* began on 9 February 1945, and it was launched on 2 April 1945. Its first voyage was across the Pacific to Melbourne, arriving on 29 May. *Vassar Victory* was launched on 3 May 1945, and left New York on 20 September on its first voyage, to France. *Wooster Victory* was laid up on 2 May 1946, while *Vassar Victory* was laid up on 4 April 1947.

Soon after both vessels were bought by Alexandre Vlasov, with *Wooster Victory* being allocated to one of his many companies, Cia Argentina de Nav de Ultramar, registered in Panama. *Vassar Victory* was assigned to another Vlasov company, Sitmar, and renamed *Castelbianco.*

The first voyage to Australia by one of these ships was that of *Castelbianco,* operating as a cargo ship, which departed the Italian port of Ancona on 16 August 1947. After a long voyage, *Castelbianco* arrived in Sydney on 23 April 1948. After loading cargo, *Castelbianco* left Sydney on 18 June, returning to Genoa on 14 October.

Meanwhile, *Wooster Victory* had been refitted at Baltimore, the troop quarters being upgraded to accommodate 900 displaced persons in segregated areas. A single deck of superstructure was added, and four sets of double-banked lifeboats installed.

Wooster Victory departed Genoa on 6 August 1948, carrying 883 passengers, being the sixth ship to carry displaced persons to Australia, and the first Sitmar voyage to carry passengers. *Wooster Victory* arrived in Sydney on 6 September, then returned empty to Europe.

Wooster Victory returned to Genoa, from where it departed on 18 October 1948 for Melbourne, carrying 893 passengers, arriving on 16 November. The vessel was then sent to Shanghai, where refugees were embarked and taken to South Africa.

Meanwhile, *Castelbianco* had also been refitted, and on 19 October left Genoa on its second voyage to Australia, this time carrying 879 passengers, arriving in Sydney on 19 November. *Castelbianco* also went to Shanghai to collect refugees, who were carried back to Europe. Both ships had black hulls at this time, and made trips to Australia on a regular basis over the next two years.

During 1950, *Wooster Victory* was extensively refitted. When the refit was completed in May 1950, the vessel was renamed *Castelverde,* and placed on a regular service from Italy to South America. In September 1950 it was transferred to Sitmar ownership. It was also at this time that the hulls of both vessels were repainted white.

On 1 February 1950, *Castelbianco* departed Naples with 885 passengers, arriving in Sydney on 2 March. On its next voyage, *Castelbianco* left from Bremerhaven on 18 April, again with 885 passengers on board, who were taken to Newcastle, arriving there on 24 May.

Castelbianco was then refitted to provide accommodation for 1,132 passengers, most in dormitories. On 4 September the vessel departed Bremerhaven for Australia, arriving in Melbourne on 30 September. *Castelbianco* made one further voyage during the year, carrying 1,101 passengers from Naples to Melbourne, arriving on 15 December.

Castelbianco made three trips to Australia during 1951, all to Melbourne. The first departed Bremerhaven on 8 February, and carried 1,019 passengers, arriving on 13 March. On the return trip the vessel called at Djarkarta to board Dutch nationals and carry them back to Europe.

Castelbianco then left Naples on 15 June, with only 703 passengers, arriving in Melbourne on 17 July. It was not until November that *Castelbianco* left Bremerhaven on its next trip to Melbourne, arriving on 27 December.

During 1952 *Castelbianco* made three more trips to Australia, arriving in Melbourne on 4 April and 3 June, and in Sydney on 31 July, but after this voyage the vessel went to the Monfalcone shipyard of Cant Riuniti dell'Adriatico for a major reconstruction. An entirely new superstructure was added, the original masts and funnel replaced, and accommodation installed for 1,200 tourist class passengers. The tonnage was increased to 10,139 gross, and prior to resuming service in 1953, the name was amended to *Castel Bianco,* and it began operating from Genoa to Central America.

Castelverde was then sent to the same shipyard, but its rebuilding was not as extensive. It was given only one deck of superstructure, which increased the tonnage to 9,008 gross, and accommodation for 800 tourist class passengers. Its name was amended to *Castel Verde,* and the vessel returned to service with a departure from Bremerhaven on 10 June 1953, carrying 964 migrants to Australia.

Castelbianco after 1950, arriving in Sydney, with a white hull

Castel Verde after being rebuilt in 1953.

Castel Verde made a further three voyages to Australia between March and October 1954, arriving in Melbourne from Bremerhaven on 11 April and 9 June, then leaving Naples on 14 September and reaching Sydney on 14 October, on its final trip to Australia.

From 1955 both ships were mainly used on the service from Italian ports to Central and South America. *Castel Bianco* also made some Atlantic voyages, two in September 1953 from Bremen to Quebec, and one in December 1956 from Bremen and Southampton to St John. Just prior to this voyage, *Castel Bianco* had made its final trip to Australia, leaving Genoa in October, arriving in Sydney on 15 November.

In 1957 *Castel Bianco* and *Castel Verde* were offered for sale. They were purchased by Cia Transatlantica Española, otherwise known as the Spanish Line. *Castel Bianco* was renamed *Begona*, while *Castel Verde* became *Montserrat*. The only external change was repainting the funnel black.

Begona was immediately dispatched on a voyage to Australia in May 1957, arriving in Sydney on 20 June, and returning to Genoa on 19 July. In mid-August 1957 *Begona* departed Trieste on its second voyage to Australia, arriving in Melbourne on 23 September, then berthing in Sydney on the morning of 27 September, departing the same evening for Genoa.

Begona was then refitted to carry 830 tourist class passengers, while *Montserrat* was altered to carry 708 tourist class passengers. In May 1958, *Begona* inaugurated a service from Southampton and Spanish ports to the West Indies and Venezuela, being joined by *Montserrat* in August.

On 6 May 1959, *Montserrat* departed Naples bound for Australia, carrying 844 migrants, including 169 Spanish men, all bachelors, who comprised the first organised group of Spanish migrants to come to Australia. The ship was delayed 14 days in Colombo with engine trouble, and when it arrived in Fremantle on 29 June, local inspectors found the lifesaving gear to be faulty, in particular several lifeboats, which had holes in them. Refused permission to sail further, all the passengers were off-loaded and forced to find their own way to their destinations. *Montserrat* remained in Fremantle until it passed inspection, and on 8 July left for Spain.

For the next 10 years, *Begona* and *Montserrat* remained on the Venezuela service, then on 11 August 1970, *Montserrat* broke down in mid-Atlantic, with 660 persons on board. *Begona* was nearby, and rescued all the passengers from *Montserrat*. Four days later a tug arrived, and towed the vessel to port. After repairs, *Montserrat* returned to service until February 1973, when it was sold to Spanish shipbreakers.

Begona also suffered a mid-Atlantic breakdown, on 10 October 1974, when it had 800 passengers on board. After several days adrift *Begona* was towed to Bridgetown in Barbados on 17 October. It was decided the engines were not worth repairing, so *Begona* was towed back to Spain, arriving at Castellon on 24 December 1974, having been sold to shipbreakers there.

Castel Bianco after rebuilding in 1953.

TOSCANA

BUILT: 1923 by AG Weser, Bremen
TONNAGE: 9,584 gross
DIMENSIONS: 480 x 62 ft (146.3 x 18.9 m)
SERVICE SPEED: 13 knots
PROPULSION: Triple expansion/twin screws

Toscana was a most unusual looking vessel, having a corrugated hull and a bulbous sponson down each side. These were intended to reduce the rolling of the ship, and were quite unsightly.

This vessel had been built for North German Lloyd as the *Saarbrucken*, with accommodation for 98 first and 142 second class passengers. It operated from Bremen to the Far East until 1935, then was purchased by the Italian Government, and renamed *Toscana*. Initially allocated to Italia Line for their South American service, it was transferred to Lloyd Triestino in 1937.

Fitted out with austere accommodation for up to 2,000 passengers, it was used on the service from Italy to East and South Africa, at this time having a thin, upright funnel and white hull. When Italy came into the war, *Toscana* was converted into a hospital ship, and was one of the few Italian flag vessels to survive the conflict. Initially taken over by the Allies, it was handed back to Italy in 1947, and restored to Lloyd Triestino.

The vessel was refitted with accommodation for 136 saloon class passengers in 2- and 4-berth cabins, and 690 third class passengers in 6-berth cabins and dormitories. It was also given a much larger funnel and the hull was painted black. *Toscana* returned to commercial service with several voyages to South Africa.

On 19 October 1948 *Toscana* departed Genoa on the first post-war voyage by a Lloyd Triestino vessel to Australia, going first to Melbourne, where it berthed on 30 November, then arriving in Sydney on 2 December. In 1949 *Toscana* was joined by *Sebastiano Caboto* and *Ugolino Vivaldi*, and this trio maintained the Lloyd Triestino service to Australia for the next two years.

During 1951 the new liners *Australia*, *Neptunia* and *Oceania* entered service, so *Toscana* was altered to carry 819 third class only. Outbound the vessel carried migrants to Australia, returning with the six holds filled with cargo. In this way the old vessel was able to maintain its place on the Australian trade for a further 10 years.

On 3 June 1952, *Toscana* lost both anchors in heavy weather off Portsea, while waiting for the seas to moderate so it could enter Port Phillip Bay, and had to remain in Melbourne until new anchors were fitted. A more serious accident was a collision on 7 March 1953 with the US Navy oiler *Cowanesque* in Suez Roads, in which one passenger on *Toscana* was killed. On 7 May 1956, the lifesaving gear was found to be faulty during an inspection in Australia, and the owner was fined.

During 1960 *Toscana* was withdrawn and laid up, then sold to a Genoa shipbreaking firm, arriving at their yard on 21 February 1962.

KOMNINOS

BUILT: 1911 by John Brown & Co, Clydebank
TONNAGE: 931 gross
DIMENSIONS: 254 x 31 ft (78.1 x 9.5 m)
SERVICE SPEED: 12 knots
PROPULSION: Triple expansion/twin screws

Quite a smart looking little vessel, *Komninos* was not really suited for a long voyage to Australia, having been designed and built as the luxury private yacht *Jeanette* for a British millionaire.

In 1910, the John Brown shipyard completed a private yacht named *Doris* for Solomon B Joel, and Sir Harry Livesay was so impressed by the vessel that he tried to have John Brown build him a copy, but without reference to the designers, G L Watson & Co. John Brown refused, so Livesay went to Watson's, and they designed a vessel in which minor changes from *Doris* were incorporated.

Sir Harry Livesay owned *Jeanette* from 1911 to 1936, when it was sold to William Lancaster, but in 1938 he sold the vessel to John Gretton. Within three months of the war starting in 1939, *Jeanette* had been taken over by the British Admiralty, and converted into an anti-submarine vessel. Renamed *St Modwen*, pennant No FYO25, it was fitted out with depth charges, and later also carried one or two small guns. The vessel was returned to its owner in 1945, and once again named *Jeanette*, but in 1946 was offered for sale.

Purchased by Cia de Nav Dio Adelphi SA, registered in Panama, the vessel was renamed *Komninos*, and was listed in Lloyds Register as a cargo ship. A number of changes were made, the most noticeable being the removal of the original clipper bow, which was replaced by a straight stem. The accommodation must have been greatly enlarged, for when *Komninos* left Marseilles bound for Australia in March 1948, there were 217 migrants aboard, consisting of 132 Greeks, 29 Palestinians, and smaller numbers of Lebanese, Poles, Italians and Britons.

Komninos arrived in Fremantle on 20 April, and a delegation of passengers complained that the ship had been horribly overcrowded, the meals monotonous, and conditions on board generally dirty. Some bed linen had not been changed throughout the voyage, and water had been rationed on the longer sectors between ports. It was also claimed that only seven lavatories were provided, of which two were unusable, while only one of the two shower baths had been in service. The only public room for passengers was a smoke room, but this could seat only 25 persons. There were three dining rooms, which were also used by the stewards to sleep in as they had no other quarters provided for them. For exercise, there was only a single narrow promenade deck.

This story was given considerable prominence in the Perth newspapers, and the British passengers also complained about the lack of personal hygiene practised by some of the others on board. Two days later, a letter was published, signed by a group of Italian passengers, refuting some of the earlier claims. They said that the captain had done all he could to make the voyage tolerable, the meals had been plain, but food was plentiful, and in fact some 20 lavatories and 10 shower baths had been available. *Komninos* remained four days in Fremantle, departing on 24 April bound for Batavia.

Later in 1948, *Komninos* was sold to an Israeli company, Ships and Vessels Ltd, and renamed *Eilath*. In 1950 it was laid up in Haifa, where it was reported on 27 December 1950 that the vessel was being broken up.

SKAUGUM

BUILT: 1949 by Germaniawerft, Kiel
TONNAGE: 11,626 gross
DIMENSIONS: 552 x 66 ft (168.1 x 20.2 m)
SERVICE SPEED: 15 knots
PROPULSION: Diesel electric/twin screws

When Hamburg-America Line ordered a pair of large cargo ships, the first was completed in 1938 as *Steiermark*. When war broke out she was converted into the commerce raider *Kormoran*, which encountered HMAS *Sydney* off the coast of Western Australia on 19 November 1941. In the ensuing battle, both ships were sunk.

The second ship was launched on 17 January 1940, and named *Ostmark*, but it was laid up in an incomplete state for the duration of the war. The British claimed *Ostmark* as a prize of war, and it was placed under the control of the Ministry of Transport, but remained idle in Kiel.

In 1948, the Ministry of Transport sold *Ostmark* to the Norwegian shipowner, Isak M Skaugen, who obtained an 18- month contract from the International Refugee Organisation to transport displaced persons and decided to have *Ostmark* completed as a passenger carrier. The work was done in Kiel by the Howaldtswerke yard, where an extra deck was built along the full length of the hull, and austere quarters for up to 1,700 persons installed in the holds, consisting of large dormitories, with toilet and washing blocks, and extra lifeboats fitted along each side.

When the work was completed, in April 1949, the vessel was renamed *Skaugum*, and nine years after being launched made its maiden voyage. *Skaugum* departed Naples on 1 May 1949 on a voyage to Melbourne, arriving on 30 May, followed by a second voyage from Naples on 4 July, also to Melbourne, and a third voyage, with 1,792 passengers, which terminated in Sydney on 28 September. In November *Skaugum* left Naples again, with 1,707 persons on board, who all disembarked at Newcastle on 29 November.

In December 1949, *Skaugum* was crossing the Indian Ocean returning to Europe empty, when another IRO ship, *Anna Salen*, developed engine trouble while outward bound with 1,570 persons on board. *Anna Salen* returned to Aden, and *Skaugum* also went there to take on board the passengers from *Anna Salen* and carry them to Fremantle.

During 1950 *Skaugum* made four voyages to Australia, each time carrying over 1,800 passengers, the first from Naples, arriving in Melbourne on 27 March, and on her return trip called at Tandjung Priok to board Dutch nationals returning to Holland. The second voyage was from Bremerhaven in June to Fremantle only, arriving on 18 July with 1,854 persons on board. The third voyage, in August, was also from Bremerhaven to Fremantle, and when she departed on 29 September, again went to Indonesia to collect more Dutch evacuees. The fourth voyage for the year was from Naples in November to Melbourne, arriving on 10 December.

Skaugum continued to operate from Naples and Bremerhaven when the IRO contract ended, carrying migrants to Australia until 1957. Returning to the Howaldtswerke shipyard at Kiel, *Skaugum* was rebuilt as a cargo ship, and also given new diesel engines. For the next seven years she operated in this capacity for I M Skaugen, then in 1964 was sold to Ocean Shipping & Enterprises, and renamed *Ocean Builder* under the Liberian flag.

Under her new name the vessel continued to operate as a tramp cargo ship, and in May 1970 returned to Australian waters again for a brief visit. This was her last time in these waters, as on 25 August 1972 she arrived in Kaohsiung, having been sold to a shipbreaking firm there.

DOMINION MONARCH

BUILT: 1939 by Swan, Hunter & Wigham
  Richardson Ltd, Newcastle
TONNAGE: 26,463 gross
DIMENSIONS: 682 x 84 ft (207.8 x 25.8 m)
SERVICE SPEED: 19 knots
PROPULSION: Doxford diesels/quadruple screws

Dominion Monarch was designed for Shaw Savill Line as much as a cargo carrier as a passenger liner, with six holds and accommodation for 517 passengers, all first class. Launched on 27 July 1938, *Dominion Monarch* went first to London to load cargo, departing on its maiden voyage on 16 February 1939, embarking passengers at Southampton next day. The liner went to Cape Town and Durban before arriving in Fremantle on 13 March. Following visits to Melbourne and Sydney, it continued to New Zealand ports, then followed the reverse route back to Britain.

Dominion Monarch was in Lyttelton when war broke out on 3 September, but voyaged back to England around South Africa as usual. *Dominion Monarch* remained in commercial operation to Australia and New Zealand until August 1940, then was requisitioned and sent to Liverpool for conversion into a troopship.

In December 1941, *Dominion Monarch* arrived in Singapore, and was put into drydock to have the engines dismantled for overhaul. When it became clear that Singapore was about to be captured by the Japanese, the ship's own engineers were able to rebuild the engines in a few days, and the ship escaped just before the island fell. Subsequently *Dominion Monarch* had a very hectic war career. By the time the war ended, *Dominion Monarch* had carried over 90,000 troops and 70,000 tons of cargo while travelling some 350,000 miles.

After the war ended, *Dominion Monarch* made several voyages repatriating troops to Australia and New Zealand, then in July 1947 was handed back to its owners, and was given an extensive refit, in which the accommodation was rebuilt for 508 first class passengers. *Dominion Monarch* left London on 17 December 1948, on its first post-war commercial voyage to Australia and New Zealand.

Dominion Monarch carried fare-paying passengers and assisted migrants to both Australia and New Zealand, but relied heavily on cargo to make its operation financially viable. Due to frequent waterfront strikes in both Australia and New Zealand, the schedule was often disrupted, which was unpopular with passengers. In 1955 Shaw Savill introduced *Southern Cross*, which carried no cargo, and such was its success a second ship was ordered, to replace *Dominion Monarch*.

Dominion Monarch departed London on 30 December 1961 on its final voyage, departing Wellington on 15 March 1962 to return to Britain. By the time the liner reached London, it had been sold to the Mitsui Group of Japan. They chartered *Dominion Monarch* to an American consortium for service as a floating hotel in Seattle during the World Fair from June to November 1962.

When the charter ended, the liner was renamed *Dominion Monarch Maru* for the voyage from Seattle to Osaka, where it arrived on 25 November 1962, at the Mitsui shipbreaking yard.

ORCADES

BUILT: 1948 by Vickers-Armstrong Ltd, Barrow
TONNAGE: 28,164 gross
DIMENSIONS: 709 x 60 ft (216 x 27.6 m)
SERVICE SPEED: 22 knots
PROPULSION: Geared turbines/twin screws

The first brand-new liner to arrive in Australia after the war was *Orcades*, built for the Orient Line to replace a liner of the same name sunk during the war. Launched on 14 October 1947, *Orcades* achieved 24.74 knots on trials. Accommodation was provided for 773 first class and 772 tourist class passengers.

The liner departed Tilbury on 14 December 1948 on its maiden voyage, arriving in Fremantle on 6 January 1949, then going on to Melbourne and Sydney, where it berthed on 13 January. For the first six years of its career, *Orcades* plied only between Britain and Australia through the Suez Canal. On the outbound voyage most of the tourist class accommodation was allocated to assisted migrants.

On 7 May 1952 *Orcades* grounded in Port Phillip Bay while leaving Melbourne in strong winds, but was pulled free later the same day. On 17 December 1954, *Orcades* left Sydney on its first voyage across the Pacific, arriving in San Francisco on 6 January 1955, then returning to Sydney. On 22 August 1955, *Orcades* left Southampton on its first voyage to Australia through the Panama Canal.

During November 1956, *Orcades* spent two weeks berthed in Melbourne, serving as a floating hotel during the Olympic Games.

Early in 1959, *Orcades* was given an extensive refit by Harland & Wolff at Belfast, during which air-conditioning was installed and a new swimming pool constructed for first class, the old one being allocated to tourist class.

Following the integration of the fleets of Orient Line and P & O in 1960, *Orcades* retained the corn coloured hull until 1964, when it was repainted white during a refit. The accommodation was altered for 1,635 passengers in one class at the same time. *Orcades* made its first voyage in this configuration from Tilbury in May 1964, but in subsequent years was used more for cruising than line voyages.

On 17 April 1972, *Orcades* was in Hong Kong on a cruise from Sydney when fire damaged the boiler room. Replacement parts were removed from *Iberia*, which was laid up in Southampton, and flown to Hong Kong to be installed in *Orcades*.

The liner was now at the end of its career, as on 3 June 1972 it left Sydney for the last time, bound for Britain. *Orcades* made a short series of cruises from Southampton, the last returning on 13 October, following which the vessel was laid up.

In January 1973, *Orcades* left Southampton bound for Taiwan, arriving in Kaohsiung on 6 February 1973 and being handed over to ship-breakers there. On 15 March 1973, work began on scrapping the liner.

MOOLTAN and MALOJA

BUILT: 1923 by Harland & Wolff Ltd, Belfast
TONNAGE: 21,039 gross
DIMENSIONS: 625 x 73 ft (190.5 x 22.3 m)
SERVICE SPEED: 17 knots
PROPULSION: Quadruple expansion/twin screws

The first P & O liners to exceed 20,000 gross tons, this pair was constructed on adjoining slipways, and spent most of their careers operating together. *Mooltan* was launched on 15 February 1923 and *Maloja* on 19 April. They were fitted out to carry 327 first class and 329 second class passengers, and looked very powerful. However, they were rather underpowered and could only manage 16 knots.

Designed for the mail service from Britain to Australia, both ships first made a return voyage to Bombay, *Mooltan* in September 1923, *Maloja* two months later. *Mooltan* made its maiden departure for Australia from Tilbury on 21 December 1923, being joined by *Maloja* on 18 January 1924.

In 1929, P & O reorganised their services, combining the Indian and Australian routes on an accelerated schedule. To attain the higher speed required, *Mooltan* and *Maloja* had exhaust turbines fitted, increasing their speed by 1 knot. This pair had originally been painted in very drab colours, black hulls and funnels and dark brown upperworks, but when the new "Strath" liners entered service with their white hulls, the upperworks of *Maloja* and *Mooltan* were repainted a light stone colour. At the same time their accommodation was altered to 346 first class and 336 tourist class.

On the day war broke out, *Maloja* was in the Red Sea, outbound to Australia. The voyage was terminated at Bombay, where the vessel was converted into an armed merchant cruiser. This included removal of the mainmast and the top half of the aft funnel. Eight 6-inch guns were also fitted, and *Maloja* was sent off to patrol the Indian Ocean. *Mooltan* was requisitioned in Britain, and converted in a similar manner, then sent to the South Atlantic. In March 1940, *Mooltan* joined the Northern Patrol, operating near the Faroe Islands.

In 1941 both vessels became troopships, later taking part in the landings in North Africa, Sicily and the Italian mainland. After the war they repatriated troops, *Mooltan* arriving in Australian waters again in August 1945. Both vessels were returned to P & O in July 1947, and refitted by Harland & Wolff, *Mooltan* in Belfast, *Maloja* in London. They were given austere accommodation for 1,030 tourist class passengers only. The aft funnel was rebuilt, but no mainmast was fitted, and they were repainted in their pre-war colours.

Relying heavily on assisted migrants to fill the ships, *Maloja* left Tilbury on 10 June 1948, followed by *Mooltan* on 26 August. They sailed independently of the mail ships, calling at Aden and Colombo en route to Fremantle and other major Australian ports. On the return trip, fare-paying passengers were carried. For some time these ships regularly called at Bombay, to collect British officials and their families returning home.

On 30 September 1953, *Mooltan* left Tilbury on its final voyage to Australia, departing Sydney on 24 November and Melbourne four days later to return to London on 7 January 1954. *Maloja* made its final departure on 5 November 1953, leaving Sydney on 2 January 1954. After a few days in Melbourne, the vessel sailed on 9 January for Adelaide and then Fremantle, departing on 16 January to reach Tilbury on 18 March.

Both liners had completed 80 round trips in peacetime to Australia. They were sold to British Iron and Steel for scrapping, *Mooltan* at Faslane and *Maloja* at Inverkeithing.

Maloja

NAPOLI

BUILT: 1940 by Harland & Wolff Ltd, Belfast
TONNAGE: 8,082 gross
DIMENSIONS: 451 x 57 ft (137.5 x 17.3 m)
SERVICE SPEED: 14 knots
PROPULSION: Diesel/single screw

Flotta Lauro was founded in Naples during 1923 by Achille Lauro, but most of his ships were lost in World War 2. Among the ships bought by Achille Lauro to rebuild his fleet was the hulk of the *Araybank*.

Araybank was the first of a series of cargo ships built for the Bank Line. Launched on 6 June 1940, it was immediately requisitioned by the British Government, and completed as a supply ship during October 1940. *Araybank* carried a contingent of Australian and New Zealand troops from Britain to Greece on its maiden voyage, then was used to transport provisions from Alexandria to Greece.

While lying in Suda Bay in Crete on 3 May 1941, *Araybank* was severely damaged during an attack by German aircraft, and had to be run aground to prevent it sinking. It was hoped that the vessel could be repaired, but on 16 May the Luftwaffe mounted a series of attacks on Allied shipping as the Germans invaded the island of Crete, and *Araybank* was abandoned by its crew, ablaze and sinking in shallow water.

During 1944, the Germans salvaged the wreck, and towed it to Trieste for rebuilding. Seized by the British in 1945, the ship was not wanted back by the Bank Line, and was bought by Achille Lauro.

Renamed *Napoli*, it was taken to Genoa in 1946 for rebuilding as an emigrant ship to carry 656 persons, 176 in cabins and 480 in dormitories. The accommodation was quite austere, and the ship still resembled a freighter on completion of the rebuilding in August 1948.

Napoli departed Marseilles on its maiden voyage on 15 September 1948, bound for Australia, reaching Melbourne on 21 October and berthing in Sydney four days later. It did not embark any passengers in Australia for the return trip, but instead proceeded to Java to take on board Dutch nationals wishing to return home, and also visited Singapore on the way back to Europe. Subsequent voyages by *Napoli* to Australia were from Genoa and Naples, and initially no passengers were carried on the return voyage.

Napoli made a total of 15 round trips to Australia, on a schedule of four voyages per year, up to 1951, when Flotta Lauro introduced two new ships to the Australian trade, *Roma* and *Sydney*. *Napoli* was transferred to a route from Italy to ports in South America. This trade also relied heavily on emigrants, for which there was considerable competition between several Italian companies.

Towards the end of 1952, *Napoli* was withdrawn from the South American trade. The passenger accommodation was then removed, and the ship resumed service as a cargo carrier only. In this guise, *Napoli* served in the Flotta Lauro fleet for almost 20 years. In April 1971 the vessel was withdrawn from service, and sold to shipbreakers at La Spezia.

RANCHI

BUILT: 1925 by Hawthorn Leslie & Co, Newcastle
TONNAGE: 16,974 gross
DIMENSIONS: 570 x 71 ft (173.7 x 21.7 m)
SERVICE SPEED: 17 knots
PROPULSION: Quadruple expansion/twin screw

Ranchi was the second completed of four two-funnelled sister ships delivered to P & O during 1925 for their service to India, the others being *Ranpura*, *Rawalpindi* and *Rajputana*. Launched on 24 January 1925, *Ranchi* made its maiden voyage in August the same year. The vessel could carry 308 first and 282 second class passengers, and remained on the Indian trade until October 1939, then was requisitioned at Bombay.

Converted into an armed merchant cruiser, with the aft funnel removed, *Ranchi* served in this capacity until late 1942, then was refitted in Southampton as a troopship, entering service in this capacity in March 1943.

Ranchi was in a Mediterranean convoy in November 1944 when it was attacked by German bombers. One bomb aimed at *Ranchi* was deflected by a wire over the forecastle head, and passed through the side of the ship without exploding. Had it not been deflected, the bomb would have struck the bridge and caused extensive damage.

As a troopship, *Ranchi* steamed 85,977 miles, and carried 54,711 personnel. After the war ended, the vessel was used to repatriate troops and released prisoners-of-war. *Ranchi* was the only one of the four sister ships to be handed back to P & O, in July 1947. *Rawalpindi* was sunk on 23 November 1939 by

the German battleships *Scharnhorst* and *Gneisenau* when serving as an armed merchant cruiser, while *Rajputana* was torpedoed and sunk by a German submarine on 13 April 1941. *Ranpura* was sold to the British Admiralty in 1942, and converted into a repair ship, surviving in this role until 1961.

Being a lone ship, and over 20 years old, *Ranchi* was considered not worth refitting for regular commercial service again. P & O accepted an offer from the British Ministry of Transport to charter *Ranchi* as an emigrant ship to Australia. Refitted by Harland & Wolff in Belfast, with accommodation for 940 persons in 8-, 10- and 12-berth cabins, the ship was repainted in the P & O pre-war colours, black hull and funnel with stone upperworks.

On 17 June 1948, *Ranchi* left London on its first voyage to Australia, being in Fremantle on 17 July, Melbourne on 22 July, and reaching Sydney on 27 July. Returning to Britain, *Ranchi* carried a limited number of fare-paying passengers. On several occasions in 1950 and 1951, *Ranchi* left Sydney empty, and in Indonesian ports boarded Dutch nationals returning home.

The four-year charter ended during 1952, and the ship also suffered some damage during a boiler fire off the Cocos Islands on 7 March that year. When the migrant charter was not renewed, P & O decided to dispose of *Ranchi*.

On 6 October 1952 *Ranchi* left London on its final voyage, departing Sydney on 3 November. On returning to London, the vessel was immediately sold to shipbreakers, and arrived at their yard in Newport, Monmouthshire, during January 1953.

SVALBARD

BUILT: 1938 by Bremer Vulkan, Vegesack
TONNAGE: 6,789 gross
DIMENSIONS: 438 x 58 ft (133.8 x 18 m)
SERVICE SPEED: 15 knots
PROPULSION: Diesel/single screw

This vessel was the second of two ships ordered by a German company, the Woermann Line, being named *Togo* when launched on 13 August 1938, and delivered on 22 September. A cargo ship with cabins for 12 passengers only, *Togo* operated from Hamburg to West Africa, with its sister ship, *Kamerun*, which is covered on the next page as *Goya*.

Togo was at sea when the war began, but in November 1939 managed to elude the British blockade and return to Germany. It was taken over by the German Navy in March 1940, and in August that year began serving as a minelayer.

In 1941 *Togo* went to the Wilton Fijenoord shipyard in occupied Holland to be fitted out as a commerce raider. The work was completed at the Oder Werke shipyard in Stettin, the vessel being armed with six 5.9-inch guns, four torpedo tubes and three seaplanes. Accommodation was installed for 16 officers and 331 crew. In December 1942 the ship was renamed *Coronel*, otherwise known as *Schiff 14*, its raider number.

Hoping to break out into the Atlantic through the English Channel, in early February 1943 *Coronel* began its dangerous voyage, but on 13 February was attacked and damaged by Allied aircraft off Gravelines, and had to put in to Boulogne the next day. After further air attacks there, the break-out attempt was abandoned, and on 2 March *Coronel* returned to Kiel. Renamed *Togo* again, the vessel was altered for duty as a night fighter direction ship, and served in this capacity in Baltic waters until the end of the war.

In August 1945 *Togo* was seized by the British as a war prize, but in 1946 was handed over to the Norwegian Government, renamed *Svalbard*, and converted to carry 900 displaced persons.

On 26 May 1948, *Svalbard* left Southampton for Australia, going only to Melbourne where it berthed on 29 June. *Svalbard* then obtained an IRO charter to transport displaced persons, and on 20 September 1948 left Bremerhaven on its first voyage in this capacity, arriving in Fremantle on 23 October, then proceeding directly to Sydney where it berthed on 29 October. The vessel returned empty to Genoa, from where it sailed again on 11 December, arriving in Sydney on 15 January 1949. During 1949 *Svalbard* made a further three voyages to Australia from Italian ports, being in Melbourne on 20 April, 27 June and finally on 8 October.

Following this voyage, *Svalbard* passed into the Norwegian Navy until 1954, then was sold to A/S Tilthorn and renamed *Tilthorn*, though this was soon changed to *Stella Marina*. In an unusual occurrence, in 1956 the vessel was sold to Deutsche-Afrika Linien, renamed *Togo*, and with most of the accommodation removed, returned to the route for which it was built.

Togo remained under the German flag again for 12 years, then in 1968 was sold to Taboga Enterprises Inc, and renamed *Lacasielle* under the Panamanian flag. This phase of its career lasted eight years, then in 1976 the vessel changed hands for the last time, going to Caribbean Real Estate SA, also a Panamanian concern, and being renamed *Topeka*. It operated along the South American coast for Linea Argomar of Columbia, but on a voyage from Tampico to Barranquilla, ran aground off Coatzacoalcos on 24 November 1984 when the anchors dragged in a storm, and became a total loss.

GOYA

BUILT: 1939 by Bremer Vulkan, Vegesack
TONNAGE: 6,996 gross
DIMENSIONS: 438 x 58 ft (133.8 x 18 m)
SERVICE SPEED: 15 knots
PROPULSION: Diesel/single screw

This vessel was the first of a pair of ships ordered by a German company, the Woermann Line, being named *Kamerun* when launched on 17 May 1938, and delivered on 28 June. With accommodation for only twelve passengers, it operated a cargo service from Hamburg to West Africa with its sister ship *Togo*, which is covered on the previous page as *Svalbard*.

When war broke out in September 1939, *Kamerun* was in Hamburg, and on 13 November 1939 was taken over by the German Navy for conversion into a repair ship, in which capacity it served throughout the war. In May 1945 *Kamerun* was ceded to the Norwegian Government as war reparations, and in 1947 the vessel was allocated to a Norwegian company, A/S J Ludwig Mowinckels Rederi, and renamed *Goya*, being fitted out initially as a cargo ship.

During 1949, Mowinckels obtained a contract from the IRO to transport displaced persons from Europe to Australia and other countries. At that time the company did not have any passenger-carrying vessels in their fleet, so they decided to convert *Goya*. It was fitted out with basic quarters for about 900 persons in segregated dormitories constructed in the cargo holds.

In March 1949, *Goya* left Genoa on its first voyage to Australia, carrying 907 passengers to Adelaide, arriving there on 2 May. This was followed by four voyages from Naples to Australia, the first terminating at Fremantle on 22 June. The next voyage took *Goya* to Sydney for the first time, arriving on 19 August, followed by a voyage to Melbourne, berthing there on 26 December.

The first voyage by *Goya* in 1950 departed Naples on 23 January, arriving in Melbourne on 28 February. Then on 17 April 1950, *Goya* left Bremerhaven for the first time bound for Australia, arriving in Melbourne on 26 May. On the return voyage the vessel stopped in Indonesia to board Dutch refugees. *Goya* made two further trips to Australia from Bremerhaven in 1950, the first departing on 17 July and arriving in Newcastle on 16 August, the second carrying 924 passengers and terminating in Melbourne on 7 November.

In March 1951, *Goya* left Piraeus on a voyage to Wellington. It made two more trips to New Zealand, but only carried 505 passengers on the last one. On 8 December 1951, *Goya* arrived in Melbourne again, but only had 446 passengers on board. This was the final voyage by *Goya* as a migrant ship.

In 1953 *Goya* reverted to being a cargo ship again. In 1961 it was sold to T J Skogland and renamed *Reina*, but the following year was sold again, to T Matiand Jr, and renamed *Svanholm*. In 1963 the vessel changed hands again, being renamed *Hilde* when bought by Skibs A/S Hilde.

In 1964 the vessel finally left the Norwegian flag when sold to Meldaf Shipping Co of Greece, being given its final name, *Melina*. It served under this name for five years, then was sold to shipbreakers in Taiwan in 1969, arriving in Kaohsiung on 19 July for demolition.

DERNA - ASSIMINA

BUILT: 1917 by Bremer Vulkan, Vegesack
TONNAGE: 5,751 gross
DIMENSIONS: 436 x 56 ft (132.9 x 17.1 m)
SERVICE SPEED: 11 knots
PROPULSION: Triple expansion/single screw

This vessel made two voyages to Australia, the first as *Derna* in 1948, the second as *Assimina* in 1951. Designed as a cargo ship, with accommodation for nine passengers, it was ordered in 1914, just prior to the outbreak of war, by Deutsche Ost Afrika Linie for their service from Germany to East Africa. Launched on 27 July 1915 and named *Kagera*, it was completed on 17 November 1917.

On 30 March 1919 *Kagera* was seized as a prize of war, and allocated to France. Initially operated by the French Government, the vessel was purchased from them in 1922 by Cie Generale Transatlantique, better known as the French Line. Renamed *Indiana*, it was placed on a cargo service from French ports to various destinations in the Gulf of Mexico, and remained in this trade for almost 20 years.

At the time of the fall of France in 1940, *Indiana* was in American waters, being seized by the United States, and laid up. In 1942 it was taken over by the United States War Shipping Administration, and used as a transport.

In 1945, *Indiana* was handed back to the French Line, and retained by them for the next three years. In 1948, *Indiana* was sold to Dos Oceanos Cia de Nav, a Panamanian registered concern, and renamed *Derna*. It was at this time that the vessel was converted to carry displaced persons, with rather austere temporary facilities being installed in the holds.

On 30 August 1948, *Derna* departed Marseilles bound for Australia, berthing in Melbourne on 5 November. The vessel remained in the port for six weeks, loading cargo for the return trip, then sailed on 16 December bound for Le Havre.

During 1949 the vessel was renamed *Assimina* by its owner, but did not make a voyage to Australia under that name for almost two years. Departing Genoa on 29 December 1950, *Assimina* arrived in Fremantle on 5 February 1951, then proceeded to Melbourne, berthing on 13 February, and finally arrived in Sydney on 19 February.

After another lengthy stay in port loading cargo, *Assimina* left Sydney on 7 March, returning to Genoa. The vessel was scheduled to make another voyage to Australia, departing Genoa in May 1951, but this did not eventuate.

Late in 1952, *Assimina* was sold to Hughes Bolckow Ltd, and arrived at their shipbreaking yard in Blyth, England, on 12 December 1952.

Assimina

CHARLTON SOVEREIGN

BUILT: 1930 by Cammell Laird & Co Ltd, Birkenhead
TONNAGE: 5,516 gross
DIMENSIONS: 366 x 57 ft (110.5 x 17.3 m)
SERVICE SPEED: 20 knots
PROPULSION: Geared turbines/twin screws

Charlton Sovereign made a single voyage to Australia with migrants. The appearance of this vessel on arrival in local waters was very different from its original design, having been the last completed of a trio of three-funnelled ferries built for Canadian National Railways. Its original name was *Prince Robert*, the other two being *Prince Henry* and *Prince David*, and they were designed for the highly competitive service between Seattle and Vancouver. Accommodation was provided for 334 first class and 70 third class passengers.

Despite all this, they failed dismally in competition with the vessels of Canadian Pacific on the same route, so in 1931 *Prince Henry* and *Prince David* were transferred to the east coast of Canada, while *Prince Robert* was laid up until the summer of 1935, when it began a summer cruise service from Vancouver to Alaska. *Prince Robert* was taken over by the Royal Canadian Navy on 26 November 1939, and rebuilt as an armed merchant cruiser. Two decks of superstructure were removed and the two forward funnels trunked into one.

On 5 February 1940, *Prince Robert* was bought by the Royal Canadian Navy, and initially served in the Pacific. In 1943 it was converted into an auxiliary anti-aircraft cruiser, seeing action in the Mediterranean, and later taking part in the Normandy landings. *Prince Robert* finished the war back in the Pacific, and was in Sydney when the Japanese surrendered. Its final task was the repatriation of released Canadian prisoners-of-war from Hong Kong, then late in 1945 *Prince Robert* was paid off, and offered for sale.

In October 1946 *Prince Robert* was bought by the Charlton Steam Shipping Co Ltd, along with *Prince David*. They were refitted as emigrant carriers in Belgium, with austere accommodation for 750 persons. *Prince Robert* was renamed *Charlton Sovereign* and its sister *Charlton Monarch*, and both were chartered by the IRO in March 1948.

On 4 August 1948, *Charlton Sovereign* departed Bremerhaven with 725 passengers for Australia, but was delayed almost a month at Gibraltar by boiler problems. After visiting Colombo, the vessel was held up 10 days in Batavia with further engine trouble, then stopped at Cairns before arriving in Sydney on 29 October, after a voyage lasting 86 days.

Remaining in Sydney for two weeks undergoing further repairs, *Charlton Sovereign* left on 15 November for Britain, where further extensive repairs were completed. *Charlton Sovereign* made five further voyages for the IRO, three to South America, one to Central America and one to Halifax, followed by a pilgrim voyage from North Africa to Jeddah, all of which were delayed by engine problems.

In April 1951, the vessel was sold to Fratelli Grimaldi, and rebuilt as a passenger liner. New engines were installed, a full superstructure added topped by two funnels, a raked bow fitted, and accommodation provided for 80 first class, 80 intermediate, and 560 third class passengers. Renamed *Lucania*, and looking very smart and modern, the vessel entered service in July 1953 operating between Italy and South America. In 1962 it was withdrawn, and sold to shipbreakers in Italy, to end a very varied career.

LUCIANO MANARA

BUILT: 1941 by Ansaldo SA, Genoa
TONNAGE: 7,121 gross
DIMENSIONS: 472 x 62 ft (143.8 x 18.9 m)
SERVICE SPEED: 14 knots
PROPULSION: Fiat diesel/single screw

Many of the ships that carried new settlers to Australia in the late 1940s are virtually unknown, and forgotten by all but those who travelled on them. *Luciano Manara* is one such ship, as it only served in a passenger-carrying capacity for a very brief period, and the facilities provided were extremely basic.

During 1941, the Garibaldi Group of Italy took delivery of three new cargo ships, named *Augistino Bertani*, *Nino Bixio* and *Luciano Manara*. They were placed under the ownership of a subsidiary company, Soc Anon Co-operativa di Navigazione, which already owned a dozen dry cargo ships and four tankers. The Italian merchant navy was decimated by the war, yet all three of these new ships managed to survive, though nothing is known of their activities during the conflict.

The Garibaldi Group set about rebuilding its fleet, and then saw the possibility of joining the booming migrant trade. It was for this purpose that *Luciano Manara* was converted, being given very austere accommodation for about 700 persons. This entailed the enlarging of the superstructure,

additional lifeboats, and the installation of basic passenger facilities in the holds. It was in this guise that *Luciano Manara* made two voyages to Australia from Italy.

The first voyage departed Italy in September 1948, and the vessel was in Melbourne on 21 October, and then continued on to Sydney. The second voyage commenced in April 1949, and again the vessel called at Melbourne, on 15 May, before continuing to Sydney. On each of these voyages it only carried about 350 persons. It appears that *Luciano Manara* was not a success as a migrant carrier, and the passengers must have had some very uncomfortable voyages.

Soon after the second Australian voyage, *Luciano Manara* reverted to being a cargo ship again, with the superstructure reduced in size and the extra lifeboats removed. In 1953 the vessel was renamed *Giuseppe Canepa*, and served under this name in the Garibaldi fleet for two years.

In 1955 the vessel was sold to Polish Ocean Lines and renamed *Malgorzata Fornalska*, then in 1965 passed to the flag of the People's Republic of China, being sold to China Ocean Shipping Co, and renamed *Chung Ming*. In 1977 its name was changed to *Hong Qi 144*, being registered in Guangzhou.

It is very difficult to trace vessels operated by the Chinese, but it is highly likely that this vessel has been scrapped.

PROTEA - AROSA KULM

BUILT: 1920 by American International Shipbuilding Corp,
 Hog Island, Pennsylvania
TONNAGE: 7,783 gross
DIMENSIONS: 448 x 58 ft (136.6 x 17.6 m)
SERVICE SPEED: 16 knots
PROPULSION: Steam turbines/single screw

This vessel was built as a standard "Hog Island-A" type transport, the name deriving from the site at which they were built. A total of 110 basic "Hog Islanders" were built there, very plain ships, with no sheer or camber. This vessel was launched on 27 October 1919, and named *Cantigny*, being owned by the US Shipping Board. Between 1920 and 1923 it served as a troopship, then in 1924 was transferred to the American Merchant Line.

Renamed *American Banker*, it operated on a cargo service between New York and London, carrying only 12 passengers. During 1926 the accommodation was enlarged to carry 80 tourist class passengers. In October 1931, American Merchant Line was absorbed into United States Line, but *American Banker* remained on its regular route. On 8 November 1939 the vessel arrived in New York from London for the last time.

In February 1940, *American Banker* was one of eight ships transferred by the US Government to a new Belgian company, Soc Maritime Anveroise. Renamed *Ville d'Anvers*, it left New York on 9 March 1940 for Liverpool, as it was too dangerous to try and reach Antwerp. When the Germans overran Belgium in May 1940, all eight ships were taken over by the Allies.

Ville d'Anvers was returned to United States Line in February 1946, but was not needed, so in October 1946 it was sold to Cia di Vapores Mediterranea, who renamed the ship *City of Athens* under the Honduran flag. Refitted to carry 200 tourist class passengers, and managed by T J Stevenson & Co of New York, *City of Athens* left New York on 11 November 1946 for Istanbul. Following a second trip to Istanbul, the vessel made a voyage to Piraeus, returning to Baltimore on 12 July 1947, and being laid up. On 13 August 1947, the vessel was sold to Panamanian Lines, a forerunner of Home Lines.

Renamed *Protea*, the vessel was sent to Genoa for an extensive refit, during which the passenger capacity was increased to 965 in one class. Operating under an IRO contract, *Protea* entered service in April 1948 with two voyages carrying migrants from Italy to South America, then on 20 August 1948 *Protea* departed Genoa bound for Australia, carrying 897 passengers. After calling at Melbourne on 23 September, the ship berthed in Sydney on 29 September. This was followed by another departure from Genoa in November with 903 passengers, which terminated in Melbourne on 23 December, while a third voyage went to Sydney, berthing on 25 March 1949, as did the fourth, arriving on 6 June.

It was not until 2 November 1950 that *Protea* left Naples on its next voyage to Australia, disembarking 1,096 passengers at Melbourne on 9 December. During 1951, *Protea* made a further trip to Australia, leaving Genoa on 19 May and reaching Melbourne on 22 June and Sydney on 3 July.

On returning from this voyage, *Protea* was sold by Panamanian Lines in August 1951 to Cia Internacional Transportadora, a new company owned in Switzerland, but registered in Panama. At first *Protea* was not renamed, and made a trooping voyage to Haiphong for the French Government, followed by two trans-Atlantic voyages under charter to Incres Line. In January 1952 it arrived in Bremen for an extensive refit, during which the accommodation was altered to 46 first and 919 tourist class. The ship was then renamed *Arosa Kulm*, and the owners adopted the name Arosa Line. On 18 March 1952, *Arosa Kulm* left Bremerhaven on a new service to Canada.

On 21 December 1954, *Arosa Kulm* left Bremerhaven bound for Australia, reaching Fremantle on 27 January 1955, Melbourne on 3 February and Sydney two days later. On the return voyage it called at Saigon, to carry French settlers back to Europe. The vessel returned to the Canadian service, then on 29 October 1955 left Bremerhaven on a second voyage to Australia, visiting the same three ports, leaving Sydney on 11 December. *Arosa Kulm* then sailed from Trieste on 18 January 1956, going only to Fremantle and Melbourne, leaving there on 20 February for Saigon again.

The fourth voyage to Australia made by *Arosa Kulm* was also its last, departing Genoa on 2 April 1956, and arriving in Fremantle on 5 May. The next day the lifesaving equipment was inspected and found to be faulty, delaying the vessel five days before it could continue to Melbourne, from where it sailed on 16 May for Auckland, arriving on 20 May. *Arosa Kulm* then crossed the Pacific, going to Boston and on to Europe.

Arosa Line was encountering financial difficulties, and on 6 December 1958 *Arosa Kulm* was arrested at Plymouth while returning from a voyage to the West Indies from Bremerhaven. The same month the three other liners owned by Arosa Line were also arrested, and on 10 April 1959 the company was declared bankrupt. *Arosa Kulm* was sold to the Belgian firm, Van Heyghen Freres, and on 7 May 1959 arrived at their yard in Bruges.

Protea

Arosa Kulm

CAMERONIA

BUILT: 1921 by W Beardmore & Co Ltd, Glasgow
TONNAGE: 16,584 gross
DIMENSIONS: 578 x 70 ft (176.3 x 21.4 m)
SERVICE SPEED: 16 knots
PROPULSION: Geared turbines/twin screws

The keel of *Cameronia* was laid on 7 March 1919, the first British passenger liner laid down after the end of World War One. Launched on 23 December 1919, it was May 1921 before *Cameronia* entered service for the Anchor Line, operating from Glasgow and Liverpool to New York. It was the first of four similar vessels built jointly for Cunard and the Anchor Line immediately after the war. The second ship was originally named *Tyrrhenia,* which was later changed to *Lancastria,* and sunk in June 1940 at St Nazaire. The third vessel, *Tuscania,* later came to Australia as *Nea Hellas,* while the fourth, *California,* was also sunk in the war.

Cameronia provided accommodation for 265 first class, 370 second class and 1,150 third class passengers, but proved to be a very unsatisfactory sea-boat. In November 1928 the lower section of the bow back to beneath the bridge was removed, and rebuilt to a new design.

In September 1935 *Cameronia* was chartered by the British Government to carry troops. During April and June 1936 the liner was out of service again, being refitted, then on 10 July left Glasgow bound for New York. *Cameronia* remained on the Atlantic trade until November 1940, when it was requisitioned as a troopship, being fitted out to carry 3,000 men.

Cameronia entered military service in January 1941. In December 1942, while on its second voyage to the North African landings, *Cameronia* was hit by a torpedo dropped from an aircraft, but was able to limp into Bone, then return to Gibraltar. The vessel took part in several other landings, including D-Day.

In May 1945 *Cameronia* was handed back to Anchor Line, but as they did not intend to resume their Atlantic service, the ship was laid up. In 1947, *Cameronia* was chartered by the British Government to carry troops to Palestine, following which the Ministry of Transport decided to use the ship on the Australian migrant trade.

In July 1948, *Cameronia* arrived at the shipyard of Barclay, Curle & Co for an extensive refit. Four of the six boilers were replaced, the machinery overhauled, and a shorter funnel fitted, while the gap between the boat deck and the bridge was filled in. Accommodation for 1,266 persons was installed in cabins with up to six berths. The vessel was managed for the Ministry of Transport by Anchor Line and painted in their colours.

On 1 November 1948, *Cameronia* left Glasgow on its first voyage to Australia, and over the next four years was to make a further 11 voyages from the Scottish port. The only unfortunate incident to mar its career occurred in June 1950, when the starboard engine broke down shortly after leaving Glasgow, and the ship had to spend several days being repaired. On most voyages the ship returned empty, but in August 1950 it went to Indonesia to collect Dutch nationals and return them home.

In October 1952, *Cameronia* departed Glasgow on its final voyage to Australia, departing Melbourne on 6 November to return to Britain. In January 1953, the liner was bought from the Anchor Line by the Ministry of Transport, and renamed *Empire Clyde.* Repainted in troopship colours, it served a further four years under the new name. In September 1957, *Empire Clyde* was sold to shipbreakers, and on 22 October arrived at their Newport yard.

RENA

BUILT: 1904 by John Brown & Co, Clydebank
TONNAGE: 1,619 gross
DIMENSIONS: 279 x 36 ft (85 x 10.9 m)
SERVICE SPEED: 16 knots
PROPULSION: Triple expansion/single screw

Migrant ships came in all sizes after the war, and one of the smallest was *Rena*, a former British ferry. Originally named *Woodcock*, it was built for G & J Burns Ltd to operate an overnight service across the Irish Sea between Ardrossan and Belfast. This was a high density service, and the vessel could carry over 1,200 passengers, though berths were provided for only about 400, most travelling in lounges or on deck. It also had a large cargo capacity, and as was usual on this route, there were also spaces for live cattle.

From 1914 to 1919 the vessel served as the armed boarding ship HMS *Woodnut*, being armed with three 12-pounder guns. In 1920, following a refit, the vessel returned to the Irish Sea trade again under its original name.

In 1922, following the merger of two Irish Sea shipping companies, *Woodcock* became part of the Burns & Laird fleet, and in 1923 the passenger capacity was shown as 1,133. In 1929 it was renamed *Lairdswood*, when a new naming system was adopted. However, the following year the vessel was sold to the Aberdeen Steam Navigation Co Ltd, being renamed *Lochnager*. With the passenger capacity reduced to 450, most in berths, it operated a regular service along the east coast of Britain from Aberdeen to London.

When war broke out in September 1939, *Lochnager* was withdrawn from service and laid up in Aberdeen, then in April 1940 was requisitioned by the Admiralty. Soon after, the vessel was sent to Molde in Norway, being attacked by German bombers as it made its way up the fjord, but escaping damage. Going on to Alesund, it suffered slight damage during a bombing raid there, then returned to Scapa Flow. *Lochnager* spent the rest of the war operating between Aberdeen and Lerwick, apart from three trips to Iceland. Late in 1945, *Lochnager* was returned to its owners, and resumed the coastal trade.

In October 1946, the vessel was sold to Rena Cia de Nav SA, of Panama, and renamed *Rena*. The new owner converted it from coal to oil-firing, and added a new deckhouse behind the mainmast. *Rena* was used to carry displaced persons, and in October 1948 left Europe with 360 persons aboard, bound for Melbourne, where it arrived six weeks later, on 29 November. *Rena* remained in Melbourne for two months, until a cargo was obtained for the return trip. On 16 January 1949, *Rena* was struck by the cargo ship *Citos*, which had broken adrift during a storm, causing some minor damage. On 22 January *Rena* finally left Melbourne, bound for Alexandria.

Rena remained in service a further three years, but did not return to Australia. Early in 1952 it was renamed *Blue Star*, but shortly afterwards was sold to shipbreakers, arriving on 26 April 1952 at their La Spezia yard.

DORSETSHIRE and SOMERSETSHIRE

BUILT: 1920–21 by Harland & Wolff Ltd, Belfast
TONNAGE: 9,787 gross
DIMENSIONS: 468 x 57 ft (142.6 x 17.4 m)
SERVICE SPEED: 12 knots
PROPULSION: B & W diesels/twin screws

Shortly after the end of World War One, Bibby Line ordered two cargo ships, the first in their fleet, intended to carry lead ore from the Namtu mines in Burma to Britain. *Dorsetshire* was launched on 22 April 1920, being delivered in August the same year, while *Somersetshire* was launched on 24 February 1921, and delivered three months later. Unfortunately, by then the mine company had built a smelter at Namtu, so the two ships were not needed. Instead, they were chartered out.

In 1927, *Dorsetshire* and *Somersetshire* were sent to the Vickers-Armstrong shipyard at Barrow, and rebuilt as troopships. Accommodation was installed for 1,450 troops, 108 troop dependants, 58 warrant officers and 112 officers. They began operating as troopers in October 1927, mainly between Britain and India, which was a seasonal service from October to April. For the rest of the year they were laid up in the River Dart, or made some trips to China.

Both vessels served as troopers until war broke out in 1939, then they were converted into hospital ships. *Somersetshire* was involved in the withdrawal from Narvik in 1940, and on 7 April 1942 was struck by a torpedo in the Mediterranean, but managed to reach Alexandria. *Dorsetshire* also saw action in the Mediterranean, being subjected to intense air attack for two days in January 1943 off Tobruk, escaping with minor damage. On 12 July 1943 it was damaged in an air attack, off the coast of Sicily.

From 1946 both ships reverted to their trooping roles, and were used in the repatriation of prisoners-of-war and other duties. *Somersetshire* was released from government service in February 1948, and *Dorsetshire* the following month. Bibby Line then obtained a contract from the Ministry of Transport to carry migrants to Australia. Both ships were given basic accommodation for 550 persons.

Somersetshire departed Liverpool on 12 November 1948 for Australia, followed by *Dorsetshire* on 10 December. Despite their slow speed, the two ships were highly successful as emigrant carriers, making four round trips per year. At times they were routed via Indonesia on the homeward voyage, to collect Dutch evacuees. In August 1952, *Somersetshire* suffered engine problems in the Mediterranean while returning to Britain.

Both ships were withdrawn from the Australian migrant trade during 1952, with *Dorsetshire* departing Melbourne for the last time on 13 July, while *Somersetshire* made its final departure from Melbourne on 6 November.

Somersetshire operated again as a troopship, carrying British troops to Kenya. *Dorsetshire* went to Aden in November 1952 as an accommodation ship for workers building an oil refinery there, and in

Somersetshire as a cargoship.

March 1953 joined *Somersetshire* again as a troopship to East Africa, but on 9 November 1953 it arrived at Liverpool for the last time, and was offered for sale. *Dorsetshire* was purchased by John Cashmore Ltd, and arrived at their Newport shipbreaking yard on 1 February 1954.

Somersetshire arrived at Liverpool on 26 January 1954, then was also offered for sale. The vessel was bought by British Iron & Steel, and arrived at the Barrow shipbreaking yard of T W Ward on 4 March 1954.

Somersetshire as a migrant ship

Dorsetshire alongside in Sydney

CHITRAL

BUILT: 1925 by A Stephen & Sons Ltd, Glasgow
TONNAGE: 15,555 gross
DIMENSIONS: 548 x 70 ft (167 x 21.4 m)
SERVICE SPEED: 16 knots
PROPULSION: Quadruple expansion/twin screws

Chitral was the sole survivor of a group of three sister ships built for P & O in 1925 to operate between Britain and Australia. The first two, *Cathay* and *Comorin*, were launched at the Barclay, Curle shipyard on the same day, 31 October 1924. *Chitral* was launched on 27 January 1925, and made its maiden departure from London on 3 July 1925. Accommodation was provided for 200 first class and 135 second class passengers.

All three served on the Australian route until 1931, when *Chitral* and *Comorin* were transferred to operate from Britain to India and the Far East. In July 1936, while anchored off Gibraltar, *Chitral* was narrowly missed by bombs from a Spanish aircraft. All three sisters were requisitioned for conversion into armed merchant cruisers in September and October 1939.

Cathay was converted in Bombay, and patrolled the Indian Ocean. *Chitral* and *Comorin* were altered in Britain, *Chitral* being armed with seven 6-inch guns and three 4-inch anti-aircraft guns. Both ships were posted to the Northern Patrol, and on 20 November 1939, *Chitral* intercepted the German cargo vessel, *Bertha Fisser*, which was scuttled by its crew to avoid capture. In April 1941, *Comorin* caught fire in the North Atlantic, and was subsequently sunk by British destroyers, while *Cathay* was bombed and sunk during the North African landings in November 1942. In April 1944 *Chitral* arrived in Baltimore to be converted into a troopship, returning to service in September, operating in this capacity until released in September 1947.

Instead of refurbishing *Chitral* to its pre-war condition, P & O elected to have it refitted for the Australian emigrant trade. The work was done in London, where accommodation for 738 persons was installed, mostly comprising cabins with between six and 12 berths, and only nine two-berth cabins. One concession to comfort was the inclusion of two outdoor swimming pools.

Chitral was painted in the old P & O colours, and on 30 December 1948 left London on its first post-war voyage to Australia. Outbound the vessel carried assisted migrants, while on the return trip fare-paying passengers were carried on behalf of P & O. On a few occasions, *Chitral* was diverted to Indonesia on the homeward voyage, to collect Dutch nationals wishing to return to Holland.

Chitral served four years as an emigrant ship, making four return trips each year. On 19 December 1952, the vessel left London on its final voyage to Australia, departing Sydney for the last time on 4 February 1953, arriving back in London on 18 March. By that time a sale had been finalised to shipbreakers at Dalmuir, with *Chitral* arriving at their yard on 1 April 1953.

Chitral berthed at Woolloomooloo in Sydney

NEA HELLAS

BUILT: 1922 by Fairfield Shipbuilding & Engineering Co, Glasgow
TONNAGE: 16,991 gross
DIMENSIONS: 580 x 70 ft (176.8 x 21.4 m)
SERVICE SPEED: 16 knots
PROPULSION: Geared turbines/twin screws

This liner was originally built as *Tuscania*, the third of four liners ordered by the Anchor Line for their trans-Atlantic services. The first of this group, *Cameronia*, made many trips to Australia after the war with migrants, while the second was transferred to the Cunard Line. Launched as *Tyrrhenia*, it was later renamed *Lancastria*, and sunk with great loss of life at St Nazaire in June 1940. The fourth unit, *California*, was also lost in the war.

Tuscania was launched on 4 October 1921, and made its maiden voyage in September 1922 from Glasgow to New York. Accommodation was provided for 240 first class, 377 second class and 1,818 third class passengers. After a mere four years' service, *Tuscania* was surplus to requirements, and put up for sale, but no buyers were forthcoming.

From May 1926 to October 1930, the vessel spent the summer months operating from London to New York under charter to the Cunard Line, and was laid up in winter. From August 1931, *Tuscania* operated on the Anchor Line service to India in winter, and spent the summer either trooping under charter, or cruising from British ports. By 1935 the accommodation had been reduced to 206 cabin, 439 tourist and 431 third class, and in 1937 the vessel was laid up, and again offered for sale.

In April 1939, the General Steam Navigation Co of Greece, better known as the Greek Line, bought *Tuscania*, which was renamed *Nea Hellas*. On 19 May 1939, the vessel left Piraeus on its first voyage to New York under the Greek flag, but within months the service was abandoned due to the war. *Nea Hellas* was taken over by the British in 1941, and used as a troopship, being managed for the Ministry of War Transport by the Anchor Line.

In January 1947, *Nea Hellas* was handed back to its owners, refitted with accommodation for 1,430 passengers in three classes, and returned to the New York trade from Piraeus in August 1947.

Nea Hellas was also available for charters, and on 24 January 1949 left Genoa bound for Australia on behalf of the IRO, carrying 1,525 passengers, and one stowaway. It arrived in Melbourne on 23 February, berthing at Station Pier. The Australian Seamen's Union placed a ban on the ship, involving tugboat crews, over the involvement of the Greek Governments in the detention and subsequent death of a Greek trade union leader. This delayed the departure of *Nea Hellas* to 26 February, when it left for Piraeus.

Nea Hellas returned to the New York trade, and in late 1954 had an extensive refit, emerging with accommodation for 70 first class and 1,369 tourist class passengers, and a new name, *New York*. In March 1955 it began operating from Bremerhaven to New York, until September 1959, when it made one voyage from Piraeus to Quebec, then was laid up until being sold to Japanese shipbreakers, arriving in Onomichi on 12 October 1961.

THE "NAVIGATORS"

BUILT: 1947–48 by S. A. Ansaldo, Genoa
TONNAGE: 8,967 gross
DIMENSIONS: 485 x 62 ft (149.2 x 19 m)
SERVICE SPEED: 15 knots
PROPULSION: Fiat diesel/single screw

In 1940 Italia Line ordered a class of six cargo ships to be built for their South American trade, the first three of which were launched in 1942, and laid up incomplete. Construction of the second trio was held up during the war, but all three were eventually launched in 1945, being named *Paolo Toscanelli*, *Ferruccio Buonapace* and *Mario Visentini*. During fitting out the names of two of the ships were changed, *Ferruccio Buonapace* becoming *Ugolino Vivaldi*, while *Mario Visentini* was renamed *Sebastiano Caboto*. Due to the great shortage of passenger berths in the immediate post-war years, each of these ships was completed with an enlarged superstructure and accommodation for 90 cabin class and 530 third class passengers.

During November 1947, *Sebastiano Caboto* reopened the Italia Line service from Genoa and Naples to Central America, and through the Panama Canal to ports on the west coast of South America as far as Valparaiso, being joined on this trade by *Ugolino Vivaldi* and *Paolo Toscanelli*.

Meanwhile, work on completing the trio of ships launched in 1942 proceeded, and they entered service in 1948 and 1949, also having been fitted out with passenger accommodation, and named *Marco Polo*, *Amerigo Vespucci* and *Antoniotto Usodimare*.

The addition of these ships resulted in a surplus of berths on the South American route, so Italia Line chartered two of the ships to Lloyd Triestino to help them on the Australian trade. The two selected were *Sebastiano Caboto* and *Ugolino Vivaldi*, refitted first to carry 100 cabin class and 735 third class passengers, most in dormitories.

The first sailing was by *Ugolino Vivaldi*, from Genoa on 12 January 1949, reaching Fremantle on 5 February, Melbourne five days later, and Sydney on 14 February. *Sebastiano Caboto* did not make its first departure for Australia from Genoa until 7 July 1949. Outbound the vessels carried a combination of paying passengers and emigrants, but for the return voyage loaded their six holds full of Australian goods and carried only a minimal number of passengers. This pair and *Toscana* enabled Lloyd Triestino to operate a regular service once again, though much of the accommodation was somewhat austere.

In 1949, Lloyd Triestino placed orders for the construction of three new passenger liners in Italy, the first of which entered service in April 1951 as *Australia*. Later in the year it was joined by *Oceania* and *Neptunia*, and their entry into the Australian service led to the withdrawal of both *Ugolino Vivaldi* and *Sebastiano Caboto* during 1951. They were returned to Italia Line, and again placed on the route to Central and South America.

Four years later a third unit of the "Navigatori" class would make several voyages to Australia, this being *Paolo Toscanelli*. The demand for berths from Italy to Australia could not be met by the regular vessels on the route, so in March 1955 *Paolo Toscanelli* was chartered from Italia Line and made the first of five voyages to Australia, being in Melbourne on 17 April and Sydney two days later.

Over the next year, this vessel made a further four voyages to Australia, the last departing Genoa in April 1956, arriving in Sydney on 27 May. On returning to Italy, *Paolo Toscanelli* was handed back to Italia Line, and resumed its place on the trade to Central and South America.

In 1958, Italia Line decided to reduce their service on this route to only three ships, which resulted in the withdrawal of the three ships that had operated to Australia at various times. All were reduced to cargo ship status, retaining accommodation for only 12 passengers. *Paolo Toscanelli* remained with Italia Line, but *Sebastiano Caboto* and *Ugolino Vivaldi* were transferred to Lloyd Triestino, and placed on a service from Italy to East and South Africa. In 1963 the remaining trio of the "Navigatori" class were also reduced to 12-passenger cargo ships, and transferred to Lloyd Triestino to join the other pair on the South African trade. In June 1968, *Sebastiano Caboto* made a voyage to Australia as a cargo ship.

During the 1970s, the Italian Government sought to rationalise the services run by the various government supported shipping lines, and this led to the withdrawal from service of all six of the "Navigatori" class ships. First to go was the only unit to be retained by Italia Line, *Paolo Toscanelli*, which was laid up at Naples on 20 October 1972. Sold to shipbreakers, the vessel arrived at La Spezia in tow on 6 February 1973. Lloyd Triestino operated the other five units until 1978, when all were disposed of within a matter of months.

Ugolino Vivaldi was laid up in Trieste on 9 February 1978, then sold to a local firm of shipbreakers in August that year. *Sebastiano Caboto* was also withdrawn during the early part of 1978, and sold later in the year to Hikma Shipping Pte Ltd, of Singapore. They did not rename the ship, but sold it on quickly to shipbreakers in Taiwan, the vessel arriving at Kaohsiung on 15 February 1979.

Sebastiano Caboto in Sydney

Sebastiano Caboto after being rebuilt as a cargo ship

OXFORDSHIRE

BUILT: 1912 by Harland & Wolff Ltd, Belfast
TONNAGE: 8,624 gross
DIMENSIONS: 474 x 55 ft (144.5 x 16.8 m)
SERVICE SPEED: 15 knots
PROPULSION: Triple expansion/twin screw

Built for the Bibby Line to operate from Britain to Burma, *Oxfordshire* was fitted with accommodation for 276 first class passengers only, and had a large cargo capacity.

On the outbreak of war in 1914, *Oxfordshire* was converted into the first British army hospital ship. It spent six months operating across the English Channel, then was involved in the Gallipoli landings, looking after many wounded soldiers from Australia and New Zealand.

The ship subsequently saw active service in many other parts of the world before being handed back to the Bibby Line on 24 March 1918. After a quick refit, it resumed the pre-war trade to Rangoon. In 1919 *Oxfordshire* was converted to oil-firing, then spent the next 20 years plying between Britain and Burma.

On 3 September 1939, *Oxfordshire* was requisitioned for its second war, again being converted into a hospital ship. Initially it was dispatched to Freetown, lying at anchor for almost three years as the local base hospital.

Oxfordshire then joined the invasion fleet for North Africa in November 1942, and served in the Mediterranean over the next two years. *Oxfordshire*

finished the war in the Pacific then repatriated released prisoners-of-war, making its first visits to Australia in this role.

On 10 July 1948, *Oxfordshire* was released from government service, and handed back to the Bibby Line. Being 36 years old, the vessel was not worth reconditioning for regular service, but instead was chartered to the Ministry of Transport.

With austere accommodation for 700 persons, *Oxfordshire* made its first migrant voyage to Australia carrying 672 passengers to Adelaide, arriving on 25 May 1949. The vessel made a further two voyages to Australia in 1949, arriving in Fremantle on 8 August, and Adelaide again on 23 November.

In February 1950 *Oxfordshire* departed Naples on a voyage to Newcastle, arriving on 12 March. Returning to Bremerhaven, it sailed on 17 April 1950, bound for Fremantle, arriving on 11 June. This was followed by two more voyages from Liverpool, the last departing in August 1950.

In October 1950 *Oxfordshire* began to carry troops between Trieste and Port Said, then in February 1951 was offered for sale. The Pan-Islamic Steamship Co, of Karachi, bought *Oxfordshire*, which was renamed *Safina-E-Arab*, and refitted to carry 101 first class, 46 second class and 1,085 third class passengers.

From June to October the vessel carried pilgrims to Jeddah, and the rest of the year traded from Karachi to ports in the Indian Ocean. After six years under the Pakistani flag, the old liner was sold to shipbreakers in Karachi early in 1958.

DUNDALK BAY

BUILT: 1936 by Bremer Vulkan, Vegesack
TONNAGE: 7,105 gross
DIMENSIONS: 452 x 56 ft (137.8 x 17 m)
SERVICE SPEED: 15 knots
PROPULSION: Diesel engine/single screw

Dundalk Bay was the only Irish-owned vessel to transport migrants to Australia, and developed a reputation as one of the worst ships to travel on. The vessel was built for North German Lloyd as the *Nurnberg*, having four sisters, *Dresden*, *Leipzig*, *Munchen* and *Osnabruck*. All five ships operated on a cargo service from Bremen to the west coast of America, and could carry 12 passengers.

Shortly after the war broke out, *Nurnberg* was taken over by the German Navy, and converted into a minelayer. Later in the war it was altered again for service as a depot ship, and sent to Copenhagen. It was here that the ship was found by the Allies in May 1945, in good condition, and immediately seized as a war prize. In 1947 it was allocated to Britain, and used briefly by the Royal Navy as a depot ship, but then offered for sale.

In 1948 the vessel was bought by H P Leneghan & Sons Ltd, of Belfast, who operated as the Irish Bay Line, and renamed *Dundalk Bay*. Having obtained an IRO contract for the carriage of displaced persons, they sent the ship to Trieste, where it was completely rebuilt as an emigrant carrier. Very austere quarters for 1,025 persons were installed in the former cargo spaces, but the superstructure was only slightly enlarged.

On 15 March 1949, *Dundalk Bay* departed Trieste on its first voyage, bringing some 1,028 displaced persons to Sydney, arriving on 16 April. *Dundalk Bay* then carried the first consignment of displaced persons to be sent to New Zealand, departing Trieste and passing through Australia en route to Wellington, where it berthed on 26 June with 941 persons aboard. The next two voyages departed Trieste on 12 August and 20 October, going to Melbourne.

In 1950 the European base for *Dundalk Bay* was changed to Naples, from where it made two sailings, the first in January to Melbourne, the second in March to Fremantle only. Returning from this trip, *Dundalk Bay* proceeded to Rotterdam, then to Bremerhaven, departing there in May on its next voyage to Australia. Passing through Fremantle on 18 June, it went directly to Sydney, arriving on 25 June, and the next day proceeded up the coast to Newcastle, where it stayed four days. *Dundalk Bay* returned to Bremerhaven, from where it made its final trip to Australia, arriving in Newcastle on 17 October.

In mid-1951, *Dundalk Bay* was refitted as a cargo ship again, and used on general tramping by Irish Bay Lines. In 1953 it was sold to Duff, Herbert & Mitchell, of London, but was not renamed until 1957, becoming *Westbay*. Under this name it spent a further five years as a tramp cargo ship. On 2 September 1962, *Westbay* arrived at the Hamburg shipbreaking yard of Eisen und Metall AG, who had purchased the ship the previous month.

CYRENIA

BUILT: 1911 by Fairfield Shipbuilding & Engineering Co, Glasgow
TONNAGE: 7,527 gross
DIMENSIONS: 447 x 56 ft (136.2 x 17 m)
SERVICE SPEED: 14 knots
PROPULSION: Quadruple expansion/twin screws

By the time the Greek liner *Cyrenia* entered the Australian emigrant trade in 1949, it was almost 40 years old. Originally named *Maunganui*, it had been delivered to the Union Steam Ship Company of New Zealand in December 1911, and in February 1912 entered the famous "horseshoe service" between Australia and New Zealand. *Maunganui* could accommodate 244 first class, 175 second class and 80 third class passengers.

In August 1914 *Maunganui* was requisitioned as a troopship, voyaging all over the world. Handed back to its owners late in 1919, it was the middle of 1922 before the vessel returned to commercial service, having been converted from coal to oil-firing. *Maunganui* then operated from Australia and New Zealand to San Francisco until 1925, when it reverted to the trans-Tasman trade again. Over the next seven years, *Maunganui* made occasional relief sailings to Vancouver and San Francisco, then in 1932 returned permanently to the San Francisco route until it was abandoned by the Union Line in 1936. It was then used as a relief ship on the Tasman routes, or for South Pacific cruises.

Maunganui was requisitioned in January 1941 and converted into a hospital ship. Over the next four years it voyaged to Egypt, South Africa and India, and then joined the British Pacific Fleet during the final assault on Japan. In 1946 it carried the official New Zealand contingent to the victory celebrations in London, and on returning to Wellington was handed back to the Union Line. Having steamed 2,184,081 miles since being built, the vessel was offered for sale.

Surprisingly, *Maunganui* was sold for further trading, to Cia Nav del Atlantico, a Panamanian concern. Leaving Wellington on 12 February 1947, it went to Greece to be refitted with rather austere accommodation for 840 passengers, the new owners having obtained an IRO contract. Renamed *Cyrenia*, the vessel was placed under the management of Hellenic Mediterranean Lines, and painted in their colours. On 6 March 1949, *Cyrenia* departed Genoa on its first voyage to Australia, arriving in Fremantle on 2 April and terminating at Melbourne on 8 April. A second voyage commenced at Genoa on 1 June, and included a call at Malta three days later, again terminating in Melbourne.

During 1950, Hellenic Mediterranean Lines bought *Cyrenia* outright, and placed it under the Greek flag, but the vessel continued to operate from Genoa to Fremantle and Melbourne. Departing Melbourne on 16 August 1950, *Cyrenia* called at Saigon to board French nationals fleeing the war-torn area. In June 1952, *Cyrenia* was taken out of service and laid up, due to a decline in the number of displaced persons seeking passages.

Cyrenia returned to service in May 1954, now operating from Piraeus to Melbourne with migrants, returning with fare-paying passengers. In December 1955 the vessel paid its only visit to Sydney, and on 1 November 1956, *Cyrenia* left Melbourne for the last time. The old vessel was then sold to shipbreakers and arrived at their Savona yard on 6 February 1957.

INDIAN PILGRIM SHIPS

BUILT: 1947–48 by Lithgows Ltd, Port Glasgow
TONNAGE: 7,026 gross
DIMENSIONS: 451 x 60ft (137.5 x 18.3 m)
SERVICE SPEED: 14.5 knots
PROPULSION: Triple expansion/single screw

This pair was delivered as *Mohammedi* in 1947 and *Mozaffari* in 1948 to the Mogul Line, which operated a mixed fleet, mostly cargo ships, but with a few vessels capable of carrying passengers, or pilgrims. This pair was given cabin accommodation for ten deluxe and 52 first class passengers, and operated from Bombay to ports in the Red Sea. During the pilgrim season, they could also carry 1,390 passengers in the 'tween decks and cargo holds to Jeddah.

In early 1949, these ships made three voyages to Australia carrying displaced persons. The first voyage was made by *Mozaffari*, which departed Naples on 22 February 1949 carrying 902 passengers to Melbourne, arriving on 24 March. *Mohammedi* left Naples on 11 April with 900 passengers, and arrived in Melbourne on 14 May, and Sydney four days later. *Mohammedi* then went to Adelaide, arriving on 29 May to load cargo, which was carried to Bombay. On its second voyage, *Mozaffari* departed Genoa on 25 April and berthed in Fremantle on 21 May. The vessel then went directly to Sydney, arriving on 31 May, then continued to Brisbane, arriving on 9 June, before heading back to Bombay.

Early in 1950, both ships were chartered again, to make a single voyage to Australia from Malta with migrants. Although the reason for this is not clear, they were renamed for the outward voyage, the change being effected at Aden as the ships were en route to Malta to collect their passengers. *Mozaffari* was renamed *Ocean Victory*, and departed Malta on 24 February 1950, calling at Port Said four days later. The vessel then called at Aden before crossing the Indian Ocean to Bombay before heading south to Fremantle, which was reached on 24 March, then on to Melbourne, arriving on 30 March. The voyage terminated in Sydney on 2 April, where all the emigrants disembarked. Next day, the name of the ship was changed back to *Mozzafari*, as which it left Sydney on 5 April bound for Port Lincoln. A cargo of wheat was loaded, and on 22 April *Mozaffari* left for India.

Mohammedi followed its sister to Malta, being renamed *Ocean Triumph*. It left Malta on 23 March 1950, arriving in Fremantle on 22 April, and Melbourne on 28 April, before terminating in Sydney on 1 May. As soon as the migrants were disembarked, the name was changed back to *Mohammedi*, and it remained in port loading cargo until 25 May, then departed for Calcutta.

At the time of these voyages, both ships had white hulls, but these were later repainted black. The pair spent the rest of their careers in the service for which they were built. *Mozaffari* was laid up in Bombay on 11 February 1977, and sold to local shipbreakers six months later. *Mohammedi* arrived in Bombay for the last time on 24 February 1978, and was also laid up. In July 1978 it was also sold to the local shipbreakers.

Mohammedi

SURRIENTO

BUILT: 1928 by Furness Shipbuilding Co, Haverton
TONNAGE: 10,699 gross
DIMENSIONS: 498 x 64 ft (151.8 x 19.5 m)
SERVICE SPEED: 17 knots
PROPULSION: Sulzer diesels/twin screws

Surriento had an unusual claim to fame, being built in Britain for the Grace Line of America, one of the very few American-owned ships to have been built in another country. Launched on 15 August 1927 as *Santa Maria*, on completion in April 1928 the vessel crossed the Atlantic to New York. A sister ship, *Santa Barbara*, was completed in August 1928. The two sisters were placed in service from New York to Central America and through the Panama Canal to the west coast of South America as far as Valparaiso. *Santa Maria* had a very boxy appearance, with a straight bow and very square superstructure topped by two squat funnels, the forward one being a dummy. Accommodation was provided for 157 passengers, all first class, which was increased to 172 after a few years. *Santa Maria* remained on the South American route until August 1940, then was sold to the US Navy.

Renamed USS *Barnett*, the vessel was refitted to transport 1,800 troops, and for protection given a single 5-inch gun and three 3-inch guns, plus some anti-aircraft weapons. *Barnett* served as a troopship until the end of 1942, then was converted into an attack transport. Returning to service on 1 February 1943, *Barnett* took part in several of the Allied landings in Europe, and was hit by a bomb off Sicily on 11 July 1943, when seven men on board were killed. In July 1946 *Barnett* was withdrawn from service, and laid up in the James River. Sister ship *Santa Barbara* served as the transport *McCawley* in the war, but was sunk in June 1943.

During 1948 the US Government held a series of auctions to dispose of many ships it no longer required, and *Barnett* was purchased at one such auction in March 1948 by the Italian shipowner, Achille Lauro. The vessel was given a brief refit in Baltimore, then voyaged to Genoa, where it arrived in July, and over the next nine months was rebuilt.

The alterations were quite radical, as a new raked bow was fitted, and the superstructure greatly extended both fore and aft, topped by two new, low funnels with raked tops. The interior of the ship was completely gutted, and new accommodation installed for 187 first class and 868 tourist class passengers. When the work was completed in May 1949, the vessel was renamed *Surriento*.

Surriento departed Genoa on 22 May 1949 on its first voyage for Flotta Lauro, going to Fremantle, Melbourne and Sydney, departing on 28 June bound for Singapore and Colombo on her return voyage. The second voyage departed Genoa on 12 August, and a third in October 1949, each time returning via Singapore and Colombo, and also calling at Naples and Marseilles. On leaving Sydney on 26 July 1950, *Surriento* went to Brisbane, leaving on 29 July for Jakarta to collect Dutch nationals, who were carried to Genoa.

During 1951 Flotta Lauro placed two more passenger ships on the Australian trade, *Roma* and *Sydney*, which enabled them to withdraw *Surriento*, and transfer it to a new service from Naples to Venezuela. In 1952 *Surriento* was refitted, during which the accommodation was altered to 119 first class and 994 tourist class.

On 19 March 1953 the vessel departed Genoa bound for Australia once again, replacing *Roma*, which had been placed on a new service from the Mediterranean to New York. Over the next three years *Surriento* partnered *Sydney* on the Australian route, then on 30 August 1956, *Surriento* left Genoa on what was destined to be its final voyage to Australia.

Arriving in Fremantle on 22 September, *Surriento* was inspected by local safety authorities, who declared that many of the lifesaving facilities on board were defective, and levied a heavy fine on Flotta Lauro. Once the defects were rectified, *Surriento* continued to Melbourne, arriving on 28 September, and Sydney, where it berthed on 3 October, departing the next day on the return voyage to Genoa. *Roma* then returned to the Australian route, and *Surriento* reverted to the Central American service again.

During 1959, *Surriento* was given another major refit, during which the superstructure was further enlarged and streamlined, two outdoor swimming pools added, and a single modern funnel fitted in place of the former pair. Internally the accommodation was altered to carry 1,080 passengers in a single class, and air-conditioning extended throughout the ship. These changes completely altered the appearance of the ship when it returned to the Central American trade in 1960, serving there for a further five years.

In 1965 *Surriento* was withdrawn, and chartered to Zim Lines for their service from Haifa to Marseilles, replacing another former Australian emigrant ship, *Flaminia*. When that charter expired in the middle of 1966, Flotta Lauro had added *Achille Lauro* and *Angelina Lauro* to the Australian service, and transferred *Roma* and *Sydney* to the Central American service, leaving no employment for *Surriento*. The old liner was laid up, then sold to shipbreakers, arriving at their La Spezia yard on 30 September 1966.

Santa Maria

Surriento

ANNA SALEN - TASMANIA

BUILT: 1940 by Sun Shipbuilding & Drydock Co, Chester
TONNAGE: 11,672 gross
DIMENSIONS: 494 x 69 ft (150.5 x 21.1 m)
SERVICE SPEED: 17 knots
PROPULSION: Busch-Sulzer diesel/single screw

This vessel was laid down as a standard C3 type cargo ship for Moore-McCormack Line, and launched on 14 December 1939 as *Mormacland*. Fitting out was almost complete when the US Government requisitioned the vessel for conversion into an auxiliary aircraft carrier for the US Navy.

Before the conversion work was finished, the lend-lease agreement had been finalised, and the vessel was handed over to the Royal Navy at Norfolk, Virginia, on 17 November 1941. Named HMS *Archer*, it was the second auxiliary aircraft carrier transferred to Britain.

During trials, *Archer* suffered numerous engine problems, and on the night of 12 January 1942, collided with and sank the Peruvian steamer *Brazos* some 200 miles off the South Carolina coast. *Archer* had a huge hole in the bow and serious flooding, so headed for safety stern first, its single propeller half out of the water. The stricken vessel arrived in Charleston on 21 January to be repaired.

On 18 March 1942, HMS *Archer* departed for active service, being based at Freetown in Sierra Leone, but was plagued by machinery defects for some time, and also had other misfortunes. In June 1942 a bomb stored on the flight deck exploded, so the vessel went to Cape Town to collect a fortune in gold ingots, which was carried to New York, arriving on 15 July. Here the machinery was finally fixed, and *Archer* gave good service for the rest of the war.

In 1945 HMS *Archer* was transferred to the Ministry of War Transport, rebuilt as a cargo ship and renamed *Empire Lagan*, under Blue Funnel Line management. On 8 January 1946, it was handed back to the Americans, and laid up pending disposal.

During 1948 the vessel was purchased by Sven Salen, a noted Swedish shipowner, and renamed *Anna Salen*. It was sent to the Bethlehem Shipyard at Baltimore for reconstruction as a bulk carrier, but when the job was almost finished, Salen obtained a contract from the IRO to transport displaced persons.

Anna Salen loaded coal in America and carried it to Italy, where it was converted to a passenger carrier, with rather basic quarters for over 1,500 persons built into the holds, as well as numerous toilet and washing blocks, and a few public rooms.

On 22 May 1949, *Anna Salen* departed Naples on its first IRO voyage, carrying 1,503 displaced persons, going to Melbourne and Sydney, where it arrived on 21 June. The second voyage was only to Fremantle, arriving on 24 August carrying 1,566 passengers, while the third voyage went to Melbourne, arriving on 30 October.

On 1 December 1949, *Anna Salen* left Naples on its fourth voyage, but in the Indian Ocean was afflicted by engine trouble, and had to return to Aden. The 1,570 passengers were transferred to *Skaugum*,

Anna Salen

which had been crossing the Indian Ocean empty on its way back to Europe. *Skaugum* arrived in Fremantle on 5 January 1950 and all the passengers disembarked. Meanwhile, *Anna Salen* limped back to Europe for repairs, which lasted six months.

On 20 June 1950, *Anna Salen* returned to service, departing Bremerhaven with 1,561 passengers on a voyage to Melbourne, arriving on 29 July. From there the vessel went to Tientsin in China to collect refugees and carry them to Europe. On its next voyage to Australia, *Anna Salen* arrived in Fremantle on 31 December 1950, with 1,522 passengers.

During 1951, *Anna Salen* made several trips to Canada with refugees, so it was 21 February 1952 before it again left Bremerhaven bound for Australia, by way of Cape Town. When the Olympic Games were held in Helsinki during the summer of 1952, *Anna Salen* operated a ferry service from Stockholm, the capacity being increased to 2,500 passengers.

Over the next two years, *Anna Salen* made further voyages to Australia and Canada, and also made several summer voyages across the North Atlantic, carrying students. During 1955, the vessel called at Saigon and also ports in mainland China during some of the return voyages from Australia.

In the middle of 1955, *Anna Salen* was sold to Hellenic Mediterranean Lines, being renamed *Tasmania*. Apart from repainting, the ship was not altered, and returned to the Australian trade, this time carrying Greek migrants.

Tasmania departed Piraeus on 23 August 1955 on its first voyage, arriving in Melbourne on 23 September. On the return trip, the vessel was again sent to Saigon, where French troops were boarded and returned home.

Over the next year *Tasmania* made several more voyages to Australia, disembarking its passengers in Melbourne. Entering Port Phillip Bay on 3 April 1956, *Tasmania* ran aground and suffered some bottom damage, which delayed its departure by eleven days. On 15 October 1956, *Tasmania* left Melbourne for the last time, as on returning to Greece the passenger accommodation was removed, and it reverted to being a cargo ship.

Early in 1961, *Tasmania* was sold to China Union Lines, of Taipei, and renamed *Union Reliance*. Placed on a regular cargo service to American ports, the vessel was passing down the Houston Ship Canal on 7 November 1961, when it collided with the Norwegian tanker, *Berean*. An explosion was followed by a fireball that rapidly engulfed both vessels, with *Union Reliance* having to be beached and left to burn out.

Totally gutted, the vessel was refloated four days later, and towed to Galveston, where the wreck was bought by a New Orleans shipbreaking firm, arriving at their yard on 28 January 1962. While in the early stages of demolition, on 19 February 1962, the vessel was swept by a second fire and totally destroyed.

Tasmania

CANBERRA

BUILT: 1913 by A Stephen & Sons, Glasgow
TONNAGE: 7,707 gross
DIMENSIONS: 426 x 57 ft (129.8 x 17.3 m)
SERVICE SPEED: 15 knots
PROPULSION: Quadruple expansion/twin screws

During the latter part of 1949, two vessels that had spent many years on the Australian coastal trade returned with migrants. The first of them was *Canberra*, which originally had been owned by Howard Smith Ltd. Launched on 9 November 1912, *Canberra* arrived in Australian waters for the first time in April 1913, and was placed in service along the east coast from Melbourne to Cairns. Accommodation was provided for 170 first class, 180 second class and 60 third class passengers.

In October 1917, *Canberra* was requisitioned and became a troopship, carrying 800 men to Egypt. It was then used to transport troops from Alexandria to Marseilles in several convoys, and later made a voyage from Britain to India and back. *Canberra* returned to Australia in September 1919, and after being refitted, resumed the east coast service in May 1920.

In February 1925 *Canberra* was laid up in Sydney, then was due to be reactivated in late June. In the early morning of 27 June a fire broke out on board and quickly spread through the ship, which was taken to Mort's Dock in Sydney for repairs, and did not return to service until May 1926.

In July 1941, *Canberra* came under the Shipping Controller, but remained on the coastal trade, though often carrying troops. In August 1947 it was returned to its owners, being in need of an extensive refit. Howard Smith did not consider this to be worthwhile, so the ship was offered for sale, and quickly purchased by Singapore-based Chinese interests. On 5 September, *Canberra* was towed out of Sydney by the tug *Roumania*, arriving in Singapore 53 days later.

By then, *Canberra* had been resold to the Goulandris Group, better known as the Greek Line. Registered under the ownership of Cia Maritima del Este SA, Panama, *Canberra* went to Greece to be refitted, and without change of name, began operating from Europe to South America.

On 31 August 1949, *Canberra* departed Naples bound for Australia with a full complement of 766 migrants. It berthed in Sydney on 5 October, and three days later left, returning to Naples on 15 November. The vessel was then extensively remodelled, with accommodation for 52 first class and 752 tourist class passengers, and for five years operated between Europe and Canada.

In 1954 *Canberra* was sold to the Dominican Republic, and renamed *Espana*. It voyaged between the West Indies and Spain carrying migrants and sugar until 1959, then was sold to shipbreakers.

COLUMBIA

BUILT: 1913 by Harland & Wolff Ltd, Belfast
TONNAGE: 9,424, gross
DIMENSIONS: 468 x 60 ft (142.6 x 18.2 m)
SERVICE SPEED: 15 knots
PROPULSION: Triple expansion/triple screws

The second former Australian coastal liner to return to local waters in 1949 was *Columbia,* better remembered as *Katoomba* of McIlwraith McEacharn Ltd. *Katoomba* was launched on 10 April 1913, and completed three months later. It was fitted with accommodation for 209 first class, 192 second class and 156 third class passengers, and arrived in Australia for the first time in September 1913, joining the coastal trade between Sydney and Fremantle.

On 2 June 1918, *Katoomba* left Melbourne with troops bound for New York via the Panama Canal, then made two Atlantic crossings before being sent into the Mediterranean. It returned to Sydney with a full load of troops in September 1919, and was then refitted, resuming the coastal trade in March 1920.

In March 1941 *Katoomba* was requisitioned for its second war, carrying troops to New Guinea. It later carried troops to Colombo, returning in April 1942, then resumed the coastal trade again. Later in 1942, *Katoomba* was again taken over, and transported troops around the South Pacific. When handed back to McIlwraith McEacharn in February 1946 it was

offered for sale, and in July 1946 was purchased by the Goulandris Group, better known as the Greek Line, being registered under the ownership of a subsidiary company, Cia Maritima del Este SA, of Panama.

Katoomba was taken to Genoa for a refit, and on 31 December 1946 made the first Greek Line post-war sailing, from Genoa to New York. The following year it began a two-year charter to French Line, operating to the West Indies. In April 1949, *Katoomba* was given another refit, during which it was converted to oil firing, and given accommodation for 52 first class and 752 tourist class passengers. It was also painted white, and renamed *Columbia.*

The first voyage as *Columbia* was to Australia, departing Genoa on 25 November 1949. Arriving in Fremantle on 17 December, it left next day for Sydney, berthing on 26 December. *Columbia* left Sydney on 30 December, returning to Naples on 29 January 1950.

Columbia was then placed on the regular Greek Line service to Canada, making two voyages from Naples, then being based at Bremerhaven. In April 1957 it began operating from Liverpool to Quebec. On 21 October 1957, *Columbia* left Quebec bound for Bremerhaven, where it was laid up. In March 1958 the vessel was moved to Piraeus, but remained idle until August 1959, then left for Japan, arriving on 29 September 1959 in Nagasaki, having been sold to shipbreakers there.

63

HELLENIC PRINCE

BUILT: 1929 by Cockatoo Island Dockyard, Sydney
TONNAGE: 6,558 gross
DIMENSIONS: 444 x 61 ft (135.3 x 18.5 m)
SERVICE SPEED: 20 knots
PROPULSION: Geared turbines/twin screws

The only Australian-built vessel to bring migrants to the country was *Hellenic Prince*, which was also one of the most unusual looking ships converted for this purpose. In 1924, the Royal Australian Navy ordered a seaplane carrier, the first to be built for them. Laid down in April 1926, it was launched on 21 February 1928, completed on 21 December that year, and commissioned into the RAN on 23 January 1929 as HMAS *Albatross*. With a complement of 450 officers and ratings, it could carry six seaplanes, which were stored in a hangar forward, and lowered into the water by a crane aft.

Unfortunately, by the time the ship was completed, seaplanes were almost obsolete in the Navy, so over the next four years HMAS *Albatross* made a few coastal voyages, then on 26 April 1933 was decommissioned. It remained idle in Sydney until 1938, then was transferred to the Royal Navy in part payment for the cruiser HMS *Amphion*, which was transferred to the RAN in October 1938 as HMAS *Perth*. HMAS *Albatross* voyaged to Britain, only to be laid up in Plymouth on 15 December 1938 as HMS *Albatross*, since the Royal Navy had no use for the ship either.

In August 1939 it was recommissioned, and converted into an aircraft repair ship, then sent to the South Atlantic Station. Early in 1942 it was refitted in America, then joined the British Eastern Fleet, remaining with them until the end of 1943, when it returned to Britain. HMS *Albatross* was then converted to do ship repairs, and recommissioned in time to take part in the Normandy landings.

Albatross was stationed off the beaches, and repaired 132 damaged vessels over a period of several months. The vessel was attacked by enemy aircraft on numerous occasions, and on 11 August 1944 was hit by a torpedo. This caused the ship to return to Portsmouth for repairs, but these stopped in 1945 when the war ended. *Albatross* was laid up at Portsmouth, then moved to Falmouth.

Offered for sale, *Albatross* was purchased on 19 August 1946 by the South Western Steam Navigation Co, who intended to convert it for the Australian emigrant trade. Work began at Chatham Dockyard, then the owners changed their minds after a considerable amount of work had been done, and early in 1947 the vessel was towed to Torbay.

Renamed *Pride of Torquay*, it spent several months serving as a storage hulk, but in late 1947 was towed to Plymouth and laid up, being offered for sale. When no buyers were forthcoming, an auction was organised for 19 October 1948, but a few days before that date, the ship was sold to China Hellenic Lines Ltd, of Hong Kong.

Renamed *Hellenic Prince*, it arrived on 20 December 1948 at the C H Bailey Ltd shipyard at Barry in Wales, to be converted for the Australian migrant trade. The work involved the original hangar being divided into two decks, and accommodation installed for 1,000 persons. Amenities provided included a 560-seat dining room, three hospitals and a cinema.

The work was due to be completed at the end of March 1949, and an IRO contract was obtained for the ship to operate between Naples and Australia at 17 knots, for voyages of between 25 and 28 days, beginning in April 1949. Unfortunately, the work took longer than anticipated, and it was 17 October 1949 before *Hellenic Prince* left Barry for Naples.

On 7 November 1949, *Hellenic Prince* left Naples on its first voyage to Australia, carrying 997 displaced persons, calling at Fremantle on 28 November, then going directly to Sydney, arriving on 5 December, returning empty to Naples.

The second voyage departed on 11 January 1950, but was quite protracted, as the vessel lost an anchor off Sicily while boarding more passengers, then was held up three days at Port Said. Crossing the Indian Ocean the vessel had to stop engines due to boiler problems, and drifted for two days, eventually reaching Melbourne on 13 February.

On its third trip, *Hellenic Prince* arrived in Melbourne on 25 April 1950, then returned by way of Indonesia, picking up Dutch nationals who were taken to Bremerhaven. This became its European terminal port for future voyages, the first departure from there being on 25 June 1950.

In September 1950, *Hellenic Prince* made its second departure from Bremerhaven, but after calling at Fremantle in 10 October, went to Wellington, arriving on 16 October, then returned to Fremantle on 2 November, and called at Jakarta on its return trip to Bremerhaven. Leaving again in December, *Hellenic Prince* arrived in Melbourne on 10 January 1951.

The vessel remained on the Australian emigrant trade until 1952, when it was chartered by the British Government to transport troops to Kenya. On 12 November 1953, the vessel was laid up in Hong Kong, and on 28 August 1954 was sold to local ship-breakers, Pacific Salvage Co Ltd.

HMAS *Albatross*

Hellenic Prince

KANIMBLA

BUILT: 1936 by Harland & Wolff Ltd, Belfast
TONNAGE: 11,004 gross
DIMENSIONS: 484 x 66 ft (147.6 x 20.2 m)
SERVICE SPEED: 17 knots
PROPULSION: H & W diesels/twin screws

Built for McIlwraith McEacharn Ltd, *Kanimbla* was the only Australian-owned liner to have any involvement in the migrant trade. Launched on 12 December 1935, it arrived in Sydney on 1 June 1936 on its delivery voyage, the largest and last liner to be built for the trade between Sydney and Fremantle. Accommodation was provided for 203 first and 198 second class passengers.

Taken over by the Royal Australian Navy on 27 August 1939, *Kanimbla* was converted in Sydney to an armed merchant cruiser, with seven 6-inch guns and two 3-inch guns. Commissioned on 6 October 1939, *Kanimbla* was posted to the China Station, based on Hong Kong, then in June 1941 transferred to the East Indies Station at Colombo.

Kanimba was converted into a Landing Ship, Infantry, in 1943, carrying 26 landing barges, and took part in numerous landings, being in Subic Bay when the Japanese surrendered. *Kanimbla* was then used to repatriate released prisoners-of-war to Australia, and later carried troops home.

On 29 November 1947, *Kanimbla* arrived in Fremantle carrying released internees and Axis prisoners-of-war, who were transferred to the American troopship *General Stuart Heintzelmann* to be returned to Europe. Meanwhile, the first group of displaced persons to arrive in Australia, 837 single men and women from the Baltic States, who had been carried to Fremantle on the *Heintzelmann*, boarded *Kanimbla* and were transported to Melbourne, where they arrived on 7 December.

In June 1948 *Kanimbla* left Sydney with the crew to bring the new Australian aircraft carrier, HMAS *Sydney*, from Britain. On the return voyage, *Kanimbla* arrived on 17 September in Genoa, where 432 Italian single male migrants were embarked and carried to Melbourne, arriving on 18 October.

Kanimbla was then released from government service, and given an extensive refit. With accommodation for 231 first class and 125 second class passengers, it resumed the coastal service again in December 1950. On 14 June 1952 *Kanimbla* ran aground in Moreton Bay, suffering serious bottom damage, and being out of service for three months. In September 1958, *Kanimbla* made a cruise to Hong Kong and Japan, and made two similar cruises in 1959 and 1960.

Kanimbla was sold in January 1961 to Pacific Transport Co Inc. Renamed *Oriental Queen*, it was placed on the pilgrim trade from Indonesia to Jeddah for three years, then early in 1964 the Japanese firm, Toyo Yusen Kaisha, chartered the vessel. Repainted in their colours, *Oriental Queen* was sent to Australia in May 1964 to serve as a cruise ship, being based in Sydney. Providing accommodation for 350 passengers in one class, it operated a mixture of Pacific cruises and longer trips to Japan and the Far East, and some trans-Tasman voyages.

In January 1967, Toyo Yusen Kaisha bought *Oriental Queen* outright, and subsequently it operated cruises out of Japan, arriving in Yokohama on 6 October 1973 at the end of its final voyage. The vessel was then sold to shipbreakers in Taiwan, arriving in Kaohsiung on 7 December 1973.

OTRANTO and ORONTES

BUILT: 1925–1929 by Vickers-Armstrong Ltd, Barrow
TONNAGE: 20,051 / 20,186 gross
DIMENSIONS: 659/664 x 75 ft (200.6/202.3 x 22.9 m)
SERVICE SPEED: 20 knots
PROPULSION: Geared turbines/twin screws

During the 1920s the Orient Line took delivery of five new liners for the Australian trade: *Orama*, completed in 1924, *Oronsay* and *Otranto* the next year, *Orford* in 1928 and *Orontes* in 1929.

Otranto was launched on 9 June 1925, and had accommodation for 572 first class and 1,114 third class passengers, slightly less than the earlier ships. On 9 January 1926, *Otranto* departed Tilbury on its maiden voyage to Australia. On returning to Britain, *Otranto* made a Mediterranean cruise, but hit rocks off Cape Matapan on 11 May 1926, suffering severe bow damage, which was repaired in Britain.

Orontes was launched on 26 February 1929, being completed in July 1929, then making a series of cruises from Britain before leaving Tilbury on 26 October on its maiden voyage to Australia. *Orontes* had a raked bow and carried a smaller number of passengers, 460 first class and 1,112 third class. By 1933 the third class accommodation on all these ships had been upgraded, and reduced to about 500 tourist class. When cruising, all the ships carried a maximum of 550 passengers in a single class.

By the beginning of 1940, all five sisters were operating as troopships, and on 1 June 1940, *Orford* was bombed by German aircraft off Marseilles, having to be beached to burn out, becoming a total loss. Only eight days later, *Orama* was caught by the German heavy cruiser *Admiral Hipper* off Norway, and sunk. On 9 October 1942 *Oronsay* was sunk by a submarine in the South Atlantic.

In 1942 *Otranto* was converted into a landing ship, and with *Orontes* was involved in the North Africa landings. Later both ships were involved in the landings in Sicily and at Salerno, surviving several intense attacks by German aircraft, *Orontes* once being straddled by five bombs.

Orontes was retained by the British Government until 1947, then went to the Thorneycroft shipyard at Southampton to be reconditioned. With accommodation for 502 first class and 610 tourist class passengers, it left Tilbury on 17 June 1948 to resume service to Australia.

Otranto was released by the British Government in August 1948, and refitted by Cammell Laird at Birkenhead, with accommodation for 1,416 tourist class passengers only. On 14 July 1949, *Otranto* left Tilbury, arriving in Sydney on 19 August. Both these ships had been repainted in their pre-war colours, and looked very dated. In 1953, *Orontes* was refitted to carry 1,410 tourist class passengers, and joined *Otranto* carrying assisted migrants.

In 1957, having completed 64 round trips to Australia in peacetime, *Otranto* was sold to Shipbreaking Industries., leaving Tilbury on 12 June 1957 bound for their Faslane yard.

On 25 November 1961, *Orontes* left Tilbury on its final voyage to Australia, departing Sydney on 12 January 1962 on the return leg. On 5 March 1962 *Orontes* arrived in Valencia, where it was broken up.

Orontes

ASTURIAS

BUILT: 1926 by Harland & Wolff Ltd, Belfast
TONNAGE: 22,445 gross
DIMENSIONS: 666 x 78 ft (203 x 23.9 m)
SERVICE SPEED: 18 knots
PROPULSION: Geared turbines/twin screws

The first of two sisters ships built for Royal Mail Line, being launched on 7 July 1925, *Asturias* left Southampton on its maiden voyage to South America on 27 February 1926. The following year it was joined by *Alcantara*, and they were, for a short time, the largest motor liners in the world, being powered by Burmeister & Wain diesels, and having two squat funnels.

Unfortunately, the engines caused excessive vibration, so in 1934 *Asturias* and her sister returned to their builder's yard, where geared turbine machinery was installed. At the same time, the vessels were lengthened 10 ft (3.2 m), and the two funnels raised. On returning to service in September 1924, *Asturias* had accommodation for 330 first, 220 second and 768 third class passengers.

Asturias was frequently used for cruises in the first eight years of her career, along with regular voyages to South America, until September 1939, when it was requisitioned, and converted into an armed merchant cruiser. Eight 6-inch guns were fitted, and at the same time the dummy forward funnel was removed.

When 400 miles from Freetown, *Asturias* was hit by a torpedo, fired by the Italian submarine *Ammiraglio Cagni*, just before midnight on 24 July 1943. The torpedo exploded in the port engine room, killing four men and disabling the ship. The tug *Zwartze Zee* towed *Asturias* to Freetown, arriving on 1 August. The ship was beached with the midships open to the sea, and eventually was declared a total loss.

However, in February 1945 the hulk was sold to the Royal Navy, and a concrete patch fitted over the hole in the side. *Asturias* was towed to Gibraltar for drydocking and further repairs, and then towed to Belfast, for rebuilding by Harland & Wolff as a troopship. In mid-1946 *Asturias* was ready for service once again, managed by Royal Mail Line on behalf of the Ministry of Transport.

On 12 October 1946, *Asturias* left Southampton for Cape Town, then went on to Australia, berthing in Fremantle on 12 November, Melbourne on 17 November and being in Sydney from 19 to 26 November before returning to Britain. During 1947 *Asturias* made two voyages to Fremantle from Southampton, the first departing on 29 August, the second on 9 November, carrying 1,612 migrants, arriving on 10 December.

In 1948 *Asturias* made three trips to Australia, and one early in 1949. *Asturias* was then refitted to carry 160 first class, 113 third class and 1,134 dormitory passengers. Still painted in troopship colours, grey hull and a yellow funnel, *Asturias* departed Southampton on 26 July 1949, carrying 1,340 migrants, and voyaged to Fremantle, Melbourne and Sydney. On the next voyage, *Asturias* left Sydney on 10 December 1949 and went to Jakarta to board Dutch nationals and carry them back to Rotterdam.

Asturias then departed Southampton on 8 February 1950, and on returning, the liner was repainted in the colours of its former owners, Royal Mail Line. The first departure from Southampton in this guise was on 10 May. *Asturias* remained on the Australian migrant trade until 1953, then was withdrawn and began transporting British troops to the Korean war zone. On 14 September 1957, the old liner arrived at Faslane, to be broken up.

Asturias

NELLY - SEVEN SEAS

BUILT: 1941 by Sun Shipbuilding & Drydock Co, Chester
TONNAGE: 11,086 gross
DIMENSIONS: 492 x 69 ft (150 x 21.2 m)
SERVICE SPEED: 16 knots
PROPULSION: Busch-Sulzer diesel/single screw

This vessel was laid down as a standard design C3 cargo ship, and launched on 11 January 1940 as *Mormacmail*. Work on the ship proceeded very slowly, then on 6 March 1941 it was taken over by the US Navy, and converted into an auxiliary aircraft carrier at the Newport News shipyard.

Commissioned as USS *Long Island* on 2 June 1941, it could carry 21 aircraft, and was armed with one 5-inch gun and a pair of 3-inch guns. USS *Long Island* served in the Pacific zone throughout the rest of the war, with its aircraft capacity being increased as demand for aircraft grew. When the battle for Guadalcanal was being fought, USS *Long Island* was sent to the area, and on 20 August 1942 flew off 19 Wildcat fighters and 12 Dauntless dive-bombers from a position 210 miles away. These were the first combat planes to land at Henderson Field on Guadalcanal, only three days after the airstrip was completed, and 13 days after the Americans had captured the area.

Long Island was decommissioned on 26 March 1946 and laid up pending disposal. On 12 March 1948 it was bought at auction by Caribbean Land & Shipping Corp, a Swiss-based organisation. Renamed *Nelly*, and registered in Panama, it was rebuilt for the emigrant trade, being given rather basic accommodation for 1,500 passengers.

Nelly made its first voyage from Naples to Australia in June 1949, arriving in Melbourne on 17 July. The second voyage arrived in Melbourne on 15 September, and the third on 14 November. On its fourth voyage, *Nelly* went to Sydney for the first time, arriving on 15 January 1950. *Nelly* arrived in Sydney again on 3 March 1950, but did not leave until 26 March, going to Jakarta to collect Dutch nationals returning home.

Nelly made more trips to Australia from Europe over the next three years, and also made some migrant voyages to Canada, leaving Southampton in January 1953 on its final voyage as *Nelly*, going only to Melbourne and being in port three days from 24 February. On returning to Bremerhaven, the vessel was withdrawn for an extensive refit.

The accommodation was extensively altered to cater for 20 first class and 987 tourist class passengers, and the bridgehouse enlarged. It was then renamed *Seven Seas*, and on 9 May 1953 left Bremerhaven for Australia once more, arriving in Fremantle on 8 June, and terminating in Melbourne on 12 June.

On its return to Bremerhaven, *Seven Seas* was chartered by Europe-Canada Line, which was jointly owned by Holland-America Line and Royal Rotterdam Lloyd. Europe-Canada Line was formed to provide cheap travel across the Atlantic, and *Seven Seas* began operating from Bremerhaven, Le Havre and Southampton to Quebec and Montreal. Towards the end of 1955, *Seven Seas* was bought outright by Europe-Canada Line, and registered in West Germany, but its service remained unchanged.

Nelly

On 30 October 1960, *Seven Seas* departed Southampton under charter to Royal Rotterdam Lloyd, visiting Fremantle, Melbourne and Sydney, then going on to Wellington and Auckland, where it berthed on 18 December.

Seven Seas returned to the Canadian trade until April 1963, when it began operating from Bremerhaven to New York. At the end of the 1963 summer season, *Seven Seas* was chartered by Chapman College to undertake study cruises for their University of the Seven Seas, visiting many countries around the world.

When this ended, the vessel went to Amsterdam, and on behalf of Holland-America Line, departed in March 1964 for Australia, passing through Fremantle on 28 April on the way to Melbourne and Sydney, from where it sailed on 6 May across the Pacific to New York. Following another season as a floating university, in March 1965 the vessel made another voyage to Australia and New Zealand on behalf of Holland-America Line.

Seven Seas then resumed its Atlantic service for the summer months, and on 18 July 1965 was disabled by an engine room fire when some 500 miles from St John, being towed there for repairs. *Seven Seas* made its final visit to Australia when, as a floating university, it departed Los Angeles on 10 February 1966, being in Sydney for two days from 8 March, then going to Fremantle and on to the Middle East, and back to New York.

Following one more summer on the Atlantic, *Seven Seas* was withdrawn in September 1966, and sold to Verolme Shipyards for duty as a floating hostel for workers at their Parkhaven yard in Rotterdam. It served in this static role for the next 10 years, until being sold to shipbreakers in April 1977. On 4 May *Seven Seas* was towed away from Parkhaven and arrived at the Ghent yard of Van Heyghen Freres the following day.

Seven Seas berthed in Sydney

HIMALAYA

BUILT: 1949 by Vickers-Armstrong Ltd, Barrow
TONNAGE: 27,955 gross
DIMENSIONS: 709 x 90 ft (216 x 27.6 m)
SERVICE SPEED: 22 knots
PROPULSION: Geared turbines/twin screws

Himalaya was the first new liner built for P & O after the war, being launched on 5 October 1948, and running trials off Arran on 24 August 1949, reaching 25.13 knots. *Himalaya* left Tilbury on its maiden voyage on 6 October 1949, reaching Sydney on 7 November.

Himalaya had an identical hull to *Orcades*, but a different superstructure. The accommodation was also very different, being for 758 first class and 401 tourist class passengers. After two round trips to Australia, *Himalaya* made two cruises from Southampton to the Mediterranean, and would be frequently used for cruising.

One problem to affect the ship was smuts from the funnel falling on the afterdecks, so in 1953 a Thorneycroft top was fitted to the funnel. While *Himalaya* was in the Mediterranean on 30 August 1956, an explosion in the refrigeration plant killed four crewmen and injured 12, causing a diversion to Malta for repairs.

In March 1958 *Himalaya* departed Tilbury on a four-month journey that went first to Australia via the Suez Canal, then from Sydney to the west coast of America and back to Sydney, returning to Tilbury on 2 June, this being the first trans-Pacific voyage by a P & O liner.

Following its next voyage to Australia, *Himalaya* made a series of eight cruises from Sydney between 25 July and 5 November 1958, then returned to Britain. In March 1959 *Himalaya* left Sydney on another trans-Pacific voyage, but on the return trip made the first ever P & O crossing from America to Japan, then came back to Sydney.

Himalaya had to enter the Garden Island drydock in Sydney on 18 August 1959 for replacement of a propeller which had been damaged in the Suez Canal, arriving 15 days late into Sydney. On returning to Britain the vessel was drydocked again to have air-conditioning installed.

In 1963 *Himalaya* was converted into a one-class liner, with tourist class accommodation for 1,416 passengers. It left Tilbury in this guise for the first time on 1 November 1963, and over the next 10 years was used increasingly for cruising, with very few line voyages. On 10 October 1969, *Himalaya* was the last P & O vessel to depart from Tilbury, as the company then moved their base to Southampton.

In the 1970s *Himalaya* was used almost exclusively for cruising, May to October from Southampton, then making a line voyage to Sydney, cruising from there the rest of the year. In April 1974, *Himalaya* voyaged back to Britain, but then left Southampton again on 16 May to return to Australia, and made another series of cruises from Sydney.

On 18 October 1974 *Himalaya* left Sydney for the last time, heading for Hong Kong. Here the passengers disembarked, and many of the fittings were removed. *Himalaya* then went to Kaohsiung in Taiwan, arriving on 28 November 1974, and being handed over to shipbreakers.

EMPIRE BRENT

BUILT: 1925 by Fairfield SB & E Co, Glasgow
TONNAGE: 13,475 gross
DIMENSIONS: 538 x 66 ft (164 x 20.2 m)
SERVICE SPEED: 15 knots
PROPULSION: Geared turbines/twin screws

This ship was built for the Donaldson Line as *Letitia*, to operate between Glasgow and Montreal. Launched on 14 October 1924, it entered service in April 1925, providing accommodation for 516 cabin and 1,023 third class passengers. Its sister was named *Athenia*, and is best remembered as the first British passenger vessel to be sunk in World War Two.

In October 1939, *Letitia* was requisitioned and converted into an armed merchant cruiser. Later the vessel was used as a troopship, and in 1944 was transferred to the Canadian Government and converted into a hospital ship. Following a period repatriating Canadian troops, *Letitia* was bought outright by the Ministry of Transport, for whom it was managed by Donaldson Line

Renamed *Empire Brent*, it was initially used to carry the war-brides and families of Canadian servicemen to their new homeland. It was while outbound on such a voyage that *Empire Brent* collided with and sank the small coaster *Stormont* in the Mersey on 20 November 1946. *Empire Brent* suffered severe bow damage, and had to be drydocked for repairs. Late in 1947, *Empire Brent* was sent to the Barclay, Curle shipyard on the Clyde to be refitted for the emigrant trade, with accommodation for 965 persons.

On 31 March 1948, *Empire Brent* departed Glasgow for Australia, with the families of servicemen aboard, arriving in Fremantle on 2 May, Melbourne on 7 May and was in Sydney from 10 to 16 May. A second voyage to Australia with migrants departed Glasgow on 13 July 1948, and it arrived in Melbourne again on 22 November on its next voyage.

During 1949 *Empire Brent* made four voyages to Australia from Glasgow, departing on 8 February, 14 May, 17 August and 30 November, on this trip calling at Fremantle and Melbourne before reaching Sydney on 7 January 1950. Its next trip departed Glasgow on 6 April 1950, and on leaving Sydney on 22 May, the vessel went to Indonesia to collect Dutch nationals wishing to return home. After one more voyage to Australia, *Empire Brent* arrived back in Glasgow on 6 December 1950, and then was laid up.

Early in 1951, the New Zealand Government chartered *Empire Brent*, which was renamed *Captain Cook*, and left Glasgow on 5 February 1952 on its first voyage to New Zealand. The vessel spent the next seven years carrying British migrants to New Zealand. Over those years the New Zealand government had been purchasing *Captain Cook* by instalments, and by 1959 owned the ship outright. It was at this time that the hull was repainted white.

Captain Cook left Glasgow on 11 September 1959 on its twenty-fifth voyage to New Zealand. The vessel then returned to Britain empty, arriving in Glasgow on 10 February 1960. The old liner was laid up at Falmouth until being sold to T W Ward Ltd, and arrived at their Inverkeithing shipbreaking yard under tow on 29 April 1960.

FAIRSEA

BUILT: 1942 by Sun Shipbuilding & Drydock Co, Chester
TONNAGE: 11,678 gross
DIMENSIONS: 492 x 69 ft (150 x 21.1 m)
SERVICE SPEED: 16 knots
PROPULSION: Doxford diesels/single screw

Fairsea was another of the converted aircraft carriers to see service in the Australian emigrant trade for many years. Although generally thought of as a Sitmar ship, *Fairsea* spent most of its career under the Panamanian flag, but had been built for service under the American flag as *Rio de la Plata*.

In February 1939, an American shipping company, Moore-McCormick Line, ordered four cargo ships, with accommodation for about 70 passengers, to operate from New York to the east coast of South America. They were to be the first American passenger vessels to be fitted with diesel machinery, in this case two 6-cylinder Doxford diesels geared to a single shaft.

Launched on 1 March 1941, *Rio de la Plata* was taken over by the US Government in October that year, and completed as an escort carrier. Handed over to the Royal Navy under the Lend-Lease agreement, it was commissioned as HMS *Charger* on 3 March 1942. Later in 1942, the vessel was returned to the Americans, and as USS *Charger* saw considerable service in the Pacific.

USS *Charger* was released from naval service on 15 March 1946, and returned to the US Government, being placed under the management of Moore-McCormick Line. The flight deck was removed, and the ship converted to carry troops, in which guise it

saw brief service, then was laid up and offered for sale. In 1949, the vessel was bought by Alexandre Vlasov, and registered under the ownership of Alvion Steam Ship Corporation as *Fairsea*, but operated by Sitmar.

The vessel was rebuilt as a passenger ship when Vlasov obtained an IRO contract to transport displaced persons and refugees to Australia, but under the terms of the contract, had to return to Europe empty.

With rather austere accommodation for 1,900 persons, *Fairsea* departed Naples on 11 May 1949 carrying 1,896 displaced persons, who disembarked at Melbourne on 9 June. The second voyage left Naples on 21 July, going to Newcastle, where the 1,896 passengers left the ship on 20 August. The third voyage, from Naples on 21 September, berthed in Melbourne on 19 October. On its fourth voyage, *Fairsea* disembarked 1,852 passengers in Sydney on 31 December 1949, while the fifth trip only went as far as Fremantle, arriving on 3 March 1950 with 1,898 passengers.

On 10 April 1950, *Fairsea* made its first departure for Australia from Bremerhaven, which became its regular home port for the next two years. Carrying 1,878 passengers, the vessel berthed in Melbourne on 23 May, returning there again on 18 August and 7 November.

On 22 January 1951, *Fairsea* disembarked 1,902 passengers in Melbourne, but on its next voyage, it was carrying only 1,393 displaced persons when it arrived in Melbourne on 24 April.

In February 1952, Sitmar opened an office in Sydney, and began offering passages to Italy on their ships. On 7 April 1952, *Fairsea* departed Amsterdam

Fairsea as first converted in 1949

and voyaged by way of the Panama Canal to Australia for the first time, but later reverted to departures from Bremerhaven. In April 1953, *Fairsea* was taken off the Australian trade, to make six round trips between Bremerhaven and Quebec, offering accommodation for 40 first class and 1,400 tourist class passengers.

When *Georgic* was withdrawn from service in 1955, *Fairsea* became the first non-British ship to be allocated to transport British migrants to Australia. It left Southampton for the first time on 6 December 1955. In February 1957, *Fairsea* crossed the Tasman for the first time to visit New Zealand, then crossed the Pacific for its first transit of the Panama Canal. In July 1957, *Fairsea* made the first of three round trips from Bremerhaven to New York, then was withdrawn for six months to undergo an extensive refit.

The appearance of the ship was changed considerably, as the superstructure was raised one deck, and the forward section plated in. Internally, the accommodation was improved, new public rooms added in a deckhouse forward, and full air-conditioning was installed. Emerging in April 1958, the tonnage had been increased to 13,432 gross. *Fairsea* offered accommodation for 1,460 tourist class passengers, and was transferred from Panamanian to Italian registry, and to the ownership of Sitmar Line.

Fairsea continued to carry British migrants to Australia under a government contract, and in 1961 was given another extensive refit, during which the accommodation was further upgraded, and capacity reduced to 1,212 in one class. On 18 December 1962, *Fairsea* departed Sydney on the first cruise to be operated by Sitmar Line, visiting Brisbane, Noumea, Tonga, Suva and Auckland. Subseqently *Fairsea* made occasional cruises from Sydney.

In 1968, *Fairsea* reverted to Panamanian registry again, the registered owners being Passenger Liner Services Inc. It still operated as a unit of the Sitmar fleet, but was due to be withdrawn in 1970.

On 14 January 1969, *Fairsea* left Sydney for New Zealand and Britain, with 986 passengers on board. On 29 January, an engine room fire disabled the vessel when it was midway between Tahiti and Panama. The freighter *Louise Lykes* arrived on the scene, and towed *Fairsea* to Balboa, where they arrived on 3 February. The passengers were flown to their destinations from Panama, while *Fairsea* was inspected to decide her future. Being one of a very few ships to have been fitted with Doxford geared diesels, spare parts were no longer available, and repairs were considered to be uneconomic, so the vessel was sold to shipbreakers in Italy. On 9 July 1969, *Fairsea* left Panama under tow by the tug *Vortice*, arriving on 6 August 1969 at La Spezia, where it was broken up.

Fairsea after rebuilding in 1957

GROOTE BEER, ZUIDERKRUIS and WATERMAN

BUILT: Groote Beer: 1944 by Permanente, Richmond, California
  Zuiderkruis & Waterman: 1944–45 by Oregon Shipbuilding
  Corp, Portland, Oregon
TONNAGE: 9,190/9,178/9,176 gross
DIMENSIONS: 455 x 62 ft (138.7 x 18.9 m)
SERVICE SPEED: 17 knots
PROPULSION: Geared turbines/single screw

These three Dutch vessels were among 413 "Victory" ships built in America, their original names being *Costa Rica Victory*, *Cranston Victory* and *La Grande Victory* respectively. Toward the end of the war, 97 "Victory" ships were completed as transports, able to carry up to 1,597 troops. Bunks were installed in the 'tween decks; and galleys, washrooms, hospital facilities and a few public rooms were added. The entire accommodation area was fitted with a ventilation system and heating. To support these additions, the hull and decks had to be strengthened, but by the time most of these ships were completed, the war was over.

Cranston Victory was launched on 5 May 1944, and on completion was operated for the US Maritime Commission by the South Atlantic Steamship Corp,

of Savannah. *Costa Rica Victory* was launched on 17 June 1944, completed three months later, and operated for the government by the American Hawaiian Steamship Corp, of New York.

Last of this trio to be launched was *La Grande Victory*, on 16 January 1945, which was managed by the Shepard Steamship Co, of Boston. All three ships were laid up in 1946, and offered for sale the following year.

Purchased during 1947 by the Dutch Government, they were renamed after the three major star formations, the Great Bear, Southern Cross and Aquarius. *Groote Beer* was placed under the management of Nederland Line, while *Zuiderkruis* and *Waterman* were managed by Royal Rotterdam Lloyd. The trio was refitted to carry troops to the Dutch East Indies, with accommodation for 276 in cabins and 575 in dormitories. They remained in this service over the next four years, then in 1951 were refitted again, for the emigrant trade.

Each vessel was sent in turn to the Nederland Dock Co shipyard in Rotterdam, where an extra deck was added, and the bridge moved forward atop an extension to the superstructure. Internally, accommodation was installed for 830 persons in cabins.

Zuiderkruis was the first to be altered, returning to service in June 1951 with a voyage from Rotterdam to New York, then was placed on a service to Canada.

Waterman in Sydney

In August it left Rotterdam with 800 migrants bound for New Zealand.

Waterman was the second of the trio to be reconstructed, but during 1951, *Groote Beer* made three voyages to Australia before being rebuilt, the first departing Rotterdam on 28 February to reach Fremantle on 21 March, Melbourne on 27 March and Sydney three days later. It then called at Surabaya on the way back to Holland.

Leaving Amsterdam on its second voyage to Australia on 26 May, *Groote Beer* followed the same route. The third voyage also left from Amsterdam, this time bound for New Zealand with 450 migrants, then going to Australia.

On 2 November 1951 *Groote Beer* arrived at Nederland Dockyard, while on 14 November, *Waterman* left Rotterdam on its first voyage to Australia, berthing in Fremantle on 9 December, Melbourne on 14 December and Sydney on 17 December. *Groote Beer* returned to service in May 1952, and on 18 June left Rotterdam on a voyage to New York, followed by a trip to Quebec. It was now being managed for the Dutch Government by Holland-America Line, with *Zuiderkruis* being transferred to the management of Nederland Line.

Over the next decade, these three ships made periodic voyages to both Australia and New Zealand, as well as being employed on various Atlantic trades. In January 1961, the Dutch Government formed their own shipping company, N V Scheepsvaart Maats Trans-Oceaan, to which these vessels were transferred, though remaining under the same management as before. Their accommodation was upgraded to tourist class, as the demand for emigrant passages was declining.

During November 1962, *Groote Beer* and *Waterman* were berthed in Fremantle to provide accommodation for visitors to the Commonwealth Games in Perth. In January 1963, *Waterman* departed Amsterdam on what was to be the last voyage to Australia and New Zealand by these vessels under the Dutch flag, as in September 1963 *Zuiderkruis* was transferred to the Dutch Navy as an accommodation ship, based at Den Helder, while *Groote Beer* and *Waterman* were sold to the Greek shipowner, John S Latsis.

Waterman was renamed *Margareta*, while *Groote Beer* became *Marianna IV*, and both were initially used for economy services in the Mediterranean and across the Atlantic.

However, on 2 December 1964, *Marianna IV* left Piraeus for Australia, arriving in Melbourne on 28 December and Sydney two days later, leaving on 2 January 1965 to return to Piraeus. For this voyage, the ship's funnel was painted in Chandris cargo line colours.

Both Latsis ships were used for student travel across the Atlantic during the summer months. On 12 July 1966, *Marianna IV* was leaving Southampton when it collided with the sand dredger *Pen Avon* off the Isle of Wight. After basic repairs, *Marianna IV* returned to Piraeus, but no further repair work was done, and the vessel was laid up in Eleusis Roads on 17 March 1967. Also during 1967, *Margareta* was withdrawn from service, and sold to the Yugoslav shipbreaking firm, Brodospas, being towed out of Piraeus on 10 November 1967 bound for Split. *Marianna IV* remained laid up until June 1970, then was sold to local shipbreakers.

Zuiderkruis remained with the Dutch Navy until being sold to local shipbreakers in Rotterdam on 29 October 1969, who then resold the ship to Spanish breakers at Bilbao, where it arrived under tow on 27 November.

Groote Beer

JOHAN VAN OLDENBARNEVELT

BUILT: 1930 by Nederland Shipbuilding Co, Amsterdam
TONNAGE: 19,787 gross
DIMENSIONS: 608 x 74 ft (185.4 x 22.8 m)
SERVICE SPEED: 17 knots
PROPULSION: Sulzer diesels/twin screws

Built for the Nederland Line service from Holland to the Dutch East Indies, and launched on 3 August 1929, *Johan van Oldenbarnevelt* was named in honour of a sixteenth-century Dutchman executed by his political enemies. The vessel had comfortable accommodation for 366 first, 280 second, 64 third and 60 fourth class passengers, and 360 crew.

On 7 May 1930 *Johan van Oldenbarnevelt* left Amsterdam on its maiden voyage to Batavia, but while passing through the North Sea Canal came into collision with the small Dutch coaster *Reggestroom*. *Johan van Oldenbarnevelt* had to return to port for repairs, sailing again several days later. In October 1930, it was joined by an identical sister ship, *Marnix van St Aldegonde.*

For the next nine years these ships operated regularly to the Dutch East Indies, but as war clouds gathered, *Johan van Oldenbarnevelt* was chartered by Holland-America Line for a single return trip to New York, departing Amsterdam on 30 August 1939. *Johan van Oldenbarnevelt* then made a return trip to Batavia, and was outward bound again when Holland was invaded.

Both *Johan van Oldenbarnevelt* and its sister were taken over by the British as troopships, the former being converted by Harland & Wolff at Belfast. Both ships retained their Dutch crews, and visited Australia several times during the war, to carry troops overseas. On 6 November 1943, *Marnix van St Aldegonde* was torpedoed and sunk off Algeria. *Johan van Oldenbarnevelt* survived the war without incident, and in October 1945 was handed back to

Nederland Line.

Refitted at Amsterdam, the vessel returned to its pre-war service from Holland to Batavia in July 1946. As the revolt against Dutch rule intensified, demand for passages out to the area declined rapidly, so in 1950 Nederland Line withdrew *Johan van Oldenbarnevelt* from the route.

Chartered by the Dutch Government to carry migrants to Australia, the liner departed Amsterdam on 5 September 1950 on its first commercial voyage to Australia, calling at Malta en route, arriving in Fremantle on 5 October, Melbourne on 10 October and Sydney two days later. Leaving on 14 October for Jakarta, it boarded Dutch nationals returning home. On 19 December the liner left Amsterdam on its second voyage, departing Sydney on 23 January 1951 for Surabaya, and then back to Amsterdam.

Johan van Oldenbarnevelt was then taken out of service for an extensive refit, to better suit it for the Australian migrant trade, being completely altered internally to carry 1,414 passengers in a single class, and the hull was repainted light grey. On 23 January 1952, the liner departed Amsterdam bound for Australia again, and after leaving Sydney called at Surabaya on the return trip. It remained on the emigrant trade to Australia for the next seven years, though from 1954 to 1958 was also used for occasional voyages across the North Atlantic, making 11 trips in all to New York or Montreal.

In August 1958 the Dutch Government terminated their charter of *Johan van Oldenbarnevelt* at the end of its final Atlantic voyage, and Nederland Line decided to place the vessel on a new round-the-world service. First it was sent back to its builder's yard for another refit, during which the accommodation was altered to cater for 1,210 tourist class passengers. This consisted of 247 two-berth cabins, 90 three-berth, 81 four-berth, 6 five-berth and 5 large dormitories.

The biggest alteration was to the external appearance of the liner, as the original squat funnels were heightened and given round tops, the mainmast

Johan van Oldenbarnevelt in the mid-1950s

Johan van Oldenbarnevelt after rebuilding in 1959

removed and the foremast shortened, and a new signal mast installed behind the bridge.

On 3 April 1959, *Johan van Oldenbarnevelt* left Amsterdam on its first voyage on the new route, calling at Southampton, then through Suez to Fremantle on 30 April, Melbourne on 5 May and Sydney on 8 May, leaving next day for Wellington, where it arrived on 13 May. The liner then continued across the Pacific to the Panama Canal and back to Amsterdam, with calls at Port Everglades and New York.

The schedule called for four trips per year, but unfortunately this new service was not a success, despite the addition of extra ports of call along the way. Nederland Line operated the route for three years, but then decided to withdraw *Johan van Oldenbarnevelt*, its final round-the-world voyage departing Amsterdam on 30 June 1962.

On 29 September the liner left Amsterdam bound for Australia and New Zealand for the last time, going as far as Wellington. *Johan van Oldenbarnevelt* returned to Sydney, and then went to Fremantle, serving as a floating hotel there during the Commonwealth Games in Perth. Leaving

Fremantle on 2 December, the liner came back to Sydney, and made two cruises to New Zealand, departing on 9 December and 23 December. Two trips between Sydney and Wellington followed.

Johan van Oldenbarnevelt had been sold to the Greek Line by the time it berthed in Sydney for the last time, on 3 February 1963, and the liner left empty the same day bound for Genoa.

Handed over to the new owners on 8 March, it was renamed *Lakonia,* and given a quick refit. Work on the interior was still in progress when it arrived at Southampton to begin a new career as a cruise liner. The first cruise departed on 24 April, going to Madeira, Teneriffe and Las Palmas.

Lakonia was on its eighteenth cruise out of Southampton when, on 22 December 1963, a fire broke out and quickly spread through the liner, which was 200 miles from Madeira. Calls for assistance were quickly answered, but of the 1,028 passengers, 128 lost their lives. On 24 December the Dutch salvage tug *Herkules* took *Lakonia* in tow, but on 29 December 1963 the liner sank 250 miles west of Gibraltar.

Lakonia

AUSTRALIA, NEPTUNIA and OCEANIA

BUILT: 1951 by Cant Riuniti dell'Adriatico, Trieste
TONNAGE: 12,839 gross
DIMENSIONS: 528 x 69 ft (161 x 21.1 m)
SERVICE SPEED: 18 knots
PROPULSION: Sulzer diesels/twin screws

Lloyd Triestino had re-established its Australian service after the war with old and chartered tonnage, but began a rebuilding programme as soon as possible, ordering seven liners. Two were for their Far East route, two for the African trade, and three for the Australian service. This trio was the first to be built, and all were launched during 1950.

The first was named *Australia* when launched on 21 May, the second *Oceania* on 30 July, the third *Neptunia* on 1 October. Accommodation was provided for 280 first class, 120 second class and 392 third class passengers, with a crew numbering 236. First class cabins were mostly 2-berth with either private or shared facilities, while second class had 2- and 4-berth cabins. Third class comprised 6 and 8-berth cabins and dormitories with up to 22 bunks in them.

Australia departed Trieste on its maiden voyage on 19 April 1951, reaching Fremantle on 11 May, Adelaide on 15 May, and Melbourne on 17 May. Departing three days later, *Australia* arrived in Sydney on 22 May, and terminated the voyage at Brisbane on 24 May. The return voyage was made along the reverse route, and the ship returned to Genoa, from where all future sailings would depart.

Oceania departed Genoa on its maiden voyage on 18 August, and *Neptunia* on 14 September, reaching Brisbane on 18 October. With the three ships in service, Lloyd Triestino was once again able to offer a regular monthly schedule operated by modern liners, and enjoyed extremely good passenger loadings over the next decade.

When the Suez Canal was closed in 1956, the vessels were routed around South Africa. *Oceania* was the first vessel bound for Australia to pass through the canal when it re-opened in April 1957.

On 15 June 1958, *Australia* made a call at Newcastle to load wool and board passengers, being the first large passenger vessel to visit that port since the war.

During 1958, each liner was withdrawn from service in turn for a refit, during which the forward well deck was filled in. At the same time, air-conditioning was extended to encompass the entire ship, and the accommodation altered to cater for 136 first class and 536 tourist class, the latter being subdivided into 304 tourist A and 232 tourist B.

The changes effected in 1958 verified the gradual drift away from first class accommodation to the more popular tourist class, and reflected the decline in the assisted emigrant trade from Italy with the removal of third class.

Neptunia

Australia arriving in Sydney

From October 1960, *Neptunia* began operating as a tourist one-class ship, but the other two were not altered in a similar way.

The three ships continued to carry good passenger loads in both directions, so in 1960 Lloyd Triestino placed orders for two large liners more than twice the size of the *Australia* trio to be built for the Australian trade. When they entered service during 1963, these three liners would be withdrawn, and transferred to Italia Line, to replace three cargo/passenger liners on the service from Italy to Central America and the west coast of South America.

Australia was the first to be withdrawn, departing Genoa for the last time on 18 January 1963, and after leaving Sydney on 21 February, made a call at Hobart on 23 February, before going back to Melbourne, Adelaide and Fremantle, from where it sailed on 4 March for Genoa. *Australia* was then handed over to Italia Line, and renamed *Donizetti*, departing Genoa on 4 June on its first voyage to Valparaiso. *Oceania* made its final departure from Genoa on 15 February 1963, leaving Sydney on 23 March, and on being handed over to Italia Line was renamed *Rossini*.

The first of the new liners, *Galileo Galilei*, entered service in April 1963, but work on the second was delayed, so *Neptunia* was retained on the route,

making its final departure from Genoa on 7 August 1963, departing Sydney on 11 September. On being transferred to Italia Line it was renamed *Verdi*.

On 16 April 1964, *Verdi* collided with the tanker *Pentelikon* in fog off Gibraltar, suffering bow damage, and having to return to Genoa for repairs.

The services to South America and Australia were heavily subsidised by the Italian Government, but by the mid-1970s the Italian Government could no longer support these shipping services, and they were abandoned. The South American service was the first to go, these three ships being withdrawn within a matter of months.

Donizetti arrived at La Spezia on 15 October 1976 to be laid up, being joined by *Rossini* on 19 November, and finally *Verdi* was laid up on 26 January 1977. All three were offered for sale, with *Donizetti* and *Verdi* being purchased by shipbreakers at La Spezia in June 1977. At the same time *Rossini* was transferred to another Italian company, Tirrenia, but they had no use for the ship, and in September 1977 it was also sold to shipbreakers at La Spezia.

These three liners had all come from the same shipyard within months of each other, spent their entire careers operating together on two different routes, and ended their careers at the same place within months of each other.

SONTAY

BUILT: 1921 by Bremer Vulkan, Vegesack
TONNAGE: 8,917 gross
DIMENSIONS: 469 x 58 ft (144.3 x 17.8 m)
SERVICE SPEED: 13 knots
PROPULSION: Triple expansion/single screw

This vessel was built to the order of Hamburg America Line, being launched on 2 June 1921 as *Bayern*. Along with a sister ship, *Wurttemberg*, it was designed as a supplementary liner for the lucrative migrant trade between Germany and North America.

Permanent cabin accommodation was provided for 16 cabin class passengers, with austere quarters for 750 third class set up in the holds for the westbound voyage. On the return trip, the temporary berths would be removed to make way for cargo. *Bayern* departed Hamburg on 13 September 1921 on its maiden voyage to New York, but only served on this route until December 1923.

Early in 1924, *Bayern* and *Wurttemberg* were transferred to another major Hamburg America Line route, from Germany to South America. *Bayern* spent the rest of its career under the German flag on this route. During 1930, a low pressure turbine was added to the existing machinery, to increase speed and economy.

On 8 December 1936, *Bayern* was sold by Hamburg America Line to Messageries Maritimes, and hoisted the French flag as *Sontay*, joining the major Messageries Maritimes trade from Marseilles to French colonies in South East Asia. The passenger arrangements were not altered, though the third class was often used by troops. From 1940 to 1945, *Sontay* operated under Allied control, being managed by Union Castle Line. On being handed back to Messageries Maritimes, *Sontay* resumed its pre-war trade to South East Asia.

On 5 August 1950, *Sontay* departed Marseilles on its only voyage to Australia, stopping at Malta to collect further migrants. *Sontay* arrived in Fremantle on 9 September, then proceeded directly to Sydney, berthing at No 1 Circular Quay on 19 September. All the migrant passengers were disembarked in Sydney during a five-day layover, then on 24 September *Sontay* left, bound for Haiphong.

Sontay spent the remainder of its career under the French flag on the trade to South East Asia. In February 1955, the vessel was sold to a Panamanian company, Wheelock Marden & Co, though not handed over until 5 June. Renamed *Sunlock*, it operated as a general cargo ship until 1959, then was sold to shipbreakers in Japan.

NEW AUSTRALIA - ARKADIA

BUILT: 1931 by Vickers-Armstrong Ltd, Newcastle
TONNAGE: 20,256 gross
DIMENSIONS: 579 x 76 ft (176.6 x 23.3 m)
SERVICE SPEED: 19 knots
PROPULSION: Turbo-electric/quadruple screws

New Australia was a most unusual looking vessel, with rather austere accommodation, but it had originally been one of the most luxurious liners in the world. Built for Furness, Withy & Co, it was launched as *Monarch of Bermuda* on 17 March 1931, and completed in November the same year.

Monarch of Bermuda was designed for the luxury service between New York and Bermuda operated by Furness Bermuda Line. It had three funnels, the last being a dummy, a high superstructure, and luxurious accommodation for 830 first class passengers only, all in cabins with private facilities.

Monarch of Bermuda departed New York on 28 November 1931 on its maiden voyage to Bermuda, berthing in Hamilton two days later. The liner soon became very popular, and was joined in 1933 by a sister, *Queen of Bermuda*. They were known as the "millionaire's ships" during the 1930s.

Monarch of Bermuda was laid up in New York in September 1939, then in November was requisitioned by the British Government and began service as a troopship, boarding 962 troops in Halifax and carrying them to Gourock. It then went to Liverpool where the luxury fittings were removed, and quarters for 1,385 men installed.

In July 1940, *Monarch of Bermuda* was one of three ships delegated to carry the bulk of the bullion of the British Government, valued at some £690 million, from the River Clyde to Halifax. In 1941 the trooping capacity was increased to 3,250, and in August 1942 the vessel was altered to carry landing craft. It took part in the North Africa landings, making three voyages with troops.

The vessel later took part in the landings on Sicily, and in 1943 the troop capacity was increased to 4,050, though 5,560 could be carried by double berthing in some of the three-tiered bunks. In July 1946 the liner was released from government service, having travelled 450,512 miles and carried 164,840 persons during the war.

Monarch of Bermuda was sent to the Palmer shipyard at Hebburn on Tyne to be refitted for a return to her pre-war service. The work was well in hand when, on 24 March 1947, a fire broke out which gutted the ship, and it was subsequently declared a total loss.

The hulk was towed away to Rosyth, and at any other time it would have been sold for scrap. However, in the immediate post-war years passenger ships were in very short supply, and the Argentine Government made a bid for the vessel, but the

Monarch of Bermuda

British Government refused to sanction the sale.

Instead, after trials had indicated that the engines were still in working order, the British Government purchased the hulk on behalf of the Ministry of Transport early in 1948. In April 1948 the vessel arrived at the Thorneycroft shipyard in Southampton, to be rebuilt to transport migrants to Australia. The cost of the rebuilding would be shared equally by the British and Australian Governments.

The badly damaged upperworks were totally removed, and a new superstructure was constructed, not as high as the original. The first and third funnels were also removed, and a single large funnel was placed amidships. A bipod mast was fitted where the forward funnel had been, but this also served as a funnel.

Accommodation for 1,600 persons was installed, with a large number of six-berth cabins, and some four-berth and eight-berth cabins. All contained two-tier metal bunks and wardrobes, but did not have washbasins, there being a large number of communal facilities. From being one of the most luxurious liners ever built, it was now the epitome of austerity. One concession to its former identity was the retention of the outdoor swimming pool aft.

The ship was renamed *New Australia*, and placed under the management of Shaw Savill Line, with the funnel painted in their colours. Rebuilding took longer and was more expensive than anticipated, and it was 18 July 1950 before trials were run, only to have a steam pipe burst, scalding nine people. Two days later further sea trials were completed

successfully, and the ship was accepted by the Ministry of Transport.

The original plan had been for the ship to make three trips a year to Australia, carrying British assisted migrants on the outward voyage, but returning empty. During the northern summer *New Australia* would operate a series of economy voyages across the North Atlantic. This idea was dropped before the ship entered service, and instead it was programmed to make four round trips a year to Australia, but rather than returning empty it would carry some fare-paying passengers.

The first voyage departed Southampton on 15 August 1950, passing through Suez to reach Fremantle on 9 September, Adelaide on 13 September, Melbourne two days later and Sydney on 18 September. The vessel then went to Jakarta to board Dutch nationals and return them home. Over the next three years, *New Australia* maintained a regular service between Southampton and Australia, carrying thousands of British migrants.

New Australia left Southampton on 28 January 1953 on a regular migrant voyage, berthing in Sydney on 1 March. It was then taken over for trooping duties, as on 5 March the men of 2 Battalion, Royal Australian Regiment, boarded the ship to be taken to Korea. *New Australia* arrived at Pusan on 21 March, where 2 RAR disembarked. Then the men of 1 Battalion, RAR, who had completed their tour of duty in Korea, boarded the ship, which returned them to Sydney on 6 April. *New Australia* then returned to Britain.

New Australia

On 7 September 1953, *New Australia* left Sydney on a regular voyage back to Southampton, but then was taken over by the British Government to carry troops to Korea. This employment continued until April 1954, when *New Australia*, having carried troops to Korea, then voyaged south to Brisbane, and then Sydney on 19 April. The vessel made a regular voyage back to Britain, and resumed its place on the migrant trade.

The vessel spent the rest of 1954 and all 1955 trading to Australia, then it was diverted to trooping duties again in 1956. *New Australia* left Southampton on 1 February with a full complement of migrants, arriving in Sydney on 4 March. The vessel then left Sydney on 8 March to go to Kure, arriving on 19 March, and then to Inchon on 26 March to board Australian troops who were returned to Sydney on 5 April. The vessel then made a regular voyage back to Britain.

New Australia left Southampton on 16 August 1957 on its final voyage to Australia, and on leaving Sydney went to Singapore, then returned to Sydney again on 31 October. Leaving on 2 November, it bypassed Melbourne, but stopped at Adelaide on 4 November, and departed Fremantle on 8 November, bound for Southampton, where it was laid up.

The migrant charter under which *New Australia* had been operating terminated on 21 September 1957, and was not renewed by the British Government, so the vessel was offered for sale. In January 1958 *New Australia* was sold to the Greek Line, and renamed *Arkadia*.

The vessel was sent to the Blohm & Voss shipyard in Hamburg for refitting, during which the superstructure was streamlined and a new, raked bow fitted. The accommodation was completely rebuilt to carry 150 first class and 1,150 tourist class passengers. Repainted white, and looking very smart, *Arkadia* left Bremerhaven on 22 May 1958 on its first voyage, to Quebec and Montreal.

This remained its regular trade, but in 1959 the vessel made some cruises out of New York, and in 1960 began cruising occasionally from Southampton. At the end of that year the vessel returned to Blohm & Voss and the accommodation was altered to carry 50 first class, and 1,337 tourist class. At the same time the after end of the superstructure was glassed in.

Arkadia alternated between Atlantic voyages and, cruises until 1963, when it departed Bremerhaven on 23 October, and Tilbury two days later, bound for Australia. The vessel arrived in Fremantle on 18 November, Melbourne five days later, and Sydney on 25 November, berthing at the Overseas Passenger Terminal in Circular Quay, leaving next day to return to Europe.

Whilst *Arkadia* was on this voyage, Greek Line suffered the loss by fire and sinking of *Lakonia*, the former *Johan van Oldenbarnevelt*. When *Arkadia* returned to Britain, it was put on the full-time cruise service from Southampton, taking over the itinerary originally scheduled for *Lakonia*.

On 21 November 1966 the vessel was laid up in the River Fal, then sold to Spanish shipbreakers, arriving at their Valencia yard on 18 December.

Arkadia

AMARAPOORA

BUILT: 1920 by W Denny & Sons Ltd, Dumbarton
TONNAGE: 8,173 gross
DIMENSIONS: 484 x 59 ft (147.6 x 18 m)
SERVICE SPEED: 13 knots
PROPULSION: Triple expansion/single screw

Amarapoora was built for P Henderson & Co, a Glasgow-based firm that traded to Burma. The vessel had seven holds, and provided accommodation for 146 first class passengers only.

In 1935, *Amarapoora* was given an extensive refit, during which the passenger accommodation was upgraded and reduced to 124 first class. All the public rooms were also refurbished and upgraded, and the forward end of the promenade deck was glassed in.

Requisitioned in September 1939, *Amarapoora* was converted into a hospital ship, and based at Scapa Flow until October 1942, when it went to Gibraltar, then to Salerno after the landings there, and finished the war based at Trincomalee.

Handed back to Henderson's early in 1946, they sold the vessel to the Ministry of Transport in June 1946. Retaining its hospital fittings, *Amarapoora* was used to repatriate released prisoners-of-war. In 1948 it was reconditioned to carry displaced persons from Italian ports to Australia under an IRO charter.

On its first voyage to Australia, *Amarapoora* disembarked 617 passengers at Fremantle on 19 April 1949, arriving back in Fremantle again on 22 July. On its next voyage, *Amarapoora* berthed in Sydney on 20 October 1949. The vessel did not return to Australia again until the following year, disembarking 631 passengers at Newcastle on 24 April 1950. On 1 August 1950 *Amarapoora* left Genoa on its last voyage to Australia, landing 634 passengers at Newcastle on 15 September.

When the IRO charter ended, the Ministry of Transport offered *Amarapoora* to the New Zealand Government to transport British migrants, and *Amarapoora* was sent to Glasgow for an extensive refit. Accommodation for 584 persons was installed, and the ship renamed *Captain Hobson*. It left Glasgow on 15 July 1952 on its first voyage to New Zealand, through the Panama Canal to Wellington.

In August 1953, *Captain Hobson* was diverted to Hong Kong to collect British troops and return them to Britain. It made several more trooping voyages from the Far East over the next two years, and in January 1955 ran aground when leaving Singapore while en route from Japan to Britain. In July 1955, *Captain Hobson* was back on the New Zealand emigrant trade again, only to return to trooping duties from August to December 1956 at the time of the Suez crisis.

In April 1957 *Captain Hobson* left Glasgow with 590 migrants aboard, but on 12 June, when two days out from Wellington, was disabled by major engine trouble. The Port Line freighter *Port Macquarie* towed *Captain Hobson* to Auckland, arriving on 18 June. The vessel limped back to Britain for repairs to be effected.

In May 1958, *Captain Hobson* left Glasgow on its twelfth and final voyage to New Zealand, arriving in Wellington on 19 July. The vessel was then sent to Bombay and laid up. In December 1958, *Captain Hobson* was sold to Japanese shipbreakers, Okushogi & Co, and arrived at their Osaka yard on 18 March 1959.

Amarapoora as an emigrant ship

BRASIL

BUILT: 1905 by A Stephen & Sons Ltd, Glasgow
TONNAGE: 11,182 gross
DIMENSIONS: 538 x 60 ft (164 x 18.4 m)
SERVICE SPEED: 17 knots
PROPULSION: Geared turbines/triple screws

Brasil was the second of a pair of sisters built for the Allan Line that made maritime history, being the first large liners to be fitted with geared turbine engines. The first ship was named *Victorian*, while the second was launched on 22 December 1904 as *Virginian*. Completed in March 1905, it departed Liverpool on 6 April on its maiden voyage to Canada, providing accommodation for 426 first class, 286 second class and 940 third class passengers.

In August 1914, *Virginian* was requisitioned by the British Government and became a troopship, but three months later was converted into an armed merchant cruiser, serving with the 10th Cruiser Squadron. In October 1915, the Allan Line was bought by Canadian Pacific, to whom *Virginian* was handed when released from government service in January 1920. The following month the liner was sold to Swedish America Line, and renamed *Drottningholm*.

In 1922 *Drottningholm* was refitted to carry 532 cabin class and 854 third class passengers, and also given new De Laval geared turbine machinery. The liner operated on the New York trade until 1940, then served during the war under the auspices of the International Red Cross. *Drottningholm* became famous as a "mercy ship", transporting over 25,000 prisoners-of-war and civilian internees being exchanged by the belligerent powers.

In March 1946, *Drottningholm* returned to the Gothenburg-New York trade, making the first post-war trans-Atlantic sailing by any company from Europe. In 1948, the vessel was sold to Home Line, registered in Panama, and renamed *Brasil* for service from Genoa to South America. During 1950, *Brasil* was transferred to operate between Naples and New York.

On 12 October 1950, under charter to the IRO, *Brasil* boarded 1,112 displaced persons in Bremerhaven, bound for Australia. After calling at Fremantle on 12 November, *Brasil* proceeded direct to Sydney, where it berthed at 13 Pyrmont on 18 November. *Brasil* left empty on 22 November, passing through Fremantle again on 28 November, and returning to Italy. The vessel was then extensively refitted, to carry 96 first class and 846 tourist class passengers.

Renamed *Homeland*, it operated from Hamburg and Southampton to New York between June 1951 and March 1952, then returned to the Genoa-New York trade. Its final voyage was to South America, returning to Genoa in February 1955, then on 29 March 1955 the old liner arrived in Trieste to be broken up.

SIBAJAK

BUILT: 1928 by Kon Maats de Schelde, Flushing
TONNAGE: 12,226 gross
DIMENSIONS: 530 x 62 ft (161.5 x 19.1 m)
SERVICE SPEED: 17 knots
PROPULSION: Sulzer diesels/twin screws

The Dutch Government encouraged emigration in the post-war years, which resulted in a number of vessels built for the Dutch East Indies trade coming to Australia, one of them being *Sibajak*, which had been built for Rotterdam Lloyd.

Sibajak was launched on 2 April 1927, and entered service in February 1928. As built it carried 200 first, 196 second, 68 third and 34 fourth class passengers, but in 1935 the vessel was refitted to cater for 200 first, 250 second and 75 third class. *Sibajak* remained on the Dutch East Indies trade until Germany invaded Holland in May 1940, when it was laid up in Surabaya. The vessel was then taken over by the British, under the management of P & O Line, but still with its Dutch crew, and used as a troopship.

In July 1941, *Sibajak* embarked Australian troops in Fremantle and carried them to Singapore in convoy US11B. Returning to Sydney, *Sibajak* carried another contingent of troops to Singapore in convoy US12B. In September 1946 the vessel visited Fremantle, Melbourne, Sydney and Brisbane, then returned to Rotterdam.

By this time the situation in the Dutch East Indies had changed, and there was little demand for passages from Holland. As a result, *Sibajak* was refitted to carry 956 passengers in one class, and then chartered to the Dutch Government to transport migrants to Australia.

On 15 April 1950 *Sibajak* left Rotterdam on its first post-war voyage as a passenger ship, going to Melbourne, from where it sailed on 22 May to Indonesia and back to Holland. Its second voyage departed Rotterdam in July, passing through Fremantle on 18 August, Melbourne on 24 August and arriving in Sydney two days later, returning again via Indonesia. This pattern was followed by the vessel for the next two years, which made four round trips each year.

In January 1952, *Sibajak* left Rotterdam on its first voyage to New Zealand, disembarking migrants at Wellington. Over the next few years *Sibajak* would make a further six voyages to New Zealand, but was mainly used on the service to Australia. Between 1952 and 1955 *Sibajak* also made nine voyages across the Atlantic, again under charter to the Dutch Government. The first of these was in April 1952, from Rotterdam to Quebec, and later it visited Halifax and New York.

Sibajak remained in the migrant trade throughout the 1950s, but by 1959 demand for such passages was declining. In 1958 a round-the-world service was started jointly by Royal Rotterdam Lloyd and Nederland Line, in which *Sibajak* participated briefly, but it was now wearing out. On 23 June 1959 *Sibajak* left Rotterdam on its final voyage to New Zealand and Australia, terminating in Melbourne. On 8 August the vessel left Melbourne bound for Hong Kong, where it arrived on 25 August and was handed over to shipbreakers.

ROMA

BUILT: 1914 by Newport News SB & DD Co
TONNAGE: 6,530 gross
DIMENSIONS: 410 x 54 ft (125 x 16.4 m)
SERVICE SPEED: 12 knots
PROPULSION: Triple expansion/single screw

Roma made only a single voyage to Australia with migrants, but has a place in maritime history due to the length of its career, which almost spans a century.

It was launched on 22 August 1914 as the cargo ship *Medina*, for the Mallory Steamship Co, an American coastal line. A sister ship, *Neches*, was also built in 1914, but sunk four years later. *Medina* was designed for a service along the west coast of America, but on completion made some trips across the Atlantic.

Medina remained in the coastal trade between the wars, the owners becoming Clyde-Mallory Line after a merger in 1932, and then AGWI Lines after a further amalgamation in 1934. *Medina* remained on the coastal trades throughout World War Two, though under government control, then was offered for sale.

In 1948 the vessel was purchased by Cia San Miguel SA of Panama, and sent to La Spezia to be converted into a passenger carrier. The original small central superstructure and tall, thin funnel were removed, being replaced by a new superstructure and a squat funnel, with a raked bow added, and basic accommodation for 950 persons.

Renamed *Roma*, the vessel was first chartered by the International Catholic Travel Committee to carry pilgrims from America to Europe for the Holy Year celebrations in Rome.

Roma then went to Bremerhaven to make a migrant voyage to Australia, leaving on 31 October 1950 with 949 passengers. The vessel made a very slow voyage, taking over five weeks before arriving in Fremantle on 9 December. *Roma* then went directly to Newcastle, where it berthed on 18 December, and disembarked all the passengers.

On returning to Europe, *Roma* was laid up and offered for sale. With the engines now worn out after 40 years' service, it seemed likely the old vessel would be sold for scrap.

However, in 1951 the vessel was bought by Giacamo Costa fu Andrea, known as the Costa Line, a privately owned Italian company. The new owners gave the ship an extensive refit, with new accommodation being installed for 925 passengers in three classes, and a larger superstructure. The old engines were removed, and replaced with Fiat diesels. Renamed *Franca C*, the vessel was placed on a regular service from Italy to Central America.

In 1953 *Franca C* was withdrawn from this trade and given another extensive refit. The superstructure was streamlined, and luxury accommodation for a maximum of 354 passengers installed, with all cabins having private facilities, and the entire ship being fully air-conditioned. *Franca C* then became one of the first permanent cruise liners, operating out of Italian ports in the Mediterranean most of the year, and was highly successful.

In 1970, despite the hull being over 50 years old, *Franca C* was given another new set of Fiat diesels, and it remained as a cruise ship in the Costa fleet until 1977. The vessel was then offered for sale, and bought by Operation Mobilisation, a Christian organization, which took over the ship in Genoa on 4 November 1977.

Renamed *Doulos*, which is Greek for "servant", the vessel was moved to Bremen for refitting, the majority of the work being done by volunteers. The new purpose for the ship would be as a floating book display, both Christian and educational titles, and as a mission ship. In this capacity *Doulos* has visited ports and islands throughout the world, and survived purely on donations and book sales. The crew comprise Christians who volunteer their services for varying periods of time, including the captain and officers, who are always professional seamen.

In 1989, *Doulos* came to Australia for the first time, visiting Devonport, Melbourne, Adelaide, Sydney, Newcastle, Brisbane and Townsville, then going north to Papua New Guinea.

The vessel returned to Australia again in the middle of 1999, spending three weeks in July berthed in Sydney, then going to several Queensland ports and on to New Guinea.

The vessel undergoes regular drydocking and maintenance, and has been brought up to all the current safety standards. It is expected *Doulos* will remain in service at least until 2010, and hopefully it may even survive long enough to celebrate a century afloat.

The migrant ship *Roma* in 1950

The same ship arriving in Sydney in July 19999 as *Doulos*

RAVELLO

BUILT: 1941 by Cant Nav Riuniti, Genoa
TONNAGE: 8,452 gross
DIMENSIONS: 473 x 63 ft (145.5 x 19.4 m)
SERVICE SPEED: 13 knots
PROPULSION: Fiat diesel/single screw

Flotta Lauro were the owners of a fleet of over 50 cargo ships and tankers when Italy came into the war on the Axis side in June 1940. At that time they had a cargo ship under construction in Genoa, which was completed in 1941 as *Ravello*, and immediately placed under Italian Government control.

Ravello was one of the very few Italian ships to survive the war years unscathed. The Flotta Lauro fleet was decimated during the war, so the company was very grateful to have *Ravello* returned to them.

During 1948, Flotta Lauro rebuilt the hulk of a British freighter into the emigrant ship *Napoli*, which was placed on a service to Australia. Meanwhile, *Ravello* was operating as a cargo ship, but the results from *Napoli* were so good that in 1949 *Ravello* was taken in hand for rebuilding as an emigrant ship as well.

The original small central superstructure was extended aft, and accommodation installed for some 480 persons. There were a few cabins in the superstructure, and several public rooms. Large dormitories were erected in the cargo holds, as well as ablution blocks. The facilities provided were austere, and the Italian migrants who comprised most of the passengers paid a minimal fare for the voyage to Australia.

At the end of November 1950, *Ravello* departed Genoa on its first voyage to Australia with passengers, arriving at Fremantle on 4 January after a very slow trip. After a week in port, *Ravello* left for Melbourne, reaching there on 15 January, and eventually arrived in Sydney on 17 January.

Having disembarked the passengers, the dormitory accommodation was removed and *Ravello* then loaded cargo. Several days later the vessel proceeded to Port Lincoln to complete loading, departing on 30 January for Genoa.

In April 1951, the vessel departed Genoa on its second voyage to Australia, calling again at Fremantle, Melbourne and Sydney, from where it departed on 1 June bound for Genoa, again with a full cargo.

On 4 August 1951, *Ravello* left Genoa on what was to be its final voyage to Australia with passengers, calling at the same ports again, and loading cargo in Sydney before leaving on 9 October to return to Genoa. By this time Flotta Lauro had introduced two further ships to their Australian service, *Sydney* and *Roma*, which could adequately cater to the passenger trade.

Ravello was transferred to the migrant service from Italy to ports in Central and South America, but this lasted only a short while, before *Ravello* was again rebuilt. The passenger accommodation was all removed, and the ship reverted to cargo status again. *Ravello* served in the Flotta Lauro fleet in this capacity until being laid up at La Spezia on 28 May 1971. In August that year the vessel was sold to local shipbreakers.

LIGURIA - CORSICA

BUILT: 1917 by Reiherstieg Co, Hamburg
TONNAGE: 7,474 gross
DIMENSIONS; 442 x 55 ft (134.7 x 16.7 m)
SERVICE SPEED: 14 knots
PROPULSION: Quadruple expansion/twin screws

This vessel made two voyages to Australia with migrants, under two names, but prior to the war it had been well known in local waters as the *Marella*, operated by Burns Philp. Built for the Woermann Line to operate between Germany and South Africa, it was launched on 6 June 1914 as *Hilda Woermann*. Completion was delayed by the war, and in 1917 the vessel was renamed *Wahehe*, only to be claimed by the British as a prize in 1918.

Placed under Shaw Savill management, *Wahehe* made three voyages to Australia between May 1919 and June 1920, as a troopship, then was purchased from the British Government in October 1920 by Burns Philp, refitted in Sydney and renamed *Marella*.

With accommodation for 165 first and 75 second class passengers, and a large cargo capacity, the vessel operated from Melbourne and Sydney to Singapore for the next 20 years. In December 1941 *Marella* was off the Queensland coast on a voyage to Singapore, which was terminated at Darwin. *Marella* then became a troopship, and spent the war years in the South Pacific. Late in 1946 the vessel was returned to Burns Philp, and resumed the trade to Singapore, leaving Sydney for the last time on 2 November 1948, having been sold.

In Singapore *Marella* was handed over to Cia Nav Baru, a Panamanian registered firm, and renamed *Captain Marcos*. Sent to Italy for refitting, all cargo spaces were converted into passenger accommodation, increasing the capacity to 929 persons. *Captain Marcos* made a voyage from Genoa to Valparaiso in October 1949, then was renamed *Liguria*, and used in the summer of 1950 to carry pilgrims from America to Europe for the Holy Year celebrations.

On 19 November 1950, *Liguria* left Bremerhaven with 950 persons aboard, bound for Australia. It was a slow voyage as the vessel suffered serious engine problems, and broke down completely on 15 January 1951 when 200 miles from Fremantle, having to be towed to port by the British India Line cargo ship *Chandpara*, arriving on 17 January. The passengers had to find their own way to their destinations, as *Liguria* spent eight months in Fremantle being repaired. After a dispute over payment for the repairs was settled, *Liguria* left Fremantle on 18 August.

The name of the ship was then changed to *Corsica*, though still under the same ownership, and on 17 December 1951 it left Limassol in Cyprus for Australia again, arriving in Fremantle on 25 January 1952, and Melbourne on 4 February, where it was arrested three days later in connection with the previous voyage to Australia. Two weeks later *Corsica* departed, and called at Adelaide on 24 February on the voyage back to Europe.

In August 1952, *Corsica* was laid up at Casablanca, and remained idle until October 1954, when it was sold to Belgian shipbreakers. On 14 November, the old liner arrived at their Ghent yard under tow.

Liguria

FLORENTIA

BUILT: 1914 by W Denny & Bros Ltd, Dumbarton
TONNAGE: 7,821 gross
DIMENSIONS: 484 x 58 ft (147.6 x 17.6 m)
SERVICE SPEED: 13 knots
PROPULSION: Triple expansion/single screw

Florentia was completed in November 1914 as the *Burma* for P Henderson & Co, otherwise known as the British & Burmese Steam Navigation Co Ltd. *Burma* was coal-fired, and had accommodation for 120 passengers, as well as a large cargo capacity. In the early 1920s, the vessel was converted to oil-firing, and partnered by *Amarapoora* and *Pegu*, operated on the trade from Glasgow to Rangoon.

It was an unspectacular career until 1940, when *Burma* was requisitioned by the British Government and converted into a troopship. The vessel was employed mainly in the Indian Ocean, running troops between Suez and India, but also made some trips to East Africa and South Africa. On 23 December 1943 *Burma* ran aground off Mombasa, and was not refloated until 10 April 1944. Following repairs, *Burma* returned to trooping duties, and was retained in this capacity until 1948.

Burma was then handed back to Henderson's, but they had no desire to use the ship again, as it was 34 years old, and the post-war trade to Burma was not as strong as in the pre-war years. *Burma* was offered for sale, and early in 1949 purchased by Cia Nav Florencia, a Panamanian concern. Renamed *Florentia*, it was converted to transport displaced persons under an IRO contract, with austere accommodation, mostly in the cargo holds.

On 15 December 1950, *Florentia* departed Malta on its first voyage to Australia, reaching Fremantle on 14 January 1951, then visiting Melbourne. Arriving in Sydney on 26 January, the vessel remained in port for three weeks loading cargo, which was carried to Port Sudan, then the vessel went to Haifa before returning to Genoa.

For this voyage, *Florentia* had a black hull, but during 1951 it was repainted white when the vessel was transferred to the ownership of Cia Florentina de Nav, and placed under the Italian flag.

In this guise, *Florentia* made two voyages to Australia, both from Genoa. The first departed in April 1951, visiting Fremantle, Melbourne and Sydney, from where it departed on 11 June. *Florentia* departed Genoa on its final voyage to Australia on 18 August 1951, calling at Fremantle on 22 September and Melbourne on 28 September before arriving in Sydney on 7 October. From there the vessel went to Port Thevenard in South Australia to load cargo, departing on 27 October bound for Cyprus.

Florentia continued to serve under that name until 1953, then was sold to the Pan-Islamic Steamship Co, a Pakistani firm that was building up a fleet of old passenger vessels for the pilgrim trade to Jeddah. Renamed *Safina-E-Nusrat*, it survived a further four years, then was sold to shipbreakers in Karachi in September 1957.

JENNY

BUILT: 1918 by Workman, Clark & Co Ltd, Belfast
TONNAGE: 7,914 gross
DIMENSIONS: 465 x 58 ft (141.7 x 17.7 m)
SERVICE SPEED: 14 knots
PROPULSION: Triple expansion/twin screws

During World War One, there were several series of ships built as replacements for losses. *Jenny* was built as *War Argus*, a "G" class British standard ship, designed as fast refrigerated cargo liners, of which 22 were ordered by the shipping controller. However, none of these ships was completed by the end of the war, as *War Argus,* the first of the series, only ran trials on 12 December 1918.

War Argus remained under government control through 1919, but then the British Government began disposing of such tonnage to enable shipping companies to rebuild their depleted fleets. *War Argus* was sold in January 1920 to the famous White Star Line, best known for their passenger liners. However, White Star also operated a large cargo fleet, and they renamed their new acquisition *Gallic*, placing it on their cargo service between Britain and Australia.

When White Star Line ceased to exist as a separate entity in 1933, their ships and services were either taken over by associated companies, or sold. In the case of *Gallic*, it was sold in 1933 to another famous British company, Clan Line, and renamed *Clan Colquhoun.* Under this name it operated a variety of cargo services, and remained in commercial operation throughout World War Two.

In 1947, the vessel was sold again, to Zarata Steamship Co, of Panama, which was part of the Greek Livanos Group, and the ship was renamed *Ioannis Livanos.* This lasted only a brief time, as in 1948 it was transferred within the Livanos Group to the ownership of Dos Oceanos Cia de Nav SA, also a Panamanian company, and renamed *Jenny.*

It was at this time that the vessel was refitted to carry passengers. Very basic temporary facilities were installed in the holds for about 290 persons, and the original three island deckhouses joined together to form a low superstructure. Just how many voyages with displaced persons or migrants this ship made is uncertain, but it is known that it made a single voyage to Australia.

This voyage departed Genoa on 20 January 1951, and it was a very slow trip, as *Jenny* did not reach Fremantle until 26 February, then arrived in Melbourne on 7 March. After a lengthy stay, the vessel continued on to Sydney, berthing on 20 March for another long stay. After the passengers were disembarked, the vessel loaded cargo, and did not depart until 17 April, bound for Egypt.

In 1952 *Jenny* was sold to an Indonesian company, Djarkarta Lloyd, and renamed *Imam Bobdjol*, which was soon changed to *Djatinegra.* After three years of further service the vessel was sold to Japanese shipbreakers late in 1955, and left Jakarta under tow of the tug *Golden Cape*, bound for Osaka.

However, on 1 December *Djatinegra* sprang a leak, and had to be beached at Lingayen, in the Philippines. Refloated on 21 February 1956, the vessel was towed first to Manila, and then to Hong Kong, where it was broken up during June 1956.

SAN GIORGIO

BUILT: 1923 by Cantiere Navale Franco Tosi, Taranto
TONNAGE: 8,955 gross
DIMENSIONS: 460 x 59 ft (140.2 x 18 m)
SERVICE SPEED: 14 knots
PROPULSION: Geared turbines/twin screws

San Giorgio made three voyages to Australia for Lloyd Triestino in 1952, at the end of its career, but it had first voyaged to Australia at the start of its career.

The vessel was built for Lloyd Sabaudo, then a major Italian shipping company, as the single-funnelled *Principessa Giovanna*, with a sister ship, *Principessa Maria*. They were designed as large cargo ships but had 'tween deck accommodation for 400 migrants. This was only used on voyages from Italy, as on the return passage a full cargo would be loaded.

In August 1923, *Principessa Giovanna* made its maiden voyage from Genoa to Australia, and with *Principessa Maria* remained on the service until 1925, when they were transferred to the South American trade. In 1932, Lloyd Sabaudo amalgamated with another large Italian company, Navigazione Generale Italiana, to form Italia Line, to which all the vessels of both their fleets were transferred.

Shortly after the merger, *Principessa Giovanna* was rebuilt, emerging with two funnels, a more extensive superstructure, and accommodation for 640 third class passengers. It continued on the South American trade, though in 1935 was used as a troopship for the Abyssinian campaign for a short period.

In 1940 the vessel became a troopship for the Italians again, but after the surrender in 1944 was taken over by the British. Under the management of British India Line, *Principessa Giovanna* served as a British hospital ship, and later as a troopship.

In 1947 the vessel was returned to the Italians, and refitted at Genoa. Renamed *San Giorgio*, it returned to the Italia Line trade to South America until 1952, then was transferred to Lloyd Triestino. Repainted in their colours, *San Giorgio* departed Trieste on 17 February 1952 for Australia, arriving in Fremantle on 25 March and Melbourne on 1 April, berthing in Sydney on 6 April. It remained in port for a week, then returned to Trieste.

A second voyage departed on 18 June, and the third on 10 October. Leaving Sydney on 28 November, *San Giorgio* was in Melbourne on 3 December, and Fremantle on 11 December the return voyage to Trieste.

A fourth voyage, scheduled to depart on 27 January 1953, was cancelled, and *San Giorgio* was instead laid up. After remaining idle through the year, in December the vessel was sold to Italian shipbreakers, arriving on 30 December at their Savona yard.

SKAUBRYN

*BUILT: 1951 by Oresundsvarvet, Landskrona and
Howaldtswerke, Kiel*
TONNAGE: 9,786 gross
DIMENSIONS: 458 x 57 ft (139.6 x 17.3 m)
SERVICE SPEED: 16 knots
PROPULSION: Gotaverken diesel/single screw

Skaubryn was ordered by Norwegian shipowner Isak M Skaugen as a shelter deck cargo ship. Launched on 7 October 1950, it was being fitted out when Skaugen obtained a contract from the IRO to transport displaced persons.

Skaubryn was moved to the Howaldtswerke yard at Kiel, where the superstructure was added, and accommodation installed for 1,221 passengers, with two-, six- and eight-berth cabins for half that number, and dormitories for the rest. Facilities provided included several lounges, three dining rooms plus a separate dining room for children, two cinemas, a 78-bed hospital, and a large playroom for young children, as well as an open-air swimming pool. *Skaubryn* achieved 17 knots during trials on 22 February 1951.

Skaubryn departed Bremerhaven on 27 February with a full complement of 1,222 migrants, arriving in Melbourne on 1 April, then returning empty to Europe. On 23 May 1951, *Skaubryn* departed Bremerhaven on its second voyage, reaching Fremantle on 20 June, and terminating in Melbourne on 25 June. On its next voyage, which arrived in Melbourne on 5 September, *Skaubryn* carried only 757 migrants, and 767 were aboard when it returned to Melbourne on 12 November.

On future voyages, *Skaubryn* departed from either Bremerhaven or Genoa, and most terminated in Sydney. However, on occasion the vessel was chartered out for other services, and on 11 June 1953 it left Bremen on a migrant voyage to Montreal, then returned to the Australian trade.

The French Government took *Skaubryn* on charter in the mid-1950s to carry troops back to France from Vietnam. In September 1956, *Skaubryn* was chartered by the Dutch Government for one round trip from Rotterdam to Halifax and New York, then in November 1956, the vessel was chartered by the British Government to transport British troops from Singapore to Britain.

For three months in 1957, *Skaubryn* was chartered to the Greek Line, the first departure for them being on 18 June from Bremen to Le Havre and Southampton and then to Quebec. Returning to Liverpool, the vessel made three round trips from Liverpool to Quebec, leaving the Canadian port for the last time on 8 September. *Skaubryn* then returned to the Australian emigrant trade once more.

On 14 March 1958, *Skaubryn* left Bremerhaven with 1,288 passengers aboard, bound for Australia. Having passed through the Suez Canal and Red Sea, the vessel was crossing the Indian Ocean when, on 31 March, a fire broke out in the engine room. Members of the crew attempted to extinguish the blaze, but were unsuccessful.

A call for help was answered by the Ellerman cargo ship *City of Sydney*. When it arrived on the scene, all the passengers on *Skaubryn* were put into lifeboats and transferred to the British ship, as fortunately the seas were smooth. One passenger suffered a heart attack while in a lifeboat, and subsequently died, but all the others reached safety. Next day the Flotta Lauro liner *Roma* arrived on the scene, and all the *Skaubryn* passengers were transferred again in lifeboats to her.

The fire destroyed the midships and forward part of *Skaubryn*, but left the stern almost untouched. On 2 April the frigate HMS *Loch Fada* arrived on the scene, and started towing the vessel to Aden. Next day the Dutch salvage tug *Cycloop* took over the tow, but *Skaubryn* sank on 6 April.

AROSA STAR

BUILT: 1931 by Bethlehem Shipbuilding Corp, Quincy
TONNAGE: 7,114 gross
DIMENSIONS: 466 x 60 ft (142 x 18.3 m)
SERVICE SPEED: 15 knots
PROPULSION: Geared turbines/single screw

Arosa Star made three trips to Australia with migrants over a 15-month period. It had been launched on 24 September 1930 as *Borinquen* for the New York & Porto Rico Steam Ship Co, fitted out with accommodation for 261 first class and 96 second class passengers, and entered service in 1931 between New York and San Juan.

In January 1942, *Borinquen* was taken over by the US Engineers Corps, and refitted to carry 1,289 troops. It made many trips across the Atlantic during the war, as well as to South Africa, and was involved in the landings in North Africa. Returned to its owners in February 1946, *Borinquen* resumed its pre-war service until 1948, when the NY & PR Line ceased trading.

Transferred to the associated Bull Line, renamed *Puerto Rico*, and refitted to carry 186 first class only, it was placed on the San Juan route again. In 1951 the vessel was laid up, then chartered to American Export Line for a brief period before being sold to Cia Internacional Transportadora, a Swiss-owned firm registered in Panama. Renamed *Arosa Star*, the vessel was extensively rebuilt, with a lengthened superstructure, glassed-in promenade deck and new raked bow. Accommodation was increased to 38 first class and 768 tourist class, and on 18 May 1954, *Arosa Star* departed Bremerhaven on its first voyage, to Montreal.

Arosa Star came to Australia under an ICEM contract, the first voyage departing Bremerhaven on 20 November 1954, arriving in Fremantle on 24 December and Melbourne five days later. It then returned to Piraeus, to make a second voyage to Australia, calling at Fremantle and Melbourne before arriving in Sydney on 4 March, leaving the next day for Malta.

Arosa Star then returned to the Canadian trade for the summer, but on 22 January 1955 left Bremerhaven on its third Australian voyage. It visited Fremantle, Melbourne and Sydney, leaving on 5 March for Auckland, arriving on 9 March. *Arosa Star* then returned to Bremerhaven through the Panama Canal, and resumed the Canadian trade.

Arosa Star spent the next two northern winters cruising from New York, but Arosa Line was sliding into deep financial trouble. On 7 December 1958, *Arosa Star* was arrested in Bermuda, and during 1959, was sold at auction to McCormick Shipping, who operated as Eastern Steamship Line.

Renamed *Bahama Star*, it was refitted for cruising from Miami to the Bahamas all year, with 600 passengers. On 13 November 1965, it rescued survivors from another elderly cruise ship, *Yarmouth Castle*, when it burned and sank off Nassau. This disaster brought about new safety regulations for cruise ships operating from American ports, and as the cost of upgrading *Bahama Star* to the new standards was prohibitive, it was withdrawn from service in 1968.

In 1969 the vessel was sold to a California group, for conversion into a floating hotel. Renamed *La Janelle*, it was anchored off Port Hueneme, but on 13 April 1970 drove ashore during a severe storm, being declared a total loss and broken up where it lay.

ROMA and SYDNEY

BUILT: Roma 1943 by Seattle-Tacoma Shipbuilding Corp,
  Tacoma
  Sydney 1942 by Western Pipe & Steel Co, San Francisco
TONNAGE: 14687/14,708 gross
DIMENSIONS: 492 x 69 ft (150 x 21.1 m)
SERVICE SPEED: 17 knots
PROPULSION: Geared turbines/single screw

These sister ships were conversions from warships to passenger vessels, having served during the war as auxiliary aircraft carriers. They were originally ordered by the US Government as standard C3-type cargo ships, for allocation to American shipping companies on completion.

The keel of the ship built at Tacoma was laid down on 5 September 1941, but shortly after construction began it was redesigned as an auxiliary aircraft carrier, being launched on 4 April 1942 and named USS *Croatan*, commissioning into the US Navy in August 1942. The keel of the second vessel was laid down on 9 June 1942, and after a similar redesign, it was launched on 7 September 1942 as USS *Glacier*, being commissioned in June 1943.

Both these ships were handed over to the British under the lend-lease agreement, *Croatan* being commissioned into the Royal Navy on 27 February 1943 as HMS *Fencer*, while *Glacier* became HMS *Atheling* on 31 July 1943. They could carry 20 aircraft, and had a pair of 5-inch guns for defence.

Fencer was part of the British Pacific Fleet that arrived in Sydney on 16 March 1945. When the war ended, both vessels were returned to the Americans, *Fencer* on 11 December 1946, *Atheling* two days later, and laid up at Hampton Roads for disposal.

In mid-1949, both vessels were bought by Flotta Lauro, having their flight decks and other wartime fittings removed by Gibbs Corporation at Jacksonville. *Atheling* arrived there on 23 September 1949, *Fencer* on 28 October.

Atheling left Jacksonville on 9 April 1950 for Trieste, followed soon after by *Fencer*, bound for Naples, where SA Navalmeccanica Cantiere converted them into passenger liners. Due to extensive use of a new non-flammable lining called marinite, they were called the "ships that cannot burn", but fortunately this claim was never put to the test. *Roma* had accommodation for 92 first and 680 tourist class passengers, while *Sydney* could carry 94 first and 708 tourist class passengers.

The ships were scheduled to make monthly departures from Genoa to Australia. *Roma* made the first sailing, in late August 1951, arriving in Fremantle on 1 October, Melbourne on 9 October, and Sydney on 14 October. It then called at Brisbane on 17 October en route to Jakarta and Singapore on the return trip. *Sydney* followed the same route in September 1951, reaching Fremantle on 17 October, then calling at Melbourne, Sydney and Brisbane.

Sydney

When *Roma* returned to Genoa in April 1953, it was transferred to the North Atlantic trade, leaving Genoa on 3 May bound for New York. *Roma* remained on this trade for over three years, being replaced on the Australian route by *Surriento*. From July to September 1953, *Sydney* operated four round trips between Liverpool and Quebec, then returned to the Australian service. On 24 January 1957, *Roma* departed Genoa bound for Australia once again, and the two sisters remained on this route for the next nine years.

As demand for passages from Italy increased, both ships were refitted in 1960, so *Sydney* could carry 119 first class and 994 tourist class passengers, while *Roma* had berths for 119 first and 1,026 tourist class. An open-air swimming pool was now provided for each class, and air-conditioning extended throughout the vessels.

In 1962 Flotta Lauro announced plans for the construction of two 30,000 ton liners to carry 1,700 passengers on the Australian trade, to replace *Roma* and *Sydney*. Before construction began, Flotta Lauro was able to purchase two second-hand liners instead, *Willem Ruys* and *Oranje*, which were rebuilt in Italy, and due to enter service in 1965 as *Achille Lauro* and *Angelina Lauro*.

In mid-1965, *Roma* was withdrawn from the Australian trade, and transferred to a service from Italy to Central America. However, serious fires on board both *Achille Lauro* and *Angelina Lauro* delayed their delivery dates, so *Roma* had to return to the Australian service again. With the new ships finally ready for service in early 1966, *Roma* made its final departure from Genoa for Australia on 4 January 1966, departing Sydney on 3 February and

Brisbane two days later on the return trip. *Sydney* left Genoa on 11 February 1966, departing Sydney for the last time on 14 March.

Both *Roma* and *Sydney* were then transferred to a service from Naples and Genoa to Barcelona, Funchal, Teneriffe and La Guaira. Unfortunately this route was not viable, so on 4 September 1967 *Roma* was withdrawn and laid up at La Spezia. It was then sold to shipbreakers at Vado, arriving there in December 1967.

Flotta Lauro then decided to place *Sydney* on the Mediterranean cruise market, but just to confuse matters, it was renamed *Roma*. The first summer season of cruising was not a success, so in 1968 the vessel was offered for sale. Another Italian concern, Aretusa SpA di Nav bought *Roma* in 1969, and operated it on seasonal Mediterranean cruises, but in October 1970 the vessel was laid up in La Spezia, and offered for sale.

Roma was bought by Sovereign Cruises, a new Cypriot flag firm formed by a British tour operator. Renamed *Galaxy Queen*, and given a major refit, on 20 March 1971 it began cruising under the new name. Numerous mechanical and other failures dogged *Galaxy Queen*, so in 1972 it was laid up, then sold again, to G Kotzovilis, and renamed *Lady Dina*, but remained laid up.

In 1973, the vessel was chartered to the Siosa Line, who had recently lost one of their vessels, *Caribia*. Renamed *Caribia 2*, it made some cruises during 1973, but was in very poor condition.

In September 1974, the old vessel was laid up at La Spezia, then disposed of to local shipbreakers, Terrestre Marittima, who began demolition work on 1 September 1975.

Roma berthed in Sydney

ORONSAY

BUILT: 1951 by Vickers-Armstrong Ltd, Barrow
TONNAGE: 27,632 gross
DIMENSIONS: 708 x 93 ft (216 x 28.5 m)
SERVICE SPEED: 22 knots
PROPULSION: Geared turbines/twin screws

Oronsay was built to the same basic design as *Orcades*, but with a more rounded superstructure and thicker mast. Launched on 30 June 1950, it was being fitted out when a fire erupted in No 1 hold on 28 October. Firemen pumped so much water, the ship began to list heavily against the wharf, and there were fears it would capsize, so a hole was cut in the side to let the water out. This incident caused only a minor delay to completion, and on 23 April 1951, *Oronsay* ran trials, achieving 25.23 knots.

Oronsay had accommodation for 668 first class and 833 tourist class passengers, the latter predominantly used by migrants on the voyages from Britain. *Oronsay* left Tilbury on its maiden voyage on 16 May 1951, reaching Fremantle on 8 June, then visiting Adelaide and Melbourne before arriving in Sydney on 18 June. Initially *Oronsay* voyaged only between Britain and Australia but on 14 February 1953 left Sydney on its first cruise, which became an occasional feature between line voyages over subsequent years.

Oronsay was the first Orient Line vessel to make a voyage across the Pacific, departing Sydney on 1 January 1954 for Auckland, where it berthed on 4 January. The liner went on to visit Suva, Honolulu and Vancouver before arriving in San Francisco on 21 January, then returning to Sydney. *Oronsay* made two further voyages across the Pacific in 1954, leaving Sydney on 21 May and 19 November. In future years, *Oronsay* would make frequent voyages in the Pacific, but it was 1956 before the vessel transited the Panama Canal to complete its first voyage around the world. On 11 October 1960, *Oronsay* left Sydney on its first cruise to the Far East, visiting several Japanese ports, Hong Kong and Singapore.

During 1960, P & O absorbed the Orient Line, but *Oronsay* retained the corn coloured hull until early in 1964, and was then the first of the Orient liners to be repainted white, departing Tilbury for the first time in the new colours on 18 April 1964. In future years, *Oronsay* would make an increasing number of cruises from Sydney, and also from Southampton.

On 14 January 1970, *Oronsay* arrived in Vancouver on a voyage to Australia, but was found to have typhoid on board. The vessel was quarantined, and anchored out in the harbour until 4 February, when it was able to leave. The cause of the outbreak was traced to sewerage pipes that had been wrongly connected during a recent refit.

From 1973 *Oronsay* spent most of each year cruising, though never altered to a one-class ship, which did not help its cruising career. On 4 August 1975, *Oronsay* left Southampton for the last time, passing through the Panama Canal and calling at ports on the west coast of America. The liner arrived in Sydney on 15 September, and the next day left on a one-way cruise to Hong Kong.

After calls at Brisbane and Manila, *Oronsay* arrived in Hong Kong on 28 September, and was destored. On 7 October 1975, *Oronsay* arrived in Kaohsiung, in Taiwan, to be broken up.

99

CASTEL FELICE

BUILT: 1930 by A Stephen & Sons, Glasgow
TONNAGE: 12,150 gross
DIMENSIONS: 493 x 64 ft (150.3 x 19.6 m)
SERVICE SPEED: 16 knots
PROPULSION: Geared turbines/twin screws

Castel Felice was the first vessel owned by Sitmar Line to have been built as a passenger carrier. Ordered by British India Line, it was launched on 27 August 1930 as *Kenya*, and completed four months later. The vessel was designed to trade across the Indian Ocean from Bombay to East Africa and Durban, with a sister, *Karanja*.

As completed, *Kenya* could carry 66 first class, 120 second class and 1,700 third class passengers. The crew was composed of British officers and engineers, Lascar seamen and firemen, and Goanese stewards.

The accommodation provided for first and second class consisted of cabins, but third class was very basic, merely open deck spaces allocated on the main and lower decks, which were well ventilated.

Third class was restricted to Indian passengers, mostly migrants going to East Africa, and to feed them there were six galleys, with special cooks provided to prepare meals according to religious requirements.

Kenya remained on the Indian Ocean trade for 10 years, then in June 1940 was requisitioned by the British Government, as was *Karanja*. Returning to Britain for the first time since being completed,

Kenya was converted into a landing ship, infantry, carrying 10 landing craft, and 1,500 troops.

To avoid confusion with a Royal Navy cruiser of the same name, the vessel was renamed HMS *Keren*. During an active war career, *Keren* took part in a number of Allied landings, including Madagascar in May 1942, and North Africa in November 1942, during which *Karanja* was sunk. *Keren* later took part in the Sicily landings and was in the Indian Ocean, preparing for operations against the Japanese, when the war ended.

British India Line did not want the ship back, so on 3 April 1946 it was purchased by the Ministry of Transport, only to be sent to Scotland and laid up in Holy Loch. For three years the vessel lay idle, then early in 1949 the Vlasov Group began negotiations to purchase the vessel. While these were in progress, on the night of 19 February 1949, *Keren* broke its moorings and was swept ashore during a severe storm. Quickly refloated, the vessel was drydocked in Glasgow for repairs.

It was at this time that a sale was finalised to the Vlasov Group, and *Keren* passed into the ownership of the Alva Steamship Co, of London. Towed to Rothesay Bay and laid up again, over the next two years the vessel underwent a number of name changes.

Initially the vessel was renamed *Kenya*, but later reverted to *Keren*, then *Kenya* again. In 1950 it was transferred to Panamanian registry, renamed *Fairstone*, and towed back to Holy Loch again, becoming *Kenya* once more in June 1950. In October

Kenya

1950 the vessel was transferred to Sitmar Line, under the Italian flag. In March 1951 it reverted to *Keren* again, and under this name finally left Holy Loch on 15 October 1950, being towed to Falmouth where the initial work of rebuilding the vessel for passenger service began.

On 10 March 1951, the vessel left Falmouth and was towed to Antwerp, where further work was done. In August the vessel was towed from Antwerp to Genoa, where the final work would be done.

During this period a raked bow was fitted, the promenade deck extended to the stern, and a new funnel fitted, along with new masts and derrick posts. The interior was completely rebuilt, with cabins for 596 cabin class and 944 third class passengers. The work was completed in September 1952, at which time the vessel was renamed *Castel Felice.*

On 6 October 1952, *Castel Felice* left Genoa on its maiden voyage, arriving in Fremantle on 1 November, Melbourne four days later, and Sydney on 7 November. It then returned to Genoa, and was placed in regular service to Central and South America, making the first departure in January 1953. In July 1954 *Castel Felice* made the first of two voyages from Bremen to Quebec, followed by several voyages from Le Havre and Southampton to New York.

On 7 October 1954, *Castel Felice* left Bremen on its second voyage to Australia, going to Fremantle and Melbourne only, then returning to Genoa to resume the South American service.

Early in 1955 air-conditioning was installed, and the accommodation altered to 28 first class and 1,173 tourist class. On 26 February *Castel Felice* left Trieste on its third voyage to Australia, then spent several months on the South American trade, ending the year with two more voyages to Australia. The first departed Cuxhaven on 21 September, the second from Naples on 1 December, followed by another departure from Naples on 3 March 1956.

Castel Felice spent the rest of 1956 and much of 1957 operating across the Atlantic, making its final departure from New York on 19 September. The vessel was then given another refit, as Sitmar had obtained a government contract to carry assisted migrants from Britain to Australia.

On 6 April 1958, *Castel Felice* made its first departure from Southampton, and spent the rest of its career on the Australian trade. Occasional voyages were extended to New Zealand, some return trips passed through the Panama Canal, and there were infrequent cruises from Sydney. In 1970 Sitmar lost the contract to carry British migrants to Australia, and it was decided to retire *Castel Felice* at the end of the year.

Preparing for its final departure from Southampton, *Castel Felice* suffered damage from a fire that broke out in the accommodation on 15 August. The damage was not repaired, and a reduced number of passengers was carried to Australia, passing through Fremantle on 16 September, then proceeding direct to Sydney.

Arriving on 26 September, the ship was destored, the crockery and linen being sent to Italy for use on the recently purchased *Fairsea* and *Fairwind.*

On 7 October 1970, *Castel Felice* left Sydney, and arrived on 21 October at the shipbreakers' yard in Taiwan.

Castel Felice

FLAMINIA

BUILT: 1922 by Merchant Shipbuilding Corp, Chester,
 Pennsylvania
TONNAGE: 8,779 gross
DIMENSIONS: 462 x 60 ft (140.5 x 18.2 m)
SERVICE SPEED: 14 knots
PROPULSION: Sulzer diesels/twin screws

This vessel was launched on 14 December 1921 as the *Missourian*, and completed in June 1922. It was one of a pair of funnel-less freighters, the other being named *Californian*. Owned by the US Government and managed by the American-Hawaiian Steamship Co, they commenced their careers operating from the west coast of America through the Panama Canal to Europe, later changed to a service from the west coast to New York.

In 1940 both vessels were among a group of 90 ships transferred by the US Government to the British Government. *Missourian* was renamed *Empire Swan*, and managed by Runciman (London) Ltd. In 1942 *Empire Swan* was transferred to the Belgian Government, then in exile in London, and renamed *Belgian Freighter*. Managed by Cie Maritime Belge, it was purchased outright by them in 1946, and renamed *Capitaine Potie*, being placed in service from Belgium to the Congo.

In May 1948 the vessel was sold to Cia Genovese d'Armamento, better known as Cogedar Line. Renamed *Genova*, it was sent to Trieste for a major rebuilding, with accommodation being installed for 800 third class passengers. An extensive superstructure was added, and a conventional funnel fitted. During 1949, *Genova* entered service from Genoa to River Plate ports, then in 1954 returned to the Monfalcone shipyard in Trieste for further alterations.

The original B & W diesels were replaced by Sulzer diesels, while the superstructure was further enlarged to allow for more public rooms, and an outdoor swimming pool. Extra cabins were also installed, and the ship could now carry 1,024 passengers in 154 cabins, most of which contained eight berths. When the rebuilding was completed in March 1955, the vessel was renamed *Flaminia*.

The first voyage by *Flaminia* was from Trieste in April 1955, and took the vessel only to Cairns, where it berthed on 30 May, departing three days later for Italy. On 16 July, *Flaminia* left Trieste on its second voyage, arriving in Fremantle on 14 August, and terminating in Melbourne on 19 August. For the next three years, *Flaminia* operated from Italian ports to Australia.

Flaminia left Rotterdam on 15 December 1958, and Bremerhaven the next day on a new service to Australia. The vessel served on this new route a further three years, departing Fremantle on 22 November 1961 on its last trip.

The vessel was then chartered by Zim Line, of Israel, for a service between Haifa and Marseilles, and while still under this charter was sold in 1963 to another Italian firm, Covena SpA, of Genoa. When the Zim charter expired in October 1964, the vessel was sold again, to Saudi Lines, being given its seventh name, *King Abdelaziz*, under the flag of Saudi Arabia.

Placed in the pilgrim trade to Jeddah, it had the misfortune to run aground on Algaham Reef, off Jeddah, on 30 April 1965. Sent back to Italy for repairs, it resumed the pilgrim trade in September 1965. Early in 1970 the old ship was withdrawn, and on 23 April 1970 arrived at Kaohsiung in Taiwan to be broken up.

ARCADIA

BUILT: 1954 by John Brown & Co, Clydebank
TONNAGE: 29,734 gross
DIMENSIONS: 721 x 90 ft (219.7 x 27.5 m)
SERVICE SPEED: 22 knots
PROPULSION: Geared turbines/twin screws

Arcadia was launched on 14 May 1953, the same day as *Orsova* of the Orient Line. Fitting out of *Arcadia* was completed first, with accommodation for 675 first class and 735 tourist class passengers.

On 22 February *Arcadia* departed Tilbury on its maiden voyage to Australia, going to Suez, Aden, Bombay and Colombo before arriving in Fremantle on 18 March, Melbourne on 22 March and Sydney two days later. On returning to Britain, *Arcadia* made a series of cruises from Southampton, the first being to the Mediterranean. When the liner was berthing at Tilbury on 26 September, it struck the tug *Cervia*, which sank with the loss of five lives.

It was not until October 1954 that *Arcadia* departed on its second voyage to Australia. By then sister ship *Iberia* had also joined the service, and the two were easily distinguishable by their funnels, *Arcadia*'s having a black domed top.

On 1 April 1959, *Arcadia* arrived at the Harland & Wolff shipyard for a major refit. Air-conditioning was extended through the ship, and cabins and public rooms upgraded and refurbished. Leaving Belfast on 11 June, *Arcadia* made several cruises from Southampton before returning to Australia.

On 22 November 1959, *Arcadia* departed Sydney on its first cruise from an Australian port. With P & O expanding their route network, *Arcadia* then left Sydney on 11 December on its first voyage across the Pacific, going to San Francisco and returning to Sydney on 19 January 1960, then going back to Britain through the Suez Canal. Throughout the 1960s, *Arcadia* combined line voyages with cruises from Britain and Australia, and also trans-Pacific voyages, some of which transited the Panama Canal.

During a refit early in 1970, the mainmast was removed, while the accommodation was converted to carry 1,372 passengers in one class. On 26 April *Arcadia* left Southampton for Sydney, then went to San Francisco. From there the liner made a series of cruises to Alaska until October, then transferred to cruises from San Francisco to Mexican port. These cruises were so successful that P & O left *Arcadia* on the west coast of America.

In October 1974, *Himalaya* was withdrawn from the Australian cruise trade and replaced by *Arcadia*. In 1975 and 1976, *Arcadia* made one return trip to Britain, with a final departure from Southampton on 8 May 1976, voyaging by way of Cape Town to arrive in Sydney on 11 June. For the next two and a half years, *Arcadia* was based permanently in Sydney, cruising to the South Pacific and Asia. The accommodation was reduced to 1,240 in one class at this time.

On 29 January 1979, *Arcadia* left Sydney for the last time, and Brisbane two days later, then headed for Manila, and on to Hong Kong. The cruise was to have terminated there, and the passengers transferred to *Sea Princess*, but that ship had been delayed so *Arcadia* went on to Singapore, berthing on 21 February.

Once the passengers had transferred to *Sea Princess*, *Arcadia* voyaged to Taiwan, arriving in Kaohsiung on 28 February, then the liner was handed over to a firm of shipbreakers.

ORSOVA

BUILT: 1954 by Vickers-Armstrong Ltd, Barrow
TONNAGE: 28,790 gross
DIMENSIONS: 723 x 90 ft (220.3 x 27.5 m)
SERVICE SPEED: 22 knots
PROPULSION: Geared turbines/twin screws

Orsova was the first large liner to be built without masts, and was also the first liner to have an all welded hull, being launched on 14 May 1953, the same day as *Arcadia*. Running trials in March 1954, *Orsova* reached 26 knots. On 17 March 1954, *Orsova* departed Tilbury on its maiden voyage to Australia, arriving in Fremantle on 9 April, then visiting Adelaide and Melbourne before reaching Sydney on 19 April. Accommodation was provided for 681 first class and 813 tourist class, and a crew of 620.

After three return voyages from Britain to Australia, *Orsova* left Sydney on 28 January 1955 to cross the Pacific to San Francisco. The liner reached Honolulu in 89 hours, at an average speed of 23.39 knots, breaking a record that had stood since 1921. On 27 April 1955, *Orsova* left Tilbury on the first round-the-world voyage to be operated by the Orient Line. This came out to Australia through the Suez Canal, then across the Pacific to the west coast of America and through the Panama Canal, returning to Tilbury on 13 July.

Orsova had begun making occasional cruises, and in 1960 went to the Vickers-Armstrong Ltd shipyard in Newcastle for a10-week refit, during which air-conditioning was installed. It was also in 1960 that Orient Line was absorbed into P & O. *Orsova* retained its corn coloured hull until 1964, when it was repainted white, arriving in Fremantle on 23 May 1964 on its first voyage in the new colours. In 1965, *Orsova* was transferred to the ownership of P & O, and the Orient Line name disappeared.

In the early 1970s, *Orsova* was used more extensively for cruising, though retaining a two-class configuration. On 25 November 1972 the liner arrived at the Vosper-Thorneycroft shipyard at Southampton for an extensive refit to upgrade the accommodation for cruising, though still in two classes. On 9 January 1973, *Orsova* departed Southampton on what was destined to be its final voyage to Australia, as on returning to Britain the vessel began a lengthy programme of cruises from Southampton. These proved to be highly successful, and a world cruise was scheduled, departing in January 1974.

Also during 1973, *Canberra* was operating a less than successful series of cruises from New York, and returned to Britain in November 1973, with a decision to be made as to its future. At one time it was considered that *Canberra* would be sold for scrap, but instead *Orsova* became a victim of its own success. The bookings for the world cruise were more than *Orsova* could handle, so *Canberra* was substituted, and then programmed to replace *Orsova* on the rest of the 1974 cruise schedule.

Orsova berthed in Southampton on 25 November 1973 at the end of its final cruise, and then was sold to Taiwanese shipbreakers. The liner made the long voyage east under its own power, and on 14 February 1974 was handed over to the shipbreakers in Kaohsiung.

AURELIA

BUILT: 1939 by Blohm & Voss AG, Hamburg
TONNAGE: 10,022 gross
DIMENSIONS: 488 x 60 ft (148.7 x 18.4 m)
SERVICE SPEED: 17 knots
PROPULSION: MAN diesel/single screw

This vessel had a long and varied career, having been ordered by Hamburg-America Line, and launched on 15 December 1938 as *Huascaran*, entering service in April 1939. At 6,951 gross tons, and primarily a cargo ship, it had accommodation for up to 58 passengers, and joined its sister *Orsono* on the trade from Hamburg to the west coast of South America via Panama.

When war broke out, *Huascaran* was taken over by the German Navy and converted into a submarine depot ship, and later a repair ship, seeing considerable service in Norwegian waters. *Huascaran* survived the war, to be seized by the Allies as a prize, and allocated to Canada.

On 2 September 1947, *Huascaran* was bought by Canadian Pacific, and refitted at a shipyard in Sorel to carry 773 passengers in one class. Renamed *Beaverbrae*, it was intended to carry migrants from Europe to Canada, and a full cargo on the return trip. The first voyage departed St John's on 8 February 1948, for Bremerhaven, and over the next six years, *Beaverbrae* made 51 round trips between Canada and European ports.

On 1 November 1954 *Beaverbrae* was sold to Cia Genovese di Armamento, better known as Cogedar Line. Renamed *Aurelia*, it went to Trieste for rebuilding as a passenger liner. The original superstructure was enlarged, and air-conditioning installed. With accommodation for 1,124 passengers, few cabins had private facilities, and amenities included a swimming pool and a theatre.

On 13 May 1955, *Aurelia* left Trieste on its first voyage to Australia, but later that year the European terminal port became Genoa. The first departure from there was on 15 November, with calls at Naples, Messina, Malta and Piraeus. *Aurelia* made four round trips per year to Australia, and in 1958 was withdrawn for further alterations.

The original MAN diesels were replaced by a new pair of the same type, and the superstructure further enlarged both fore and aft, though passenger numbers were not increased. *Aurelia* then entered a new service to Australia from Bremerhaven, the first departure being on 12 June 1959.

In June 1960, *Aurelia* made a round trip from Bremerhaven to New York under charter to the Council of Student Travel, and in each year up to 1969 made between two and five return trips to New York under similar charter, during the northern summer months. On the Australian trade, *Aurelia* began calling at Southampton, the first visit being on 14 September 1961.

On 9 December 1964, *Aurelia* left Rotterdam, and after calling at Southampton crossed the Atlantic to go through the Panama Canal, and across the Pacific to Auckland and then Sydney, returning through Suez. After two more voyages on this route, *Aurelia* reverted to the Suez route in both directions, with an extension to Auckland, the first of these voyages leaving Rotterdam on 8 December 1965.

The original appearance of *Aurelia* on the Australian trade

The closure of the Suez Canal in 1967, combined with a decline in the migrant trade to Australia, eventually brought about the end of the Cogedar Line service to Australia. On 23 September 1968, *Aurelia* left Rotterdam on its final voyage, going around South Africa in both directions, departing Sydney for the final time on 29 October.

On returning to Europe, *Aurelia* was refitted as a cruise ship, with the accommodation reduced to 470 passengers. The work took longer than expected, and the first three sailings had to be cancelled, but finally she left Southampton on her first cruise on 5 February 1969.

This cruise programme finished in May 1969, and *Aurelia* then made six round trips to New York. Returning to cruising from Southampton again in September, loadings were poor, so the vessel was offered for sale.

Aurelia was purchased by Chandris Cruises in September 1970, and renamed *Romanza*. Chandris installed 238 new cabins, most with private facilities, for 650 passengers in one class. On 1 April 1971 *Romanza* left Venice on its first Chandris cruise.

Romanza usually spent April to October cruising in the Mediterranean, and also cruised in the Indian Ocean from South African ports over several years between November and March.

On 17 October 1979, *Romanza* ran aground on Dhenousa Island in the Aegean Sea, and suffered considerable bow damage. Refloated two days later,

it was towed to Piraeus for repairs, and returned to the Mediterranean cruising circuit. During the 1980s *Romanza* spent periods laid up, and in 1988 was under charter as a floating hotel in the Canary Islands.

In late 1991 *Romanza* was sold to Cypriana Holidays, of Limassol. Renamed *Romantica*, the vessel returned to service in the Mediterranean in May 1992 for Paradise Cruises, operating two short cruises a week from Limassol, one going to Port Said in Egypt, the other to Ashdod in Israel. This lasted until 1994, when the ship was arrested, and laid up in Greece.

Romantica was released during 1997, and purchased by Med Duchess Lines, which operated as New Paradise Cruises. Without a change of name, the vessel resumed operating short cruises from Limassol on 1 August.

Early in the morning of 3 October 1997 a fire broke out in an engine room control panel and quickly spread to other parts of the ship. The 487 passengers were evacuated, and *Romantica* was towed to Limassol and run aground, totally gutted. The wreck was refloated on 15 October, and anchored off Limassol. During a storm in February 1998, the wreck of *Romantica* broke adrift, and was blown aground on a beach. In March 1998, the wreck of *Romantica* was refloated, and moved to Larnaca. It was made seaworthy, and on 11 April was towed away, bound for Alexandria, where it was broken up.

Aurelia after alterations in 1959

SOUTHERN CROSS

BUILT: 1955 by Harland & Wolff Ltd, Belfast
TONNAGE: 20,204 gross
DIMENSIONS: 604 x 78 ft (184 x 23.9 m)
SERVICE SPEED: 20 knots
PROPULSION: Geared turbines/twin screws

In 1952, Shaw Savill & Albion decided to build a new passenger liner, which would carry no cargo at all, unlike all their previous vessels, to inaugurate a round-the-world service. The design of the new ship produced a number of other breaks with tradition, in particular locating the engines aft. On 17 August 1954 the vessel was launched by Queen Elizabeth and named *Southern Cross*, the first British merchant vessel to be launched by a reigning monarch. Work on fitting out the liner took six months, during which 405 cabins were installed for 1,160 passengers, all tourist class. After running trials in late January 1955, *Southern Cross* was handed over to Shaw Savill on 23 February.

On 29 March 1955, *Southern Cross* left Southampton on its maiden voyage, going across the Atlantic and through the Panama Canal, then to Tahiti, and on to Wellington, arriving on 2 May. On 9 May, *Southern Cross* berthed in Sydney, visited Melbourne two days later, and Fremantle on 16 May.

The liner then crossed the Indian Ocean to Cape Town, and back to Southampton. Three cruises were made from Southampton before the ship departed on its second voyage to Australia, in the reverse direction to its maiden voyage.

Southern Cross was scheduled to make four voyages around the world each year, taking 76 days for the trip at an average speed of 20 knots, having a reserve of 2 knots in case of delay. Within a short time it was clear *Southern Cross* was a great success, as the engines-aft design gave passengers much more open deck space, and public rooms were not obstructed by funnel casings.

Consequently, a second ship of similar design was built, entering service as *Northern Star* in July 1962. From this time, *Southern Cross* operated only in a westward direction, with *Northern Star* proceeding eastward. However, by the end of the 1960s, demand for liner passages was declining, and *Southern Cross* began making more cruises.

In May 1970, *Southern Cross* was extensively overhauled and refurbished, then spent several months cruising from Southampton. A line voyage was made to Sydney, from where another series of cruises was operated.

Returning to Southampton in May 1971, *Southern Cross* completed another programme of cruises. In August 1971, *Southern Cross* left Southampton on its final voyage around the world, returning to Southampton in November, and being laid up there, moving to the River Fal in April 1972.

In 1973 *Southern Cross* was sold for £500,000

to Cia de Vapores Cerulea, a Greek company, but registered in Panama. Renamed *Calypso*, it went to Piraeus for a major refit, which cost £10 million. The interior of the ship was stripped out, and new cabins with private facilities installed, to accommodate 950 passengers in one class.

The indoor pool on the lowest deck became a discotheque, while a new pool was built on the sun deck forward of the bridge, this area being fully enclosed, the only major external difference.

Calypso entered service as a full-time cruise ship in April 1975, being based again at Southampton, under charter to a British company, Thomson Tours. During 1976 *Calypso* was based in Rotterdam, and also Leith, while 1977 found it back at Southampton. At the end of 1977 the Thomson charter ended, and *Calypso* was then operated by its owner under the banner of Ulysses Cruises.

Calypso spent most of 1978 cruising in the Mediterranean, then at the end of the year went to South Africa for a short season. Returning to the Mediterranean in February 1979, *Calypso* cruised there until the end of the year, then on 16 December 1979 left Piraeus for Miami.

Under charter to Paquet Cruises, *Calypso* operated out of Miami to the Caribbean until May 1980, then transferred to the west coast of America, cruising out of Los Angeles to Vancouver and Alaska. This series ended in September, and on 29 September 1980, *Calypso* was chartered to Western Cruise Line, a subsidiary of the Gotaas-Larsen Group. Renamed *Azure Seas*, the swimming pool forward on the sun deck was removed, and the deck enclosed to form a large new public room, used as a casino, with an open observation deck above. In November 1980, *Azure Seas* began operating cruises from Los Angeles to Ensenada in Mexico, departing every Monday and Friday evening.

In October 1987, the fleets of Eastern Cruise Line, Western Cruise Line and Sundance Cruises were combined into a new company, Admiral Cruises, under which banner *Azure Seas* continued to operate until 1992, when Admiral Cruises went out of business. *Azure Seas* was then renamed *Ocean Breeze*, and began making short cruises out of Miami in the fleet of Dolphin Cruise Line. In 1998, Dolphin merged with Premier Cruise Line, but *Ocean Breeze* continued to operate as before until 2002, when Premier Cruise Line went bankrupt.

Ocean Breeze was sold to Imperial Majesty Cruise Line, and began making two-night cruises from Fort Lauderdale to Nassau until being withdrawn from service in June 2003, and soon after sold to a Bangladesh shipbreaking firm. The vessel anchored off Chittagong on 5 October 2003, but on 13 October a leak developed, flooding the engine room and causing a 20-degree list to starboard. The ship was kept afloat by pumps until 8 November, when it was beached and subsequently broken up.

Azure Seas leaving Los Angeles in 1986

IBERIA

BUILT: 1954 by Harland & Wolff Ltd, Belfast
TONNAGE: 29,614 gross
DIMENSIONS: 718 x 90 ft (219 x 27.5 m)
SERVICE SPEED: 22 knots
PROPULSION: Geared turbines/twin screws

Iberia was the final unit in the P & O post-war passenger ship rebuilding programme, the keel being laid down on 8 February 1952. Launched on 21 January 1954, nine months were spent fitting out, then *Iberia* achieved a maximum of 24.9 knots on trials, being handed over to P & O on 10 September 1954. Accommodation was provided for 673 first class and 733 tourist class passengers, with a crew of 711.

Iberia could be distinguished from its sister *Arcadia* by the funnel, which was topped by a smoke deflector. On 28 September 1954, *Iberia* departed Tilbury on its maiden voyage, passing through Suez to reach Fremantle on 22 October, then Adelaide and Melbourne before berthing in Sydney on 1 November.

On 14 March 1956, *Iberia* left Tilbury for Australia, but en route from Aden to Colombo, collided with a tanker, *Stanvac Pretoria*, during the night of 27 March. *Iberia* suffered extensive damage to the port side, but was able to complete the voyage to Sydney, arriving on 16 April. Workmen spent 17 days repairing the damage while *Iberia* was berthed at Pyrmont.

Iberia was used for occasional cruises from Southampton, and during 1958 made a cruise to New York. On 15 December 1959, *Iberia* left Tilbury on its first voyage around the world, passing through the Panama Canal and visiting West Coast ports and Honolulu before arriving in Sydney, and returning to Britain through Suez. On 19 January 1960 *Iberia* left

Sydney on its first cruise from an Australian port, 14 days around the South Pacific. In January 1961 *Iberia* was given a refit, during which air-conditioning was extended throughout the accommodation, which was also upgraded and refurbished.

Iberia was always plagued by engine problems, which grew worse during the 1960s. During one voyage to Britain late in 1969, there was a fire in the funnel while *Iberia* was berthed at Pago Pago, followed a few days later by engine trouble that made the vessel a day late into Honolulu. Shortly after leaving Acapulco the starboard engine failed, but was repaired by the engineers, then while taking on bunkers in Curacao, some oil escaped into the first class baggage room. *Iberia* reached Southampton a week late, and was drydocked for an overhaul. On the next voyage, a power failure blacked out the ship only three days out from Southampton, but this was repaired and the voyage continued.

At one time a plan to re-engine *Iberia* was considered, but not accepted. In the early 1970s, with the rising price of oil, P & O was forced to prune their fleet. Despite being the youngest of the liners under consideration, *Iberia* became the first victim due to the engine problems.

Thus on 5 November 1971, *Iberia* departed Southampton on its final voyage to Australia, and made a short series of cruises from Sydney. The final departure from Sydney was on 16 March 1972, returning to Southampton on 19 April. *Iberia* was then withdrawn from service, and soon after sold to Taiwanese shipbreakers. On 27 June 1972, *Iberia* left Southampton with a small crew aboard, and only two lifeboats. Voyaging around South Africa, it arrived in Kaohsiung on 5 September, and shortly after was scrapped.

ORANJE

BUILT: 1939 by Netherlands Shipbuilding Co, Amsterdam
TONNAGE: 20,551 gross
DIMENSIONS: 656 x 84 ft (199.9 x 25.5 m)
SERVICE SPEED: 21 knots
PROPULSION: Sulzer diesels/triple screws

Named in honour of the Dutch Royal Family, *Oranje* was launched by Queen Wilhelmina on 8 September 1938. When completed on 27 June 1939, *Oranje* was the highest powered motorship in the world, achieving 26.5 knots on trials. Its first voyage was a cruise from Amsterdam to Madeira.

Accommodation on *Oranje* was divided between 283 first class, 283 second class, 92 third class and 52 fourth class passengers. A striking feature of the ship was the shape of the hull, which flared out, the beam at the waterline being 17 ft (5.17 m) wider than at the promenade deck.

On 3 September 1939, Britain and Germany declared war, but on 4 September *Oranje* departed on schedule for its maiden voyage to the Dutch East Indies. Instead of following the regular route through the Mediterranean, the vessel went around Africa, with a call at Cape Town. On arrival in Batavia, it was decided to lay the vessel up at Surabaya, where it arrived in December 1939.

Following the German invasion of Holland in May 1940, *Oranje* was handed over to the British. In February 1941, it was offered to Australia as a hospital ship. On 31 March 1941, *Oranje* arrived in Sydney, and was converted at Cockatoo Island.

Oranje entered service on 1 July 1941 as the second hospital ship in the Royal Australian Navy, painted all white with a wide red band around the hull, and red crosses on the hull and funnel, which were lit up at night. *Oranje* operated 41 voyages as a hospital ship until November 1945, following which the vessel returned to its home port of Amsterdam.

Oranje was refitted, and in July 1947 returned to the Dutch East Indies trade, but the push for independence from Holland was growing into open rebellion. The Nederland Line and Royal Rotterdam Lloyd decided to pool their resources on the Dutch East Indies service, with *Oranje* and *Willem Ruys* operating a joint service.

Indonesia gained full independence in 1949, but *Oranje* and *Willem Ruys* remained on their regular trade. In December 1957, the Indonesian Government seized all Dutch possessions in the islands, and terminated relations with the Dutch. This brought about an immediate cessation of the joint Nederland Line-Royal Rotterdam Lloyd service to Indonesia, and *Oranje* was laid up pending a decision on its future.

In November 1958, *Oranje* left Amsterdam on its first commercial voyage to Australia, passing through the Suez Canal and arriving in Fremantle on 30 November, Melbourne on 5 December, and Sydney two days later. On returning to Holland in January 1959, the vessel was refitted at Amsterdam, the accommodation being altered to 323 first class and 626 tourist class passengers.

In March 1959, *Willem Ruys* joined the Australian trade, and in conjunction with *Oranje* began a new round-the-world service. *Oranje* made four voyages a year westabout, with calls at Port Everglades, Tahiti, Auckland and Wellington, Sydney and Melbourne, Fremantle, Singapore, Penang, Colombo and Port Said.

This service was maintained for four years, then the two Dutch companies decided to withdraw, and dispose of their liners. On 4 May 1964, *Oranje* left Amsterdam on its final voyage, being in Melbourne on 3 June, and departing Sydney on 10 June, then being laid up in Amsterdam on its return. On 4 September 1964, *Oranje* was sold to Flotta Lauro, and renamed *Angelina Lauro*.

ANGELINA LAURO

REBUILT: 1966 by Cant del Tirreno, Genoa
TONNAGE: 24,377 gross
DIMENSIONS: 674 x 83 ft (205.5 x 25.5 m)
SERVICE SPEED: 21 knots
PROPULSION: Sulzer diesel/triple screws

On 4 September 1964, *Oranje* was sold to Flotta Lauro, renamed *Angelina Lauro,* and sent to Genoa for a major rebuilding. A raked bow was fitted, the superstructure extended, and the lower decks enclosed. The mainmast was replaced by two cargo derricks, and a signal mast fitted above the bridge. An unusual feature was the new funnel, with its angled top, known as an "angel's wing", and lattice work on the sides and back.

The accommodation was rebuilt to carry 189 first class and 946 tourist class passengers, with an additional 377 berths classified as interchangeable. Over 90% of the cabins had private facilities. Air-conditioning was extended throughout the accommodation, and a new swimming pool with a sliding glass cover added for first class passengers, the two existing pools being allocated to tourist class passengers.

Several new public rooms were added as well, those for first class being located at the forward end of the saloon deck, with tourist class having the after end of the deck. Some facilities were shared between the classes, including the chapel and the two-deck-high cinema. The work was almost finished when, on 24 August 1965, a fire broke out on board. Six shipyard workers lost their lives in the blaze, and the completion of the vessel was put back six months.

Angelina Lauro was handed over to Flotta Lauro in February 1966, and on 6 March, the liner departed Bremerhaven, then called at Southampton before proceeding through the Suez Canal, arriving in Fremantle on 29 March, Melbourne on 2 April, and Sydney on 5 April, terminating the voyage at Wellington on 8 April, and returning to Europe by the reverse route.

After 1967, *Angelina Lauro* had to voyage around South Africa, and on 28 September 1968 left Sydney on her first homeward voyage across the Pacific, going around Cape Horn, with calls at several South American ports. Late in 1969, *Angelina Lauro* made her first cruise from Australia, and in 1970 also made some cruises from Southampton. From 1971 the vessel began making regular voyages around the world, and the number of cruises she operated was increased.

In April 1972, *Angelina Lauro* departed Southampton on her final voyage to Australia, leaving Melbourne on 14 May, and Sydney on 17 May. The liner was then refitted for full-time cruising, the passenger capacity being reduced to 800. From November 1972, *Angelina Lauro* was based on San Juan for regular seven-day cruises in the Caribbean, being managed for Flotta Lauro by another Italian company, Costa Line.

On 10 October 1977, Costa Line took *Angelina Lauro* on charter for three years. On 30 March 1979, *Angelina Lauro* was berthed in St Thomas during a cruise, when a fire broke out in the aft galley, and rapidly spread to engulf the whole ship. The weight of water poured into the ship left it sitting on the shallow bottom, with a 25-degree list to port.

Declared a total loss, the wreck was refloated on 6 July, and sold to shipbreakers in Taiwan, leaving St Thomas under tow on 30 July. In the middle of the Pacific *Angelina Lauro* began taking water on 21 September. Gradually the list worsened, and on 24 September 1979, *Angelina Lauro* sank.

FAIRSKY

BUILT: 1942 by Western Pipe & Steel Co, San Francisco
TONNAGE: 12,464 gross
DIMENSIONS: 502 x 69 ft (153 x 21.2m)
SERVICE SPEED: 17.5 knots
PROPULSION: Geared turbines/single screw

Fairsky was the second converted aircraft carrier that Sitmar Line placed in passenger service to Australia. The vessel had originally been laid down on 7 April 1941 as a standard C3 type cargo ship for the Isthmian Steam Ship Co, of New York, being named *Steel Artisan* when launched on 27 September 1941. Three months later, the incomplete vessel was taken over by the US Government, for conversion into an auxiliary aircraft carrier.

Intended to join the US Navy as the USS *Barnes*, it was one of a number of such vessels transferred to the Royal Navy under the lend-lease agreement, being commissioned on 30 September 1942 as HMS *Attacker*.

In its new role, the ship could carry 18 aircraft, and initially served as a convoy escort in the North Atlantic. Later it was used to provide air cover during the landings at Salerno in September 1943, and in the south of France in August 1944. HMS *Attacker* finished the war in the Pacific, then on 6 January 1946 was handed back to the Americans.

Laid up and offered for sale, the vessel was purchased by National Bulk Carriers, of New York, and in February 1947 work commenced on its conversion into a cargo ship. The flight deck and other military fittings were removed, but then the work stopped, and the vessel was laid up again.

In 1950 the vessel was bought by Navcot Corp, an American company established by Alexandr Vlasov, founder of Sitmar. Renamed *Castelforte*, it remained laid up for another two years.

In 1952, *Castelforte* was transferred to the ownership of Sitmar Line. *Castelforte* was sent to the Newport News shipyard for conversion into a reefer ship, destined for the lucrative meat trade from South America to Europe. The conversion work had barely begun when the reefer ship idea was abandoned, and the ship was again laid up. In 1953 its name was amended to *Castel Forte*. It was February 1957 before the ship moved again, this time going to the Bethlehem Steel shipyard in New York to commence conversion into a passenger ship, after Alexandr Vlasov obtained a four-year contract for the ship to transport British migrants to Australia.

A new superstructure was constructed atop the hull in New York, then in December 1957, the vessel crossed to Genoa where the internal fitting out was completed.

Accommodation for a maximum of 1,461 passengers in one class was installed, though only seven of the 461 cabins had private facilities, these being located on the sun deck. Of the cabins, 192 were fitted with two berths, five had three berths, and 261 were four berth, with three having six berths.

HMS *Attacker*

A full range of comfortable public rooms was provided, most being located on boat deck, which also had an outdoor swimming pool aft. One deck below were the three dining rooms. The entire interior of the ship was air-conditioned.

Renamed *Fairsky* early in 1958, and registered in Liberia under the nominal ownership of a Sitmar subsidiary, Fairline Shipping Corp, on 26 June 1958, *Fairsky* left Southampton on its first voyage, with 1,430 passengers on board. Arriving in Fremantle on 21 July, the vessel berthed in Melbourne on 27 July and Sydney on 29 July, *Fairsky* left the next day for Brisbane, where it berthed on 1 August, then retraced the route back to Southampton.

On some voyages back to Britain, Fairsky went north to Singapore and then Colombo. It was not until December 1961 that *Fairsky* made its first visit to a New Zealand port, Auckland, and in September 1964 made its first cruise, from Sydney to Tonga and Fiji.

Fairsky remained on the migrant trade until 1970, though in the 1960s some return voyages were made through the Panama Canal. After the closure of the Suez Canal, *Fairsky* voyaged out around South Africa, and in November 1969 suffered engine trouble between Southampton and Cape Town. It spent several days there being repaired, and eventually reached Fremantle 12 days late.

When Sitmar lost the British migrant contract to Chandris in 1970, *Fairsky* continued to operate regular voyages from Britain to Australia until February 1972, when it was laid up in Southampton.

On 8 November 1973 *Fairsky* returned to service, departing Southampton for Australia again. On 2 June 1974, the vessel left Southampton for the last time, following which it began permanent cruises from Sydney. In this role *Fairsky* enjoyed a great deal of success, operating from both Sydney and Darwin.

On 12 June, *Fairsky* departed Darwin on a cruise, but while leaving Jakarta on 23 June, struck a sunken wreck. Badly holed forward, *Fairsky* was beached on a sandbar to prevent it sinking. A concrete patch was placed over the hole, and on 9 July *Fairsky* entered drydock in Singapore.

The damage was so severe it was not worth repairing, so *Fairsky* was offered for sale, and purchased in December 1977 by Fuji Marden & Co, for breaking up in Hong Kong. Arriving there under its own power on 18 December, *Fairsky* was laid up in Junk Bay. In March 1978, the vessel was sold to Peninsular Shipping Corp, from the Philippines.

Towed to Mariveles, and converted into a floating casino and hotel, it was renamed *Philippine Tourist*, and berthed in Manila South Harbour. On the night of 3 November 1978, the ship was swept by fire, and completely gutted. The wreck was sold back to Fuji Marden & Co, being towed back to Hong Kong, arriving on 24 May, and soon after was scrapped.

Fairsky

WILLEM RUYS

BUILT: 1947 by Kon Maats de Schelde, Flushing
TONNAGE: 21,119 gross
DIMENSIONS: 631 x 82 ft (192.4 x 25.1 m)
SERVICE SPEED: 22 knots
PROPULSION: Sulzer diesels twin screws

The keel of this liner was laid down on 25 January 1939, and it was scheduled to enter service during 1941. Work continued on the vessel until Holland was invaded by the German Army in May 1940, at which time the hull was complete, and the engines installed. When the Germans retreated, they tried to destroy the incomplete vessel with dynamite, but Dutch resistance workers removed the charges.

The ship was launched on 1 July 1946 as *Willem Ruys.* This honoured the memory of both the man who founded Rotterdam Lloyd, and his son, who was executed by the Nazis in August 1942. The christening was performed by his widow.

On 21 November 1947, *Willem Ruys* was delivered, and on the same day the company name was granted the prefix "Royal" by Queen Wilhelmina. On 2 December 1947, *Willem Ruys* departed Rotterdam on her maiden voyage, going through the Mediterranean and Suez Canal to Malaya, Singapore and Batavia. Accommodation was provided for 344 first class, 301 second class, 109 third class and 86 fourth class passengers, but only the first class public rooms were air-conditioned.

In December 1957, the Indonesian Government seized all Dutch possessions in the islands, which resulted in the immediate cessation of passenger services from Holland, and the laying up of *Willem Ruys.* In May 1958 it was chartered to Holland-America Line for two round trips to New York, then made two voyages to Montreal from Rotterdam for Europe-Canada Line. Royal Rotterdam Lloyd then decided to place the ship on a round-the-world service to Australia, so on 20 September 1958, it arrived at the Wilton Fijenoord shipyard for a refit.

About 100 new cabins were installed, and air-conditioning extended through the accommodation for 275 first class and 770 tourist class passengers, but some cabins had extra berths if required, so the maximum capacity was 1,167. Fin stabilisers were fitted, several open sections of deck plated in, and the forward funnel heightened, the work being completed in February 1959.

Royal Rotterdam Lloyd and Nederland Line linked to operate a round-the-world service using *Willem Ruys* and *Oranje. Willem Ruys* was allocated the eastabout sailings, departing on its first voyage from Rotterdam on 7 March 1959, with a call at Southampton, then through the Suez Canal to Fremantle, Melbourne and Sydney on 6 April, returning via New Zealand, Tahiti and the Panama Canal. *Willem Ruys* was scheduled to make four round trips per year.

In 1964, Royal Rotterdam Lloyd decided to abandon their round-the-world service, and on 16 October 1964, *Willem Ruys* left Rotterdam on its twenty-sixth and last voyage.

The liner left Melbourne on 14 November, and Sydney three days later, returning to Rotterdam in December. It had been announced during the year that *Willem Ruys* had been sold to Flotta Lauro, and in January 1965 they took delivery of the liner, which was renamed *Achille Lauro.*

ACHILLE LAURO

REBUILT: 1966 by Cant Nav Riuniti, Palermo
TONNAGE: 23,629 gross
DIMENSIONS: 643 x 82 ft (196 x 25.1 m)
SERVICE SPEED: 22 knots
PROPULSION: Sulzer diesels/twin screws

Willem Ruys was handed over to Flotta Lauro on 6 January 1965 in Rotterdam, renamed *Achille Lauro,* after the founder of the company, and sent to Palermo for an extensive rebuilding. A raked bow was added, the superstructure extended forward and modernised, both masts removed and a new signal mast fitted behind the bridge. The most notable alteration was the two new funnels.

Internally, the old accommodation was stripped out, and new cabins installed for 270 first class and 917 tourist class passengers, plus 394 interchangeable berths, and 150 children's beds.

On 29 August 1965, when the conversion was almost finished, *Achille Lauro* was swept by fire following an explosion aboard, which caused considerable damage. Repairs set back the delivery date to March 1966.

Achille Lauro departed Rotterdam on 7 April 1966 on its first voyage, going to Southampton and then Genoa, from where it sailed on 13 April. The vessel called at Fremantle, Melbourne and Sydney, then went to Wellington, where the voyage ended on 14 May. It then retraced the route to Europe with an additional call at Singapore.

On 28 September 1968, *Achille Lauro* left Sydney, and after calling at Wellington, proceeded around Cape Horn, and called at Rio de Janeiro on the way back to Europe. *Achille Lauro* made five trips a year to Australia up to 1969, then began making occasional cruises from Sydney and Rotterdam.

In May 1972, *Achille Lauro* went to Genoa for an overhaul, during which the bridge structure and forward accommodation areas were swept by fire on 19 May, which put the liner out of service for five months while repairs were effected. During 1972, Flotta Lauro decided to withdraw from the Australian trade. *Achille Lauro* departed Rotterdam on 13 October 1972, and cruised from Sydney until February 1973 when it returned to Europe.

In April 1973, *Achille Lauro* began cruising in the Mediterranean from Genoa in the summer, and out of Durban, South Africa, from November to May.

On 7 October 1985, *Achille Lauro* was seized by terrorists off Alexandria. The ship was held for two days, during which one of the American passengers was shot, then the terrorists surrendered to Egyptian authorities.

On 14 January 1987, *Achille Lauro* returned to Australian waters, when it arrived in Fremantle, having been chartered by Motive Travel for one month in connection with the America's Cup races. The liner had come direct from South Africa with 600 passengers on board, of whom 382 were migrants to Australia. On 16 February, *Achille Lauro* departed Fremantle for South Africa, and then back to Europe to resume its Mediterranean cruising schedule.

In January 1990, *Achille Lauro* returned to Australia again on a voyage from South Africa. After calling at Fremantle and Melbourne, it arrived in Sydney on 28 January, then made a cruise, leaving again on 8 February, on a voyage to Europe. The liner returned to Australia for a series of cruises from Sydney between January and May 1991, and the same period in 1992. This was the last time *Achille Lauro* would be seen in local waters.

On 30 November 1994, when *Achille Lauro* was in the Indian Ocean off the coast of Somalia, a fire broke out in the engine room, which eventually spread through the ship. On 2 December the burning liner was taken in tow, but sank later that day.

GUMHURYAT MISR

BUILT: 1928 by Cammell Laird & Co, Birkenhead
TONNAGE: 7,830 gross
DIMENSIONS: 437 x 59 it (134.5 x 18.1 m)
SERVICE SPEED: 12.5 knots
PROPULSION: Geared turbines/twin screws

Glumhuryat Misr was originally named *Lady Nelson*, the first completed of a group of five liners built for Canadian National Steamships, the others being named *Lady Somers*, *Lady Rodney*, *Lady Hawkins* and *Lady Drake*. With accommodation for 130 first class and 32 second class passengers, they operated from Halifax to the West Indies.

Remaining in commercial service after the war started, on 9 March 1942, *Lady Nelson* was torpedoed whilst alongside at Castries in St Lucia, and settled on the shallow bottom. Refloated on 26 March, it was towed to Mobile, and converted into the first Canadian hospital ship, with 515 beds. Three sister ships were sunk during the war, and in November 1946, the two survivors were handed back to Canadian National Steamships.

Lady Nelson resumed the pre-war service in August 1947, but in December 1952 was withdrawn, and sold in February 1953 to Khedivial Mail Line, of Egypt. *Lady Nelson* was renamed *Gumhuryat Misr*, and refitted in Alexandria to carry 118 first class and 115 tourist class passengers in cabins, plus hundreds of pilgrims in the 'tween decks. During the pilgrim season it operated to Jeddah, being laid up or chartered at other times.

On 15 August 1956, *Gumhuryat Misr* departed Piraeus with 914 Greek migrants on board. The ship was refused entry to Colombo until the owner forwarded payment for the harbour dues. Leaving Colombo, *Gumhuryat Misr* headed for Fremantle, where 47 migrants were to disembark. Arriving in Gage Roads on 16 September, with little fresh water left in the tanks, the local port authorities had not been advised of the vessel's arrival in advance, so no arrangements had been made for health, migration and customs clearances, nor had the owner appointed any agents in Australia.

For 30 hours, *Gumhuryat Misr* rode at anchor off Fremantle. An agent was hurriedly appointed, and money forwarded from Egypt to cover port costs, then on the evening of 17 September, the vessel finally berthed. An inspection of the lifesaving equipment resulted in seven of the 21 lifeboats being found unserviceable. *Gumhuryat Misr* was held in port, awaiting further payments from Egypt to allow for repairs to be carried out, which did not commence until 21 September.

The repairs to the lifeboats were completed on 23 September, and at noon the next day, *Gumhuryat Misr* departed for Melbourne, where it berthed on 30 September. The bulk of the passengers disembarked, then the vessel went on to Sydney, arriving on 3 October, and remaining at 24 Pyrmont for eight days. Some 4,000 tons of flour was loaded, with more being taken on back in Melbourne during a 10-day stay at Victoria Dock. After passing through Fremantle again, *Gumhuryat Misr* went to Port Sudan to unload the cargo, then returned to Egypt.

During 1960, all Egyptian shipping companies were nationalised as The United Arab Maritime Co, and *Gumhuryat Misr* was renamed *Al Wadi*. On 18 December 1965, it was badly damaged in a collision, and laid up in Alexandria, until sold to local shipbreakers during 1968.

QUEEN FREDERICA

BUILT: 1927 by Wm Cramp & Co, Philadelphia
TONNAGE: 16,435 gross
DIMENSIONS: 582 x 83 ft (177.3 x 25.4 m)
SERVICE SPEED: 20 knots
PROPULSION: Geared turbines/twin screws

Queen Frederica was one of four American-built liners to be bought by Chandris Line in the 1960s, and all were designed by the same man, William Francis Gibbs. In fact, *Queen Frederica* was the first liner he designed, as *Malolo* for Matson Line.

Launched on 26 July 1926, *Malolo* was very advanced for the time. Accommodation was provided for 457 first class and 163 cabin class passengers, the majority of cabins being on the outside, and almost all first class had private facilities. Public rooms were spacious and finished in wood panelling. A new feature was an indoor swimming pool, one of the first on a ship.

Special attention was paid to safety, with a double bottom and 12 watertight bulkheads. The value of these was proved on trials, as on 25 May 1927, the Norwegian freighter *Jacob Christensen* collided with *Malolo*. Water flooded into the engine rooms, but *Malolo* remained afloat, being towed into New York, and put into drydock. The collision delayed delivery of *Malolo* until October 1927, when it was handed over to Matson Line, and on 16 November left San Francisco on its maiden voyage to Honolulu.

On 21 September 1929, *Malolo* left San Francisco on a cruise around the Pacific, going to Japan, Hong Kong, Manila, Singapore, Bangkok, and Australia, visiting Fremantle, Melbourne and Sydney. *Malolo* then went to Auckland, Suva, Pago Pago and Hawaii en route back to San Francisco, arriving there on

20 December. This cruise was repeated at the same time in 1930 and 1931.

At this time, *Malolo* had a chocolate-brown hull, in common with other Matson ships, but in 1931 the company took delivery of the first of three new liners, *Mariposa*, *Monterey* and *Lurline*, all of which had white hulls, and *Malolo* had its hull repainted white to match them. In 1937, *Malolo* was withdrawn for an extensive rebuilding, which considerably altered its appearance. The lifeboats were raised two decks, and much of the open promenade space enclosed to provide more staterooms, including Lanai suites that were a feature on the new Matson liners. Accommodation was altered to 693 first class only, and the liner was renamed *Matsonia* prior to returning to service, with a departure from San Francisco on 14 January 1938.

Matsonia remained on the Hawaiian trade until 21 November 1941, then was requisitioned by the US Navy as a transport. Quickly refitted to carry over 3,000 troops, it was scheduled to leave San Francisco on 8 December for Manila, but the attack on Pearl Harbor changed this. The men and equipment destined for the Philippines were off-loaded, and instead ammunition and plane parts were taken aboard, along with 3,277 troops, and on 16 December *Matsonia*, in company with *Lurline* and *Monterey*, left San Francisco bound for Honolulu. *Matsonia* spent the next four years trooping in the Pacific, with several visits to Australian ports.

In April 1946, *Matsonia* was returned to Matson Line, having carried 176,319 persons during the war, and travelled 385,549 miles. Following a quick refit, *Matsonia* resumed the Hawaiian trade on 22 May 1946 from San Francisco, and maintained a lone-ship service until April 1948, when it was replaced

Malolo as built

by *Lurline*. *Matsonia* was then offered for sale, and bought by Mediterranean Lines, a Panamanian flag subsidiary of Home Lines.

At the Ansaldo shipyard in Genoa, the vessel was refitted to carry 349 first class, 203 cabin class and 626 tourist class passengers, though the external appearance was almost unaltered. Renamed *Atlantic*, it left Genoa on 14 May 1949 on its maiden voyage to New York, remaining on this route until February 1952, then was transferred to a new route from Southampton and Le Havre to Canada. During the winter months, *Atlantic* made cruises from New York to the Caribbean.

In 1954, Home Lines formed a Greek flag subsidiary, National Hellenic American Line, and on 23 December 1954 *Atlantic* was transferred to this company, and renamed *Queen Frederica*. The accommodation was altered to 132 first class, 116 cabin class and 931 tourist class, and on 29 January 1955 left Piraeus bound for New York. It remained on this route for several years, apart from seasonal cruises from New York.

On 15 December 1958, *Queen Frederica* departed Naples with migrants bound for Australia. Reaching Fremantle on 8 January 1959, the liner continued to Melbourne, berthing on 12 January, and arriving in Sydney on 15 January. Next day it left on the return voyage, calling again at Melbourne and Fremantle to collect passengers, returning to Piraeus and Naples.

At the end of 1960, *Queen Frederica* was given an extensive refit, during which the after end of the superstructure was extended and the lower promenade deck plated in, while accommodation was increased to 174 first class and 1,005 tourist class passengers. The liner then began operating to Canada again, from Cuxhaven, and remained on this route until November 1965, when it was sold to Chandris Line.

Unaltered apart from new funnel colours, *Queen Frederica* left Piraeus on 10 December 1965 for Australia, arriving in Fremantle on 28 December, then proceeding directly to Sydney, berthing on 3 January 1966. It departed the next day for Piraeus, and a scheduled second trip to Australia was cancelled. Instead, Chandris placed the vessel on the North Atlantic trade again, from Piraeus to New York, with cruises in the winter months.

Queen Frederica did not return to Australia until November 1966, having departed Southampton on 22 October. Following this voyage it made a short series of cruises from Sydney. These were repeated in the summer of 1967–68, when the liner made its final appearance in Australian waters. From 1968, *Queen Frederica* began operating cruises in the Mediterranean under charter to Sovereign Cruises, until it was laid up in the River Dart on 22 September 1971.

In June 1972, *Queen Frederica* was moved to Piraeus, then given a refit prior to returning to service in April 1973 with weekly Mediterranean cruises from Palma de Mallorca, under charter to Blue Seas Cruises. In November 1973, the liner was laid up again, and in May 1977, *Queen Frederica* was sold to shipbreakers at Eleusis.

Queen Frederica in Chandris colours

ORIANA

BUILT: 1960 by Vickers-Armstrong Ltd, Barrow
TONNAGE: 41,915 gross
DIMENSIONS: 804 x 97 ft (245.1 x 29.6 m)
SERVICE SPEED: 27.5 knots
PROPULSION: Geared turbines/twin screws

The largest, and last, passenger liner to be built for the Orient Line, *Oriana* was launched by Princess Alexandra on 3 November 1959. A year later it reached 30.64 knots during trials in poor weather conditions. Accommodation was provided for 638 first class and 1,496 tourist class passengers. With its high speed and huge capacity, *Oriana* was able to reduce the passage time to Sydney by a week, and thus replace two older vessels on the route.

Oriana was too large to berth at Tilbury, so became the first Orient Line vessel to be based on Southampton. Its maiden voyage departed on 3 December 1960, via the Suez Canal to Fremantle, Melbourne and Sydney, berthing on 30 December. On 5 January 1961 *Oriana* left Sydney on a cruise to Hobart, Wellington and Auckland, then made a circle-Pacific voyage with calls at Vancouver, San Francisco and Los Angeles. Returning to Sydney, *Oriana* voyaged back to Britain through the Suez Canal.

Oriana spent the early years of its career engaged mostly on the mail service between Britain and Australia via Suez, with occasional cruises and circle-Pacific voyages. On 3 December 1962 *Oriana* collided with the aircraft carrier USS *Kearsage* off Los Angeles, but suffered only minimal damage.

In March 1964, *Oriana* eclipsed the record established in 1936 by *Awatea* for the journey between Auckland and Sydney, with a 45 hour 24 minute passage at an average speed of 27.76 knots.

When completed, *Oriana* was given the regular Orient Line corn-coloured hull, but during 1964 the hull was repainted white. *Oriana* made its first cruise from Southampton in July 1964, and on 2 October the same year, left Sydney on a cruise to Japan to coincide with the Tokyo Olympic Games. On 31 March 1965, *Oriana* was transferred to the ownership of the P & O Line.

While transiting the Panama Canal in September 1969, *Oriana* struck the side-suffering damage to one propeller, but a more serious incident occurred on 11 August 1970. While departing Southampton a fire broke out in the electrical switchboard, which fortunately was quickly extinguished, but *Oriana* had to return to its berth where repairs took two weeks to complete.

With the demand for passages by sea between Britain and Australia declining, *Oriana* was used increasingly for cruises from both Southampton and Sydney. In 1973, the accommodation was modified to carry 1,500 passengers in one class as a cruise ship.

For most of the year the liner was based on Southampton, then in November voyaged to Sydney for a three-month season of cruises in the South Pacific. This schedule was followed for eight years, until 1981. Following its arrival in Sydney on 22 December that year, *Oriana* remained permanently on the Australian cruise trade.

On 14 March 1986, *Oriana* left on its final cruise, returning to Sydney on 27 March, and being laid up. On 21 May the vessel was sold to a Japanese company, Daiwa House Sales, who stated the vessel would be used in a static role as a cultural and tourist centre at Beppu, on Kyushu Island, in the Oita Prefecture.

Towed by the oil rig service vessel *Lady Lorraine*, *Oriana* left Sydney Harbour on the afternoon of 28 May. On reaching Japan, *Oriana* was handed over to the new owner, and sent to the Hitachi Zosen shipyard

Oriana with a corn coloured hull

Oriana with a white hull

at Sakai for conversion to suit it for its new role. This involved the removal of all the original accommodation, and the installation of a variety of facilities, including conference rooms, exhibition hall, cinema, lounges, and bars and restaurants. On 26 June 1987, *Oriana* arrived under tow at Beppu Port.

On 1 August, the new look *Oriana* was opened to the public for the first time, and immediately began drawing large crowds. The owner needed to attract at least 1.5 million visitors a year to the ship, despite charging the quite high entrance fee of ¥2,500 per adult, to make the venture economic. For several years everything went well, but in the early 1990s the number of visitors began to decrease, and in 1994 the ship was offered for sale.

In 1995, *Oriana* was sold to Chinese interests, and towed to Qinhuandao to operate as a floating hotel. This venture failed quite quickly, so in 1998 the liner was moved to Shanghai, being berthed in the centre of the city, but only survived a year before closing. In 2000 *Oriana* was sold again, and towed to the popular tourist Chinese tourist destination of Dalien. After being extensively refurbished, the liner again began operating as a floating hotel and entertainment centre, and seemed to be successful.

On the night of 17–18 June 2004, gale force winds swept through the area, and *Oriana* was torn from its mooring, and after drifting a short distance, sank in shallow water, with a heavy list to port, which flooded the lower decks, but left the superstructure above water. Once cracks in the hull had been sealed, the liner was refloated in May 2005, and left Daliaen, for a scrapyard in Zhangiagang in Eastern China's Jiangsu Province.

Oriana in Shanghai in September 1999

120

PATRIS

BUILT: 1950 by Harland & Wolff Ltd, Belfast
TONNAGE: 16,259 gross
DIMENSIONS: 595 x 76 ft (181.3 x 23.3 m)
SERVICE SPEED: 18 knots
PROPULSION: B & W diesels/twin screws

Patris was the first liner to be operated by D & A Chandris, who bought it from Union-Castle Line. Launched on 25 August 1949, it was christened *Bloemfontein Castle,* and completed in March 1950. *Bloemfontein Castle* had been built to meet an anticipated rush of migrants to South Africa, so was fitted out to carry 721 passengers in one class, unlike any other Union-Castle liner. It was also the only liner in the fleet to have only one mast, and had a large cargo capacity, much of it refrigerated. Placed on an independent schedule from London to Cape Town and Beira, *Bloemfontein Castle* departed on its maiden voyage on 6 April 1950.

Bloemfontein Castle was always the odd ship in an otherwise well-balanced fleet, being the only Union-Castle liner to operate without partners. The expected rush of migrants did not materialise, so the liner had to rely on regular passengers to a large extent.

On 8 January 1953, *Bloemfontein Castle* answered a call for help from the Dutch liner *Klipfontein*, which was sinking off the Mozambique coast, and rescued 116 passengers and 118 crew. This was the only highlight in an otherwise unremarkable career under the British flag, and in 1959 *Bloemfontein Castle* was offered for sale. In October the vessel was purchased by Chandris Line, and arrived in Southampton on 9 November at the end of its final voyage, then was delivered to Chandris later that month.

Renamed *Patris,* it went to Smith's Dock at North Shields for a short refit. Externally the vessel was not altered, apart from new hull and funnel colours, but internally the accommodation was altered to carry 36 first class and 1,040 tourist class passengers. After a short time this was changed to 1,076 in one class. On 14 December 1959, *Patris* departed Piraeus on its maiden voyage to Australia, arriving in Fremantle on 2 January 1960, Melbourne on 7 January and Sydney on 9 January. The return voyage departed Sydney on 12 January, following the reverse route back to Piraeus.

Patris remained on this route for several years. On the morning of 16 April 1960, it ran aground in the Suez Canal during a sandstorm, but was quickly refloated without damage the same evening. The large refrigerated cargo spaces were utilised to transport meat to Greece, and on 9 January 1961, *Patris* made the first of several calls at Geelong to load mutton. It was also during 1961 that *Patris* made two return trips to Greece via Brisbane and Singapore, and in October paid its first visit to Wellington. Later the vessel also made occasional cruises from Sydney.

With the closure of the Suez Canal in 1967, *Patris* was forced to voyage around Africa to Australia, which it did for five years. On the night of 18 June 1971, *Patris* was leaving Sydney Harbour when it collided with the collier *Rickie Miller* off Goat Island. The smaller ship was able to continue to its wharf, while *Patris* went to the Bank Anchorage for repairs to the bow, eventually leaving Sydney on 20 June.

Early in 1972 *Patris* was placed on a new service, from Australia to Djibouti in the Red Sea. It was thought this would attract passengers to a faster service to Europe, with passengers flying to their destinations from Djibouti, but after several voyages

Bloemfontein Castle

the service was abandoned. On 6 October 1972, *Patris* inaugurated another route, from Sydney to Singapore via Melbourne and Fremantle, which was designed to compete with the booming "ship-jet" trade between Fremantle and Singapore.

On Christmas Day 1974, Darwin was almost destroyed by Cyclone Tracy. With most of the population homeless, Chandris offered *Patris* to provide temporary accommodation, and on 15 February 1975 it arrived in the Northern Territory port. *Patris* remained there nine months, then left on 13 November 1975, returning to Piraeus for an extensive overhaul.

Chandris had decided to convert *Patris* into a car ferry, for which purpose the lower decks were gutted to provide garage space for about 250 cars, and large doors cut in the sides. The accommodation was altered to carry 1,403 passengers, and on 17 June 1976, *Patris* began operating between Patras and Ancona. This was a seasonal trade, and the vessel was laid up in October. Returning to service in 1977, it began a new service from Patras to Venice in June, again being laid up in October. This was repeated in 1978, then in 1979, *Patris* was sold to Karageorgis Line, and renamed *Mediterranean Island.*

The vessel remained in the ferry trade between Greece and Italy, then in 1981 was renamed *Mediterranean Star.* On 28 August 1982, on a voyage from Patras to Ancona, *Mediterranean Star* was disabled by a major engine room fire. All passengers and many crew abandoned the ship in lifeboats, while remaining crew eventually managed to extinguish the blaze. The vessel was sent to Perama for repairs, but these were not effected immediately, and the ship was idle for several years.

In May 1986, *Mediterranean Star* was chartered to Star Navigation Co Ltd, and began cruising from Piraeus to Rhodes, Limassol and Alexandria. Returns from this programme were very poor, and in October 1986, the liner was laid up again. During 1986, reports had appeared in the Australian press that *Mediterranean Star* had been chartered by newly formed Scandic Line, to cruise from Sydney during 1987 as *Scandic Star,* but that did not happen, as Scandic Line went out of business in 1986. Instead *Mediterranean Star* remained idle in Piraeus until August 1987, then was sold to Pakistani shipbreakers, and under the name *Terra* was towed to Karachi to be scrapped.

Patris

CONTE GRANDE

BUILT: 1928 by Stablimento Technico, Trieste
TONNAGE: 23,842 ,gross
DIMENSIONS: 667 x 76 ft (203.3 x 23.8 m)
SERVICE SPEED: 20 knots
PROPULSION: Geared turbines/twin screws

Conte Grande made a single voyage to Australia on behalf of Lloyd Triestino, at the end of a long career. *Conte Grande* was launched on 29 June 1927, and completed in February 1928, having accommodation for 1,720 passengers in three classes. Its maiden voyage left Genoa on 3 April 1928 for New York, joining a sister ship, the British-built *Conte Biancamano*. This pair had been built for Lloyd Sabaudo, who operated a wide network of services, including one to Australia from 1921 until 1932, which eventually was taken over by Lloyd Triestino.

In January 1932 the Italian Government reorganised the numerous Italian shipping companies into a few large concerns. Lloyd Sabaudo was merged with Navigazione Generale Italiana and the Cosulich Line to form Italia Line. *Conte Grande* and *Conte Biancamano* remained on the New York route until 1933, when they were transferred to the South American trade.

When Italy entered the war in 1940, *Conte Grande* was in Brazilian waters, and was laid up at Santos. Seized by the Brazilian Government on 22 August 1941, it was then sold to the United States on 16 April 1942. Refitted as a troopship, and renamed *Monticello*, it served as such until March 1946, then was laid up.

In July 1947, the liner was handed back to Italy, and given an extensive refit, during which a raked bow and new funnels were fitted. With accommodation for 215 first class, 333 cabin class and 950 tourist class passengers, it returned to the service from Genoa to South America in July 1949 as *Conte Grande*, once again partnered by *Conte Biancamano*.

In the summer of 1956, *Conte Grande* and *Conte Biancamano* were returned to the New York trade for several months, following the sinking of *Andrea Doria*, and over the next few years both liners operated to New York during the peak summer season.

At the end of 1960, *Conte Grande* was chartered by Lloyd Triestino for one voyage, with the funnels repainted in their colours. On 15 December, *Conte Grande* departed Genoa with 1,600 passengers on board, all in one class, comprising emigrants and fare-paying passengers. After calling at Fremantle on 7 January 1961, and Melbourne on 11 January, the liner arrived in Sydney on 13 January, remaining in port for two days. On the return voyage, it called again at Melbourne, then went to Adelaide, being there on 19 January, before passing through Fremantle on 22 January, to arrive back in Genoa on 14 February.

Conte Grande then returned to the South American trade, once again in Italia Line colours. *Conte Biancamano* had been withdrawn from service in April 1960, and subsequently sold to shipbreakers. In August 1961, *Conte Grande* arrived in Genoa at the end of its final voyage, and on 7 September the old liner anchored off La Spezia, where it was subsequently broken up.

Conte Grande in Sydney Harbour in January 1961

MONTE UDALA

BUILT: 1948 by Cia Euskalduna, Bilbao
TONNAGE: 10,170 gross
DIMENSIONS: 487 x 62 ft (148.5 x 19 m)
SERVICE SPEED: 16 knots
PROPULSION: Sulzer diesels/single screw

New settlers have come to Australia from every European country in the post-war years, and *Monte Udala* made two voyages to Australia with Spanish migrants.

This vessel was the second completed of a series of six cargo ships, known as the "Monasterio" class, ordered by Empressa Nacional "Elcano". All were eventually redesigned while building into passenger-cargo liners, and sold to two other Spanish companies, Cia Transatlantica Espanola, and Naviera Aznar, who purchased the first four vessels to be completed. The Aznar ships were named *Monte Urbasa*, *Monte Udala*, *Monte Urquiola*, and *Monte Ulia*, while the others became *Covadonga* and *Guadalupe*.

Launched on 1 May 1946, work on fitting out *Monte Udala* proceeded very slowly, due to the time taken to redesign the ship, and a shortage of materials. It was not until July 1948 that it was finally handed over to Aznar Line.

Fitted with accommodation for 62 first class, 40 second class and 290 third class passengers, the first class quarters were of a very high standard, while second class consisted of 10 four-berth cabins, and third class was dormitories for migrants from Spain.

Monte Udala was placed in service from Spanish ports to Buenos Aires and other cities in the River Plate estuary.

Aznar Line had never had any connection with the Australian trade, so it was surprising when *Monte Udala* departed Bilbao in December 1959, carrying 400 migrants to Melbourne, berthing there on 20 January 1960. All the migrants disembarked, then on 27 January *Monte Udala* moved across the bay to Geelong, where a cargo of wheat was loaded. On 2 February *Monte Udala* left Geelong, returning to Spain and resuming its regular trade to South America.

In December 1960, *Monte Udala* departed Santander on its second voyage to Australia, arriving in Melbourne on 19 January 1961, remaining in port loading cargo until 7 February, then returning to Spain. This was the final visit to Australia made by *Monte Udala*, which then spent the rest of its career on the South American trade.

During the late 1960s, *Monte Udala* ceased carrying passengers, but continued to operate to South America as a cargo ship. The vessel was on a voyage from Buenos Aires to Spain when, on 8 September 1971, water was found to be leaking into the engine room.

The crew was unable to stop the inrush of water, but as the ship was close to the Brazilian coast, rescue ships were soon on the scene. The crew abandoned ship, and were picked up by a passing freighter. *Monte Udala* finally rolled on its side and sank.

CANBERRA

BUILT: 1961 by Harland & Wolff Ltd, Belfast
TONNAGE: 45,270 gross
DIMENSIONS: 820 x 102 ft (249.9 x 31.1 m)
SERVICE SPEED: 27 knots
PROPULSION: Turbo-electric/twin screws

Canberra was destined to be the last, and largest, liner that P & O would build for the Australian trade. Laid down on 27 September 1957 and launched on 16 March 1960, fitting out took 14 months, so it was 18 May 1961 before the vessel ran trials, averaging 29.27 knots.

Unable to use the usual P & O berth at Tilbury because of its size, *Canberra* was based on Southampton, departing on 2 June 1961 on its maiden voyage to Australia via the Suez Canal. *Canberra* provided berths for 548 first class and 1,650 tourist class passengers,

Slowed by engine trouble while crossing the Indian Ocean from Colombo to Fremantle, *Canberra* arrived 31 hours late on 23 June, then continued to Melbourne and Sydney, arriving on 29 June. *Canberra* reached Auckland on 4 July, going on to Suva, Honolulu, Vancouver, San Francisco and Los Angeles, then back to Sydney via Honolulu again, returning to Britain by way of the Suez Canal.

During the first year of operation, *Canberra* suffered continual mechanical problems, and on 2 June 1962 entered the King George V Drydock in Southampton for a six-week overhaul. In addition to fixing the engines, additional ballast was added forward to keep the bow deeper in the water, making for a smoother passage. Returning to service, *Canberra* made a short cruise from Southampton, followed by two cruises from Southampton to New York.

Canberra spent most of its first 10 years on the Australian trade, apart from occasional cruises. The mechanical problems continued, and on 4 January 1963 the liner was completely disabled off Malta by an engine room fire, which destroyed the main starboard switchgear. *Canberra* limped to Valetta, where the passengers disembarked, then returned to the builder's yard for repairs that lasted four months, returning to service again on 24 May.

During 1964, *Canberra* made four cruises from Southampton to New York, and early in 1966 made its first appearance in Asian waters. After calling at Yokohama on 15 March, then Kobe and Nagasaki, on 22 March *Canberra* became the first vessel to berth at the new Ocean Terminal in Hong Kong.

In July 1967, *Canberra* was in the Mediterranean on a voyage from Britain when rumours that Egypt and Israel were about go to war prompted P & O to order the captain to divert around Africa. On the day *Canberra* was scheduled to transit the Suez Canal, Israel and Egypt went to war, and all ships in the canal were trapped there for seven years.

At the end of 1972, *Canberra* was withdrawn from the Australian trade, and refitted to carry 1,500 passengers in a single class as a cruise ship. P & O decided to base the ship on New York, offering regular cruises to the West Indies, the first of which departed on 31 January 1973. Response from the Americans was so poor that, after just two cruises, *Canberra* was laid up at Wilmington in Delaware on 24 February. At the end of March, the vessel resumed its cruise schedule, but was not a success, and in November 1973 returned to Southampton and an uncertain future.

For a while it appeared that *Canberra* might go to the shipbreakers' yards. However, P & O had scheduled a world cruise, departing Southampton in January 1974 using *Orsova*, which was overbooked, so *Canberra* made this voyage, and *Orsova* went to the breakers' yard instead.

On returning from the world cruise, which included calls at Australian and New Zealand ports, *Canberra* took over the cruises originally scheduled for *Orsova* out of Southampton, and was very successful. Each January, *Canberra* departed Southampton on a three-month cruise around the world, which included calls at Auckland and Sydney during mid-February. The itineraries for these cruises varied, with some including Japan and the Far East, while others took the vessel around Africa.

On 2 April 1982, *Canberra* arrived in Naples, nearing the end of a world cruise, as Argentine forces invaded the Falkland Islands. On 5 April the vessel was requisitioned by the British Government, but it did not reach Southampton for another two days. As soon as the passengers had disembarked, workmen swarmed aboard, erecting two helipads and converting the liner for a combat role within 48 hours. Some 2,500 troops streamed aboard, and on the evening of 9 April, *Canberra* left Southampton, initial destination Ascension Island.

After all the rush, *Canberra* spent over two weeks waiting at Ascension, then headed south in a convoy. On 21 May, *Canberra* anchored in San Carlos Bay, and within hours was under attack by Argentine aircraft, but miraculously avoided damage, although one of the escorting warships was sunk.

The same night, *Canberra* slipped out to sea again, steaming in boxes until being sent to South Georgia to take on board troops from *Queen Elizabeth 2*. On 2 June, *Canberra* returned to San Carlos Bay to disembark these troops and their stores, which took two days, but air attacks were fewer during this period. Returning to sea again, *Canberra* awaited further orders, which came 10 days later, when the Argentine forces finally surrendered.

Canberra was directed to enter San Carlos Bay once again. This time the liner took on board 1,121 Argentine prisoners-of-war, then went to Port Stanley to take on more, until there was a total of 4,167 Argentinians aboard. *Canberra* then departed for the Argentine port of Purto Madryn, where the troops disembarked. Returning to the Falklands, *Canberra* entered San Carlos Bay for the fourth time, to embark British troops returning home, and on 25 June the liner left Falkland waters for the last time. Returning to Southampton on 11 July, *Canberra* had been away 94 days, and covered some 25,245 nautical miles without any mechanical malfunction.

Canberra spent the next two months in dock, then on 11 September, left Southampton on a cruise. In November, *Canberra* left Southampton on a voyage to Australia, reaching Sydney on 21 December. For the first time in many years, *Canberra* was scheduled to make five cruises from Sydney to the South Pacific, then in March 1983 returned once more to Southampton. Subsequently *Canberra* continued to make an annual round-the-world cruise, departing Southampton each January, and spending two days in Sydney in mid-February.

In 1988, *Canberra* underwent a major refit, intended to enable the liner to continue in service for a further 10 to 15 years. The liner continued to spend most of each year cruising out of Southampton, with an annual world cruise, the final such voyage departed Southampton in January 1997. *Canberra* arrived in Sydney for the last time on 22 February, departing the next day. On returning to Britain, *Canberra* continued cruising out of Southampton, making its final departure on 10 September, then being withdrawn from service when it returned on 30 September 1997.

Canberra was sold to shipbreakers in Pakistan, leaving Southampton for the last time on 10 October, and arriving off the breakers' yard at Gadani Beach on 28 October.

NORTHERN STAR

BUILT: 1962 by Vickers- Armstrong Ltd, Newcastle
TONNAGE: 24,733 gross
DIMENSIONS: 650 x 83 ft (198.1 x 25.5m)
SERVICE SPEED: 20 knots
PROPULSION: Geared turbines/twin screws

Southern Cross was such a successful ship for Shaw Savill Line, they ordered a second vessel of the same type for their round-the-world service. Launched on 27 June 1961 as *Northern Star*, it had tourist class accommodation for 1,412 passengers, and carried no cargo. *Southern Cross* had alternated the directions of its voyages, but when *Northern Star* entered service, it operated the eastward voyages, while *Southern Cross* travelled westward.

On 10 July 1962, *Northern Star* departed Southampton on its maiden voyage, but on 16 July the starboard engine had to be stopped due to a fault in the high pressure turbine, which had to be disconnected. Four days later the port engine suffered an identical problem. After making calls at Cape Town and Durban, *Northern Star* reached Fremantle two days late, on 11 August, then went on to Melbourne and Sydney, where it remained for six days undergoing engine repairs.

Departing Sydney on 24 August, *Northern Star* arrived in Wellington on 28 August, and after a call at Auckland, visited Suva and Papeete. Four days after leaving Tahiti, both engines had to be stopped again, and the high pressure turbines disconnected. *Northern Star* continued through Panama, and limped into Southampton nine days late. Repairs were effected before the vessel sailed on its second voyage, on 18 October. However, engine problems were to continually plague this ship, and bring about its early demise.

Northern Star settled into a pattern of four round-the-world trips a year, with occasional cruises from both Southampton and Sydney. In December 1965, the funnel of *Northern Star* was repainted a deep green with a thin black top, and a four-pointed gold star on either side. In 1966 the funnel was returned to the regular Shaw Savill colours, but the star remained.

As demand for line voyage passages declined in the late 1960s, *Northern Star* began making more cruises, and by 1971 was scheduled for only two round-the-world voyages during the year. These were broken up by cruises out of Sydney, and the ship cruised from Southampton between voyages.

The mechanical problems continued, and on 12 June 1973 a minor boiler explosion off Venice during a cruise sent the ship limping back to Southampton once again for repairs.

From November 1973 to March 1974, *Northern Star* cruised out of Sydney, then went back to Southampton for another programme of cruises. Returning to Sydney again at the end of 1974, *Northern Star* again operated a series of South Pacific cruises.

By now the engine and boiler problems had become very serious, resulting in one cruise being cancelled to enable further repairs. The liner went back to Britain for a final season of cruises, the last returning to Southampton on 1 November 1975.

Having been sold to shipbreakers in Taiwan, *Northern Star* left Southampton for the last time on 7 November, arriving in Kaohsiung on 11 December 1975.

GALILEO GALILEI and GUGLIELMO MARCONI

BUILT: 1963 by Cant Riuniti dell'Adriatico, Monfalcone
TONNAGE: 27,905 gross .
DIMENSIONS: 702 x 94 ft (213.9 x 28.6 m)
SERVICE SPEED: 24 knots
PROPULSION: Geared turbines/twin screws

This pair was constructed together on adjoining slips at Trieste, the first being launched on 2 July 1961 as *Galileo Galilei*, while *Guglielmo Marconi* when launched on 24 September 1961. These ships would be best known under their abbreviated names of *Galileo* and *Marconi*.

Galileo was scheduled to make its maiden departure on 16 February 1963, but it was not until 22 April that the liner left Genoa, arriving in Fremantle on 9 May, Melbourne on 13 May and Sydney two days later, leaving on 19 May to follow the reverse route home.

Marconi was scheduled to enter service on 10 June 1963, but fitting out lasted two years. Three round trips had to be cancelled before the vessel made its maiden departure from Genoa on 18 November. *Marconi* passed through Fremantle on 5 December, Melbourne on 9 December, and berthed in Sydney on 11 December.

These ships reduced the passage time from Genoa to Sydney from 31 days to 23 days, and between them they could carry more passengers than the trio they replaced. Depending on demand, first class berths could vary between 156 and 289, while tourist class could carry from 1,358 to 1,594 passengers. The only amenity shared by both classes was the cinema. The first class dining room could seat 149 persons, while that in tourist class had a 774 person capacity.

Up to 1967, both ships voyaged in each direction through the Suez Canal, but when it was closed, they had to make the longer passage around South Africa. On 7 October 1968, *Galileo* left Sydney on the first voyage by these ships across the Pacific, passing through the Panama Canal and back to Genoa. Over the next six years both ships made several round-the-world voyages each year. In the early 1970s, one of them would make an annual Christmas cruise from Sydney, but neither ship was ever engaged in cruising for any extended period.

The world oil crisis of the 1970s had an impact on the careers of these liners. *Marconi* had been programmed to depart Sydney on a cruise on 18 December 1973, but this was cancelled, and the ship lay in port until 3 January 1974, then left on schedule for Italy. A year later, *Galileo* was on a voyage to Australia around South Africa when, on 13 January 1975, it struck a reef off the coast of West Africa, and had to divert to Monrovia. Inspection showed extensive hull plate damage, so *Galileo* returned to Genoa on 24 January, and was drydocked for repairs, returning to service in March.

The service was heavily subsidised by the Italian Government, but costs were rising so fast that the charge to the public purse was becoming excessive, so the government decided to change the subsidy system. As a result, on 20 October 1975, *Marconi* departed Genoa on its final voyage to Australia, passing through Cape Town to arrive in Fremantle on 16 November, Melbourne on 20 November and Sydney two days later. Departing on 23 November, *Marconi* arrived in Auckland on 26 November, then went across the Pacific and through the Panama Canal to reach Genoa on 30 December. *Marconi* was then transferred to Italia Line, and joined their service to South America, departing Naples for the first time on 20 January 1976.

This left *Galileo* to carry on the Australian trade alone, and it was programmed to remain in service through 1977. However, at short notice the departure

Galileo Galilei

from Genoa on 26 May 1977 was cancelled. This meant that its final voyage to Australia had been from Genoa on 12 March, departing Sydney on 13 April and Auckland on 16 April for the return trip through the Panama Canal, arriving back in Genoa on 19 May.

Also during May 1977, the Italia Line service to South America was terminated, with *Marconi* returning to Naples on 7 June. The Italian Government had decided that both ships were to be transferred to the American cruise market.

Galileo and *Marconi* were refitted at the Cantiere Navale Riuniti shipyard in Palermo, with passenger capacity reduced to 900 in one class. It was planned that one of the ships would be based in North America, while the other would cruise in the Mediterranean from April to October, then switch to the Caribbean for the rest of the year.

Marconi commenced a series of cruises from New York to the Caribbean on 27 December 1978, but could not pass the US Health Service inspections. In July 1979 it failed for the seventh time, and the operators were ordered to cease selling berths on the ship.

Galileo had entered Mediterranean cruise service in April 1979, and was due to cross to Port Everglades in October. However, *Marconi* was sent to the Florida port to take over the cruises scheduled for *Galileo*, which was laid up in Genoa. *Marconi* made its first departure from Port Everglades on 20 October, but again failed to pass the US Health Service tests. *Marconi* resumed service on 22 December 1979, but on 12 January 1980 was taken out of service, and returned to Genoa.

In June 1981, *Galileo* returned to service under charter to Chandris Line, cruising in the Mediterranean until October, then was laid up again. Late in 1983, both ships were sold. *Galileo* went to Chandris, and with its name officially changed to *Galileo*, in June 1984 began cruising from American east coast ports.

Marconi was bought by Costa Line, and given an extensive rebuilding, as well as having the engines and boilers overhauled. The work was done by the.Mariotti shipyard in Genoa, and lasted over a year. New accommodation for 984 passengers was installed, along with new public rooms, and the superstructure was extended.

Renamed *Costa Riviera*, the vessel was based at Port Everglades, making its first cruise on 14 December 1985, and operated regular weekly departures throughout the year.

Late in 1989, *Galileo* was extensively rebuilt at the Lloyd Werft shipyard in Bremerhaven, and then transferred to a newly formed Chandris subsidiary, Celebrity Cruises, being renamed *Meridian*. The vessel resumed cruising from east coast ports of America in March 1990.

In 1993, *Costa Riviera* was transferred within the Costa Group to American Family Cruises, being renamed *American Adventure*. This venture aimed at attracting more families to cruising, but did not attract enough passengers, so in 1994 the vessel was returned to the Costa fleet, renamed *Costa Riviera*, and resumed cruising out of Port Everglades.

In September 1997, *Meridian* was sold to a Singapore company, Metro Holdings, who operated as Sun Cruises. Renamed *Sun Vista*, it began making weekly cruises out of Singapore on 30 November 1997. On the evening of Thursday, 20 May 1999, *Sun Vista* was in the Strait of Malacca south of Penang, when a switchboard in the engine room caught fire. Within two hours the flames were out of control and spreading rapidly. Passengers and crew abandoned the ship, and at 1.22 am, local time, on Friday, 21 May, *Sun Vista* rolled over on its side, and sank.

Costa Riviera continued to cruise out of Port Everglades until it was withdrawn from service on 16 November 2001, and laid up. Sold early in 2002 to Indian shipbreakers, the vessel was renamed *Liberty* for its final voyage to the breakers' yard at Alang.

Costa Riviera

FLAVIA

BUILT: 1947 by John Brown & Co, Clydebank
TONNAGE: 15,465 gross
DIMENSIONS: 556 x 70 ft (169.8 x 21.3 m)
SERVICE SPEED: 18 knots
PROPULSION: Geared turbines/twin screws

Flavia was originally built for the Cunard Line and named *Media*, being launched on 12 December 1946, and completed eight months later, the first British passenger liner to be built after World War Two. It was joined in April 1948 by a sister ship, *Parthia*. They provided comfortable accommodation for 250 first class passengers only, and had a large cargo capacity.

Media entered service on 20 August 1947 with a departure from Liverpool for New York. *Media* and *Parthia* operated a secondary service on this route, and remained under Cunard Line ownership until 1961, when both were sold.

Bought by Cia Genovese d'Armamento, better known as Cogedar Line, in July 1961, *Media* did not complete its final Cunard voyage until 30 September, at Liverpool. On being handed over, the vessel was renamed *Flavia*, and sent to Genoa to be rebuilt. The original superstructure was removed and a new one built, a raked bow added, and all cargo areas removed. Accommodation for 1,224 passengers in 378 cabins was installed, comprising 152 two-berth, 221 four-berth and 5 eight-berth, the majority having private facilities. When the rebuilding was completed, *Flavia* bore no resemblance to its appearance as *Media*.

On 2 October 1962, *Flavia* departed Genoa on its first voyage, arriving in Fremantle on 30 October, and being in Melbourne from 5 to 7 November before reaching Sydney on 9 November. Departing next day, *Flavia* retraced its course, but went on to Bremerhaven. In future this would be its European terminal, the first departure from there being on 22 December 1962.

Flavia also made occasional cruises from Australia, the first being from Sydney on 8 April 1963 to Japan and the Far East, returning on 10 May. Later in 1963, *Flavia* began operating a round-the-world service, from Bremerhaven, Rotterdam and London through the Panama Canal to Tahiti, Auckland, Australian ports, and back through Suez.

With the closure of the Suez Canal in 1967, *Flavia* had to divert around South Africa, but the following year Cogedar Line withdrew from the trade. On 23 July 1968, *Flavia* left Rotterdam on its final voyage to Australia, and after a cruise from Sydney, left there on 18 October, and Melbourne two days later. On its return to Europe, *Flavia* was chartered to Atlantic Cruise Line, and began cruising from Miami on 20 December 1968.

In 1969, *Flavia* was sold to the Italian shipping company, Costa Line, but not renamed. With the accommodation upgraded and reduced to 850, *Flavia* began operating short cruises from Miami to the Bahamas. In July 1977 it went to South America for a series of cruises, then in April 1978 began cruising in the Mediterranean. In September 1978, *Flavia* returned to the short cruise circuit from Miami again.

In 1982, *Flavia* was withdrawn, and sold to the C Y Tung Group of Hong Kong. With its name altered to *Flavian*, the vessel arrived in Hong Kong on 25 October 1982, and was laid up. In 1986 it was sold to Lavia Shipping SA, of Panama, and renamed *Lavia*, but remained laid up off Lantau Island.

On 7 January 1989, while undergoing a refit, *Lavia* caught fire, and was completely gutted, being run aground on a sandbank, where it heeled over on one side. The wreck was sold to Taiwanese shipbreakers, and after being refloated, it was towed to Kaohsiung, arriving there on 19 June 1989.

CHUSAN

BUILT: 1950 by Vickers-Armstrong Ltd, Barrow
TONNAGE: 24,161 gross
DIMENSIONS: 673 x 84 ft (205.1 x 25.6 m)
SERVICE SPEED: 22 knots
PROPULSION: Geared turbines/twin screws

Chusan did not appear in Australian waters until 1963, having been built for the P & O service to the Far East and Japan. It was the second liner built for P & O after the war, the first being *Himalaya*, and in many ways *Chusan* was a smaller version of that liner.

Launched on 28 June 1949, and completed one year later, *Chusan* was fitted out with accommodation for 475 first class and 551 tourist class passengers. On 15 September 1950, *Chusan* left Tilbury on its maiden voyage, which was a return trip to Bombay. On 7 November *Chusan* made its first departure for Singapore, Hong Kong and Japan.

One problem to arise on these early voyages was smuts from the funnel falling on the afterdeck. To rectify this, a Thorneycroft smoke deflector was added to the top of the funnel in 1952.

Chusan combined line voyages with cruises from Britain, on which it became very popular. On 12 June 1953, as *Chusan* was heading down the English Channel at the start of a cruise from Tilbury, it collided with a cargo ship in fog near the South Goodwin lightship. Though not seriously damaged,

Chusan returned to Tilbury for repairs, sailing again three days later.

During a refit in 1959, the accommodation was slightly reduced, to 464 first class and 541 tourist class. As P & O expanded its network of services across the Pacific, in 1960 *Chusan* made the first P & O voyage around the world. The liner followed the normal route to Japan, then crossed the Pacific to the west coast of America, and through the Panama Canal, the entire trip lasting 12 weeks.

With demand for passages to the Far East declining, on 6 June 1963, *Chusan* left Tilbury on its first voyage to Australia, arriving in Sydney on 10 July. Next day *Chusan* left on a three-week cruise to Tahiti, then returned to Britain. Subsequently, the liner came to Australia several times a year, and also operated some more cruises.

Chusan continued making occasional voyages to the Far East until 1970, when the route was abandoned by P & O. During the summer of 1970, and again in 1971, *Chusan* made four cruises from Amsterdam, for the European market. *Chusan* seemed to be quite successful, and very popular whenever it made cruises, so it was a great surprise when P & O decided to withdraw the vessel in 1973. The final departure from Southampton was on 12 May 1973, on a voyage to Australia. *Chusan* then made a one-way cruise to Hong Kong, and after destoring, crossed to Taiwan, arriving in Kaohsiung on 30 June 1973, and being handed over to shipbreakers.

BRETAGNE – BRITTANY

BUILT: 1952 by Ch de Penhoet, St Nazaire
TONNAGE: 16,335 gross
DIMENSIONS: 581 x 73 ft (177 x 22.3 m)
SERVICE SPEED: 18 knots
PROPULSION: Geared turbines/twin screws

The second of a pair of liners built for Soc Generale de Transports Maritimes, *Bretagne* was launched on 20 July 1951, completed in January 1952, and departed Marseilles on 14 February 1952 for its maiden voyage to South America, joining its sister ship *Provence*. Accommodation was provided for 149 first class, 167 tourist class and 974 third class passengers.

On 18 November 1960, Chandris Line signed a 12-month charter agreement for *Bretagne*, with an option to purchase. The liner was sent to Genoa for refitting, during which an additional 242 cabins were installed, so that the ship could carry 150 first class and 1,050 tourist class passengers.

The existing public rooms were also upgraded, while a new restaurant and a playroom for young children were added. Air-conditioning was extended to all parts of the accommodation, and a second swimming pool installed.

Bretagne was originally scheduled to leave Piraeus in May 1961 on a voyage to Australia, but instead it was chartered out for a season of cruising from New York in the summer of 1961.

During this period, Chandris was negotiating to purchase the liner, and on 20 September 1961 the deal was finalised. At that time the vessel was in Southampton, preparing for its first voyage to Australia, which departed on 22 September, and went via South Africa.

Bretagne arrived in Fremantle on 19 October, then Melbourne, berthing on 24 October, reaching Sydney two days later. The return voyage went to Brisbane, docking on 29 October, continuing around the north of Australia to Singapore and back to Southampton through the Suez Canal. The second voyage departed Southampton on 30 November, and went through the Mediterranean and Suez Canal.

On its third voyage, *Bretagne* made a special call at Geelong on 5 March 1962 to load cargo, being one of the largest passenger vessels ever to visit that port. On returning from the third voyage, *Bretagne* was renamed *Brittany* in early April 1962, and under that name left Southampton on 10 April for Australia.

After returning to Southampton, *Brittany* crossed to New York for another series of cruises, then on 12 September left Southampton again bound for Australia. This was followed by a departure on 22 November, then on 28 January 1963, *Brittany* left Southampton for Australia again.

Leaving Sydney on 2 March, the liner called at Melbourne and Fremantle, then passed through Suez and called at Piraeus. While in the Mediterranean, *Brittany* suffered serious engine trouble, and returned to Piraeus on 28 March 1963. The passengers were flown to their destinations, and the ship sent to the Hellenic Shipyard at Scaramanga for repairs.

The work was nearly completed when, on 8 April while the vessel was in drydock, a fire broke out in the engine room and quickly spread to the accommodation. Before firemen could properly attack the blaze, *Brittany* had to be floated out of the drydock, but by then the fire had a firm hold, and the ship was beached in Vasilika Bay to burn out. Early in 1964, the wreck was sold to shipbreakers at La Spezia, arriving there under tow on 31 March 1964.

Bretagne

ELLINIS

BUILT: 1932 by Bethlehem Shipbuilding Corp, Quincy
TONNAGE: 24,351 gross
DIMENSIONS: 642 x 79 ft (195.7 x 24.2 m)
SERVICE SPEED: 20 knots
PROPULSION: Geared turbines/twin screws

When Chandris Line realised that *Brittany* was a total loss, they immediately sought a replacement, and selected the Matson liner *Lurline*. In 1932, Matson Line took delivery of three sister ships, the first two built for the trans-Pacific trade to Australia as *Mariposa* and *Monterey*. The third vessel was launched as *Lurline* on 18 July 1932, and completed in December the same year. With superb accommodation for 475 first class and 240 cabin class passengers, it was designed to operate on the service between California and Hawaii.

Prior to entering this trade, *Lurline* made a cruise around the Pacific, which departed New York on 12 January 1933, and San Francisco on 27 January, and included calls at Auckland and then Sydney on 19 February, returning to San Francisco on 24 April. The liner then began its regular service to Hawaii. In February 1934, *Lurline* again visited Australia and New Zealand during a South Pacific cruise, but spent the rest of the 1930s on the service to Honolulu.

Lurline was two days out of Honolulu bound for San Francisco when the Japanese attacked Pearl Harbor on 7 December 1941. *Lurline* reached its destination two days later, and was immediately taken over by the US War Shipping Administration. The luxury fittings were stripped out, and quarters for 3,292 troops installed in just four days. *Lurline* then joined a convoy bound for Honolulu which also included *Mariposa* and *Monterey*. After several

similar trips, *Lurline* was despatched to Pago Pago and Australia, travelling alone and relying on its 22 knot maximum speed to outrun any lurking Japanese submarines.

Lurline spent the war years on active duty in the South Pacific region. In 1943 it began carrying American troops from San Francisco to Brisbane, and in April 1944 took Australian Prime Minister John Curtin and his party to America to meet President Roosevelt. Between September 1944 and June 1945, *Lurline* made five return trips to Australia, then was sent to France to board American troops and carry them to the Pacific, but before they arrived the Japanese surrendered.

On 11 September 1945, *Lurline* left Brisbane for San Francisco carrying 3,560 passengers, including 500 war brides and 200 children. The liner continued to voyage to Australia, repatriating troops and taking war brides to San Francisco, until 29 May 1946, when it was handed back to the Matson Line, going to the United Engineering Co shipyard at Alameda for a refit.

Restoring *Lurline* to its former glory took two years, during which the cost soared to US$20 million. With accommodation for 484 first class and 238 cabin class, *Lurline* returned to service on 15 April 1948, when it left San Francisco for Honolulu.

Lurline quickly regained its pre-war popularity on the Hawaiian trade. In June 1957, the accommodation was altered to 722 first class, and soon after *Lurline* began making cruises again. On 7 January 1958, *Lurline* left San Francisco carrying 575 passengers on a 73-day, 15-port cruise to the South Pacific and Orient, which included calls at Auckland and Wellington before arriving in Sydney on 31 January. Departing on 2 February, *Lurline* returned to San

Lurline

Francisco on 19 March. Subsequently *Lurline* made several short cruises each year, though a scheduled cruise to Australia in 1959 was cancelled, and in January 1960 the liner went to Tahiti.

By 1962, the Matson service to Hawaii was starting to lose money. On 3 February 1963, *Lurline* arrived in Los Angeles from Honolulu with serious problems in the port turbine. It continued to San Francisco on one engine, and then was laid up, as repairs were considered too expensive.

Lurline was offered for sale, being purchased by Chandris Line on 3 September 1963. Renamed *Ellinis*, it left San Francisco on 6 September, and went to Smith's Dock at North Shields in England for refitting. The superstructure was streamlined, the foremast removed and replaced by twin derricks, and a signal mast added above the bridge. Two new funnels were fitted, and a new raked bow. Internally, new cabins and extra berths in existing cabins increased capacity to 1,668 passengers in one class.

Ellinis left North Shields on 21 December 1963, bound for Piraeus, from where it departed on 30 December for its first voyage to Australia. Passing through Fremantle on 16 January 1964, *Ellinis* arrived in Melbourne on 20 January, and Sydney two days later, then continued to Auckland, and on across the Pacific to Tahiti before passing through the Panama Canal, then going to Southampton, arriving on 4 March. This was to be the European terminal port for future voyages to Australia, though in later years some voyages would be extended to Rotterdam. For the next 10 years, *Ellinis* made regular line voyages to Australia, with occasional cruises, and for several years was employed on an eastward round-the-world route.

On 25 April 1974, *Ellinis* was on a cruise to Japan when major problems developed in one engine, and it completed the cruise at reduced speed. This delayed the departure of the next voyage to Europe, which took over six weeks to reach Southampton, instead of less than five. *Ellinis* then continued to Rotterdam.

When the liner went to a local shipyard, it was found that the defective engine was out of alignment, and could not be repaired. At that time, its former sister *Mariposa*, which had been operating as *Homeric*, was being broken up in Taiwan, so Chandris Line bought one of its engines. It was transported to Rotterdam and installed in *Ellinis*, which then returned to service in March 1975.

During the summer of 1975, *Ellinis* made Mediterranean cruises from Cannes, then in November 1975, voyaged to South Africa for three cruises from Cape Town to South America. It cruised in the Mediterranean for much of 1976, so it was not until March 1977 that *Ellinis* appeared again in Australian waters. It made a cruise to Japan from Sydney, then returned to the Mediterranean.

On 30 August 1977, *Ellinis* left Southampton on its final voyage to Australia, then spent six months cruising out of Sydney, the last being to Japan in April 1978. On 18 May, *Ellinis* departed Sydney for the last time, calling at Auckland three days later, on the way back to Britain. For the summer months of 1978 and 1979, *Ellinis* cruised in the Mediterranean, and was laid up in Piraeus during the winter.

In 1980, *Ellinis* again cruised during the summer, but when the season ended, was laid up at Perama on 14 October 1980. For the next six years *Ellinis* remained idle. Some mechanical parts were removed and installed in *Britanis*, and various plans for further use were occasionally put forward, but all came to naught.

On 3 December 1986, *Ellinis* was towed away from Perama, bound for the scrap yard in Taiwan. The vessel began taking water off Singapore on 11 March, and developed a 15 degree list to starboard. After this was rectified, *Ellinis* arrived in Kaohsiung on 15 April 1987, where scrapping commenced two months later.

Ellinis

FAIRSTAR

BUILT: 1957 by Fairfield SB & E Co, Glasgow
TONNAGE: 21,619 gross
DIMENSIONS: 613 x 78 ft (186.9 x 23.8 m)
SERVICE SPEED: 18 knots
PROPULSION: Geared turbines/twin screws

Well known in Australia for over 30 years as a Sitmar liner, this vessel was ordered by the Bibby Line, a British company that had been involved in trooping for the government for many years. Launched on 15 December 1955 and named *Oxfordshire*, it was destined to be the last vessel built to transport troops. A sister ship, *Nevasa*, was owned by British India Line.

Oxfordshire was handed over to Bibby Line on 13 February 1957, and began a 20-year contract as a troopship. *Oxfordshire* could carry 1,000 troops in dormitories, plus 500 officers and dependents in cabins. The cabins could also be divided up into 220 first class, 100 second class and 180 third class when fare-paying passengers were carried.

In 1962, after a mere five years' service, the trooping career of *Oxfordshire* came to a sudden end. The British Government decided that all future troop movements would be by plane, and the contract with Bibby Line was terminated. On 19 December 1962, *Oxfordshire* arrived in Southampton at the end of its final voyage, then went to Falmouth to be laid up, being offered for sale or charter.

In May 1963, Sitmar Line took the vessel on a six-year charter, with an option to purchase. The vessel went to the Wilton-Fijenoord shipyard in Holland, to be refitted for the Australian emigrant trade. This involved a major enlargement of the superstructure, and the installation of extra cabins in the original troop and cargo spaces.

A dispute arose between Sitmar and Bibby Line regarding some of the alterations being made to the vessel, so in March 1964, Sitmar decided to exercise its option, and purchased *Oxfordshire*, which was then renamed *Fairstar*. The conversion work continued, but Sitmar then had a dispute with the Dutch shipyard, so in April 1964, *Fairstar* was moved to Southampton, where the conversion was completed by Harland & Wolff.

Fairstar provided accommodation for 1,870 passengers in one class, and on 19 May 1964, left Southampton on its first voyage to Australia. Fremantle was reached on 12 June, followed by Adelaide on 17 June and Melbourne the next day, with *Fairstar* arriving in Sydney for the first time on 21 June.

On the outbound voyages, the bulk of passengers on *Fairstar* were British migrants on assisted passages, while the return trip was made with fare-paying passengers. Voyages were regularly made out and back through the Suez Canal, with four return trips each year.

In January 1965, *Fairstar* made a three-day cruise from Sydney on charter to Massey Ferguson, this being the first Australian business convention held on a ship. On 22 December 1965, *Fairstar* left Sydney on its first commercial cruise, which lasted 22 days. In subsequent years, *Fairstar* made an annual Christmas cruise from Sydney.

The closure of the Suez Canal in 1967 resulted in *Fairstar* being diverted around South Africa, and eventually it began making round-the-world voyages, returning to Britain through the Panama Canal. In 1970, Sitmar lost the British migrant contract to Chandris Line, but *Fairstar* remained on the regular trade to Australia for a while, relying on fare-paying passengers. Eventually the demand for

such passages was insufficient to keep the vessel in service all year.

In July 1973, *Fairstar* made a voyage to Australia and New Zealand, then returned to Sydney to commence a programme of cruises, which lasted until April 1974. It then voyaged to Southampton, and cruised from there for several months, but with only limited success. On 13 November 1974, *Fairstar* departed Southampton for the last time, travelling via Cape Town to Sydney and Auckland, then returning to Sydney to enter year-round cruising, carrying a maximum of 1,280 passengers, with the first departure being on 23 December 1974.

For over 20 years, *Fairstar* cruised from Sydney throughout the year. Most trips were around the South Pacific islands, but there were also occasional longer cruises to the Far East and Japan. These finished temporarily in 1982, but from 1986 *Fairstar* made one cruise each year to Singapore, where it was drydocked and overhauled. During the 1988 refit, the funnel of *Fairstar* was repainted in the new colours adopted by Sitmar Cruises that year, dark blue with a swan-like "S" in red and white on either side.

Sitmar Cruises was sold to the P & O Group in July 1988. All the other vessels in the fleet were transferred to Princess Cruises and renamed, but *Fairstar* retained its name, and continued to operate out of Sydney under the control of a new company, P & O-Sitmar Cruises.

In June 1991, *Fairstar* underwent its annual drydocking in Singapore, during which the funnel was repainted white, though retaining the swan-like emblem. On 17 June, with 1,130 passengers on board, *Fairstar* left Singapore to cruise back to Sydney. Almost immediately the vessel began suffering mechanical problems, and on the morning of 19 June the engines stopped.

The vessel drifted all day and night, with no air-conditioning or lights, and the next day was taken in tow. Two days later, *Fairstar* was towed into Vung Tau, in Vietnam, where the passengers were disembarked and driven to the Ho Chi Minh City airport to be flown to Singapore, and then to Australia.

Fairstar was then towed back to Singapore for repairs, then returned empty to Sydney, arriving on 24 July. The ship was still suffering mechanical problems, and it did not resume cruising out of Sydney until 6 August.

Fairstar continued to cruise to the South Pacific islands, with an annual trip to Singapore, and during the refit there in July 1993 the funnel logo was changed, to feature a white dolphin across two blue circles. Over the next three years *Fairstar* suffered from occasional mechanical problems, and in June 1996 it was announced that the liner would be withdrawn from service in January 1997. The cruises over the next six months were all booked out, then on 21 January 1997, *Fairstar* left Sydney on its final cruise, returning on 31 January.

Fairstar was sold to shipbreakers in India, and on the evening of 12 February, with its name changed to *Ripa*, the vessel slipped quietly out of Sydney Harbour for the last time. It arrived off the shipbreaking beach at Alang on 10 April, and soon after was run ashore to be broken up.

AUSTRALIS

BUILT: 1940 by Newport News SB & DD Co
TONNAGE: 26,485 gross
DIMENSIONS: 723 x 93 ft (220.4 x 28.4 m)
SERVICE SPEED: 22 knots
PROPULSION: Geared turbines/twin screws

Australis was the most notable of all the ships Chandris Line purchased for their service from Europe to Australia, having been built as *America* for the United States Line. Designed by William Francis Gibbs, its keel was laid on 22 August 1938, and the liner launched by Mrs Eleanor Roosevelt on 31 August 1939. When completed in July 1940, *America* had accommodation for 543 cabin class, 418 tourist class and 241 third class passengers, but could not operate to Europe because of the war. Instead the vessel was sent cruising, departing New York for the first time on 10 August for the Caribbean.

One problem to arise early in her career was smuts falling on the afterdeck, so both funnels were raised about 15 ft (5 m), to retain a balanced appearance. *America* continued to operate cruises until 15 July 1941, then was taken over by the US Navy and converted into a troopship.

Fitted out with quarters for 8,175 men, the vessel was renamed USS *West Point*, and allocated pennant number AP23. Entering service in November 1941, *West Point* joined a convoy from Halifax, bound for Egypt, but was rerouted to Singapore via Cape Town.

By the time Singapore was reached, the Japanese were closing in, and *West Point* was frequently attacked by aircraft while anchored off the island. Eventually, it went to Bombay to disembark the troops, then to Suez to collect Australian troops and rush them to Singapore, returning to Bombay with civilian evacuees. *West Point* then proceeded

to Fremantle, Adelaide, Melbourne and Auckland, where American troops were embarked and carried to Noumea.

West Point had a very active war career, visiting many ports in the Pacific, Europe, Africa and South America, steaming over 500,000 miles and carrying 505,020 persons. *West Point* was released by the government on 22 July 1946, and handed back to United States Line.

Returning to its builders' yard, the liner was refitted for commercial service, with accommodation for 516 first class, 371 cabin class and 159 tourist class passengers. Given back its original name, *America* left New York on 14 November 1946, with 972 passengers aboard, for its first commercial voyage across the Atlantic, calling at Cobh, Southampton and Le Havre. After three voyages, the French terminal port was changed to Cherbourg, but in May 1948 it again began calling at Le Havre. From October 1951, the voyages were extended to Bremen.

During 1961, cabin and tourist class were combined into a single tourist class for 530 passengers, and incentive fares offered. *America* managed to remain competitive for a while longer, but just before departure time from New York on 14 September 1963, an inter-union dispute resulted in the engineers going on strike. The 900 passengers were left stranded, and *America* was towed to Hoboken and laid up.

It was 7 February 1964 before *America* returned to service, being programmed to operate 13 Atlantic voyages and three short summer cruises during the year, but on 9 October 1964 *America* left New York on its final voyage, departing Bremen on 19 October to return to New York on 27 October. The vessel was then laid up at Newport News. During 18 years on the Atlantic, *America* carried 476,462 passengers while making 288 voyages.

America

137

On 5 November came the announcement that *America* had been sold to Chandris Line, with the Greek flag being raised on 17 November, at which time the vessel was renamed *Australis*. On 18 November, *Australis* left Newport News for Piraeus, where Chandris' own shipyard set about converting the liner for the Australian trade. The accommodation was more than doubled, to 2,258 passengers in one class, and air-conditioning installed. External changes were minor, though the superstructure was extended aft, and the hull painted white.

On 21 August 1965, *Australis* departed Piraeus on its maiden voyage to Australia, reaching Fremantle on 6 September, Melbourne on 13 September, and Sydney two days later. It then crossed the Tasman to Auckland and on to Tahiti, through the Panama Canal, calling at Port Everglades on 3 October before terminating the voyage at Southampton. On 16 October, *Australis* left Southampton on its second voyage to Australia and New Zealand, but went to Wellington, then returned to Melbourne and back to Britain via the Suez Canal.

Australis remained on the regular trade between Britain and Australia through Suez until the canal was closed in 1967, then was diverted around South Africa, with calls at Cape Town and Durban. Occasionally, *Australis* made cruises from Australia during the summer. During a refit in 1968, the mainmast was removed, as well as a pair of king posts aft, while a short signal mast was added on the after funnel, and the hull was repainted light grey. In 1969, *Australis* was transferred from Greek to Panamanian registry.

On 22 October 1970, a fire broke out in the galley when *Australis* was between Auckland and Suva. The crew managed to control the blaze, but not before the galley was badly affected, and water damaged 40 cabins and the ballroom. Temporary repairs were effected in Suva, and *Australis* was able to continue its voyage on 30 October.

In 1970, Chandris Line secured the lucrative contract to transport British assisted migrants to Australia, but over the next few years the number being carried decreased, as more were choosing to travel by airplane. By 1976, *Australis* was the only liner offering regular sailings between Britain and Australia. It was also during 1976 that *Australis* was returned to Greek registry.

On 18 November 1977, *Australis* departed Southampton for the final time, carrying among the passengers 650 British assisted migrants, the last to be transported to Australia by sea. The voyage terminated in Sydney on 17 December. *Australis* had been chartered to operate a "rock and roll cruise" from Sydney, but this was cancelled due to lack of patronage. Instead the vessel left Sydney for Auckland, arriving on 20 December, then went to the small port of Timaru to be laid up.

Early in 1978 the liner was bought by a newly formed company, America Cruise Line, for US$5 million. On 23 April 1978, it left Timaru for New York, arriving on 19 May and going into drydock. The ship was completely refurbished internally, while the hull was repainted dark blue and the funnels the

Australis with a white hull

Australis with a light grey hull after 1968

same blue with a red band. Once again the vessel was named *America*, though the new owner was forced to change its name to Venture Cruise Line, to avoid confusion with another company.

On 30 June 1978, *America* left New York on a three-day cruise to nowhere, with 950 passengers aboard, but workmen were still swarming over the ship and many cabins and public rooms were out of use. Six hours out, *America* turned back, and anchored off Staten Island to disembark 250 disgruntled passengers in lifeboats. *America* made a second cruise from New York, with 641 passengers, but the next two cruises had to be cancelled while faulty plumbing was repaired. On 18 July, *America* was arrested by the District Court, then two days later Venture Cruise Line ceased operations, and *America* was laid up in Brooklyn.

On 28 August, *America* was put up for auction, and the surprise successful bidder was Chandris Line, who bought back the liner for US$1 million. It left New York for the last time on 6 September, bound for Piraeus, arriving on 12 September. Chandris refitted the ship for their cruise service, during which the dummy forward funnel was removed, and replaced by a mast. The vessel was renamed *Italis*, and on 28 July 1979 left Genoa on the first of three Mediterranean cruises, then was laid up on 12 September 1979 at Perama.

Italis was sold to Inter Commerce Corp., a subsidiary of Hilton Hotels, for conversion into a floating hotel to be based at Lagos, but apart from being renamed *Noga*, the liner remained idle at Perama. In 1984 the liner was sold again, to a Panamanian concern, Silver Moon Ferries, and renamed *Alferdos*, but remained idle at Perama.

The long period of idleness had a most destructive effect on the hull of the liner, and on 29 October 1988 *Alferdos* began taking on water, and developed a list, having to be run aground near Piraeus to prevent it sinking. Once the leaks were repaired, the vessel returned to its layup berth.

In October 1992 *Alferdos* was bought for US$2 million by Chaophraya Development Transport Company, of Bangkok, who planned to tow it to Phuket and convert it into a five-star floating hotel. On 17 February 1993 the vessel was moved to Hellenic Shipyards at Skaramanga for an overhaul, during which the ship was renamed *American Star*.

It was expected the tow would take about 100 days, going around South Africa. A large Ukrainian flag tug, *Neftegaz 67*, arrived in Piraeus in mid-December 1993, and on the afternoon of 31 December tug and tow departed Piraeus. On Saturday, 15 January, when the tug and liner were off the Canary Islands, they were hit by a Force 12 gale, causing the towline to break. Left at the mercy of wind and sea, *American Star* drifted overnight, but during the following day an emergency towline was connected. Within a few hours this towline also broke. *American Star* continued to drift, and early on the morning of Tuesday, 18 January 1994, was driven aground at Playa de Jurado Garcei, on the west coast of the island of Fuerteventura.

Constantly battered by pounding seas, within two days the hull of the liner split into two pieces just aft of the funnel. The wreck remained where it was, and over a period of time was gradually smashed to pieces by the sea.

OCEAN MONARCH

BUILT: 1957 by Vickers-Armstrong Ltd, Newcastle
TONNAGE: 25,971 gross
DIMENSIONS: 640 x 85 ft (195 x 26 m)
SERVICE SPEED: 20 knots
PROPULSION: Geared turbines/twin screws

Ocean Monarch was built for Canadian Pacific as *Empress of England,* being launched on 9 May 1956, and entering service in April 1957 between Liverpool and Montreal, joining its sister *Empress of Britain.* Accommodation was provided for 160 first class and 898 tourist class passengers. By the early 1960s, both *Empress of England* and *Empress of Britain* were spending much of each year cruising.

In February 1970, *Empress of England* was sold to Shaw Savill Line. Renamed *Ocean Monarch,* on 14 April it left Southampton on a line voyage to Australia, which terminated in Sydney on 15 May. With an Expo being held in Japan in 1970, *Ocean Monarch* made two cruises there from Sydney, the first departing on 22 May and the second on 27 June. The vessel then went back to Britain, and was sent to the Cammell Laird shipyard for a major refit.

The superstructure was extended aft, adding a new swimming pool and open deck areas. All cargo-handling gear was removed, and new cabins built into the former cargo holds, while existing cabins were refurbished, so the liner could carry 1,372 passengers in one class. *Ocean Monarch* made a cruise from Southampton, departing on 16 October, following which the ship left for Australia again on 5 November.

For several months, *Ocean Monarch* cruised out of Sydney, then returned to Britain in May 1972 for a season of cruises from Southampton. In October 1972, the vessel returned to Australia again, having been scheduled to make just two long cruises from Sydney during the 1972–73 summer season. This was revised to a longer programme of short cruises, which was not appreciated by some of the crew. Just as the ship was about to depart on 22 January 1973, 191 stewards, seamen and pantrymen walked off the ship. For three days the vessel remained in dock at Sydney, then sailed without the striking crew, the passengers helping out with shipboard chores where possible. The dissatisfied crew members were flown back to Britain, and new staff brought out to replace them.

Ocean Monarch eventually spent the rest of 1973 cruising from Sydney, and into 1974, then departed in May to return to Britain once again. By this time it was suffering from frequent engine problems, and the cruise programme from Southampton was often disrupted.

In November 1974, the liner returned to Sydney for another season of cruises, but the mechanical defects were now a major concern. Early in 1975, a cruise was cancelled so that *Ocean Monarch* could be drydocked in Sydney, but all efforts to rectify the faults failed, and Shaw Savill announced that the vessel would be withdrawn from service.

On 26 April 1975, *Ocean Monarch* was due to leave Sydney for the last time, but shortly before sailing time, crew started hurling bottles, cans and other missiles from the ship. Police had to be called to restore order, and the ship was detained in Sydney overnight.

Returning to Southampton in May, *Ocean Monarch* was offered for sale, and soon purchased by Taiwanese shipbreakers. On 13 June the liner slipped quietly out of Southampton, arriving in Kaohsiung on 17 July, where it was handed over to Chi Shun Hwa Steel Co. Ltd, who commenced demolition of the ship on 12 October 1975.

BRITANIS

BUILT: 1932 by Bethlehem Shipbuilding Corp, Quincy
TONNAGE: 18,254 gross
DIMENSIONS: 632 x 79 ft (192.6 x 24.2 m)
SERVICE SPEED: 20 knots
PROPULSION: Geared turbines/twin screws

When *Britanis* first arrived in Australia in March 1971, it was in fact the return of a vessel that had regularly visited the country in the 1930s. At that time it was named *Monterey*, being the second of three sisters built during 1931–32 for the Matson Line. *Monterey* joined *Mariposa* on the trade from California to New Zealand and Australia, while *Lurline* voyaged only to Honolulu.

Monterey was launched on 10 October 1931, and handed over to Matson on 20 April 1932. It left New York on 12 May on its delivery voyage to San Francisco, then made its maiden voyage across the Pacific. *Monterey* had accommodation for 472 first class and 229 cabin class passengers, and made six round trips each year.

Monterey was taken over by the US Maritime Commission in San Francisco on 3 December, and converted to carry 2,950 troops. After the attack on Pearl Harbor, 3,349 troops were crammed aboard, and with *Matsonia* and *Lurline*, *Monterey* left San Francisco on 16 December for Honolulu, returning with casualties, women and children.

Monterey was then further converted to carry 3,841 troops, and embarked 3,674 men to be carried to Australia. The vessel called at Brisbane, Fremantle, Adelaide and Melbourne on a 62-day voyage. *Monterey* then made a voyage from San Francisco to Adelaide, returning through the Panama Canal into the Atlantic, to spend a year ferrying troops to Europe. On most of these trips over 6,000 men were carried, many of whom had to sleep on the deck.

In November 1942, *Monterey* took part in the landings on North Africa, making four trips to Casablanca, and in June 1943 finally returned to San Francisco again. After another voyage to Brisbane, *Monterey* went back to the Atlantic, and on two trips from New York carried 6,855 soldiers to Oran, and then 6,747 to Naples.

Monterey returned to the Pacific late in the war, making several visits to Brisbane. After the war, *Monterey* was used for some time to return American troops home, then on 15 June 1946 left San Francisco on a voyage to Sydney, arriving on 2 July. On returning to San Francisco, *Monterey* was handed back to its owners on 26 September 1946.

Monterey was sent to the United Engineering shipyard at Alameda to be refitted for commercial service again, but on 11 July 1947 work stopped, and *Monterey* was laid up. On 6 August 1952, the vessel was sold to the US Maritime Commission, then towed to Suisun Bay and laid up again.

The only Matson liner to return to full service after the war was *Lurline*, which resumed the Honolulu route in April 1948. On 3 February 1956, the Matson company bought back *Monterey* from the US Government, and it went to the Newport News shipyard for conversion. A raked bow was added and the funnels modernised, while accommodation was installed for 761 first class passengers. Renamed *Matsonia*, the vessel joined *Lurline* on the Hawaiian trade, departing Los Angeles on 11 June.

On 5 September 1962 *Matsonia* was laid up in San Francisco. *Lurline* continued to operate, but

Matsonia

in February 1963 she suffered engine trouble. As a result, *Lurline* was laid up, then in September 1963 sold to Chandris Line, and renamed *Ellinis*. Meanwhile, *Matsonia* was reactivated, and resumed its place on the service to Hawaii.

In a confusing move, *Matsonia* was then renamed *Lurline* by Matson, and remained on the Honolulu trade for a further seven years. From 1966, the liner was also used for cruises to other islands of Hawaii, and in March 1969 went to the Caribbean, followed by a cruise to South America early in 1970. However, *Lurline* was losing money to such an extent it was offered for sale, and purchased on 27 May 1970 by Chandris Line. *Lurline* arrived in San Francisco for the last time on 25 June 1970, then five days later was handed over to the new owner, renamed *Britanis*, and sent to Piraeus to be converted by Chandris' own shipyard for the Australian trade.

The foremast was removed and replaced by samson posts, and a new signal mast installed on top of the bridge, while the funnels were given raked backs and dome tops. The upper deck was extended forward to allow for extra cabins, and a number of other cosmetic changes made. New cabins were installed, while most existing cabins were given extra berths, requiring new staircases and a further lift. Accommodation was increased to 1,655 passengers in one class, but surprisingly the Hawaiian decor and names were retained for many of the public rooms.

On 21 February 1971, *Britanis* departed Southampton on its first voyage to Australia, carrying a large number of British migrants. More passengers joined the ship in Piraeus. *Britanis* berthed in Fremantle on 17 March, Melbourne on 23 March, and Sydney two days later.

Leaving the next day, *Britanis* voyaged across the Tasman to Auckland, continuing eastward to Tahiti then passing through the Panama Canal, and calling at Lisbon before arriving back in Southampton. *Britanis*

was scheduled to make four round-the-world trips each year, in conjunction with *Ellinis* and *Australis*, along with an occasional cruise.

Britanis spent only three years on this trade, and on 23 October 1974, left Southampton on its final voyage to Australia, passing through Melbourne on 21 November, arriving in Sydney on 23 November. Leaving the next day, *Britanis* headed across the Pacific and through the Panama Canal, with the voyage terminating at San Juan, from where the passengers flew to Europe.

Britanis then began full time cruising, in the Caribbean during the winter, and from European ports in the summer. In 1981, *Britanis* began making short cruises out of American ports in the summer, and proved very popular. In September 1987, *Britanis* made a 47-day cruise around South America that was repeated over the next six years.

During 1994, *Britanis* began suffering engine problems, which brought its cruising career to an end in October. The following month the liner arrived at Guantanamo Bay in Cuba, having been chartered as a static accommodation ship for military and civilian personnel. The ship was damaged by a fire in December 1994, but remained in Cuba until October 1995, then moved to Tampa, Florida, to be laid up. In 1998 the vessel was sold and renamed *Belofin I*, but remained idle at Tampa, and in June 2000 it was sold to shipbreakers in India.

On 3 July 2000, the old liner was towed out of Tampa, heading south to pass around Africa. As tug and tow were approaching the Cape of Good Hope on the night of 20 October, *Belofin I* began taking on water through a leaking stern gland, and the ship took on a 30-degree list to starboard. On the afternoon of 21 October, 50 miles west of Cape Town, *Belofin I* had to be cut loose by the tug. Shortly afterwards the old liner rolled over on its starboard side, then sank stern first.

Britanis

LE HAVRE ABETO

BUILT: 1952 by A & C de la Loire, St Nazaire
TONNAGE: 12,177 gross
DIMENSIONS: 538 x 64 ft (163.9 x 19.6 m)
SERVICE SPEED: 17 knots
PROPULSION: Sulzer diesels/twin screws

Early in 1968, the Fir Line, based in Hong Kong, announced they would be inaugurating a passenger service between Colombo and Melbourne for the express purpose of bringing Ceylonese migrants to Australia. The vessel they would be using was *Le Havre Abeto*, which they had bought the previous year.

This vessel was built as *Charles Tellier* for a French firm, Cie Sudatlantique, being launched on 2 December 1951. It left Bordeaux on 2 August 1952 on its maiden voyage to Buenos Aires. Accommodation was provided for 110 first class and 326 third class passengers, and there was also a large cargo capacity.

In November 1962 the service operated by Cie Sudatlantique was taken over by another French company, Messageries Maritimes, but *Charles Tellier* remained on its original service to South America, without any change of name.

In 1967, *Charles Tellier* was sold to Cia de Nav Abeto SA, registered in Panama, which traded as the Fir Line. Renamed *Le Havre Abeto*, the vessel was primarily to be used in the pilgrim trade between Indonesia and Jeddah, so it was quite a surprise when it made a voyage to Australia.

Departing Colombo in early July 1968, *Le Havre Abeto* arrived in Fremantle on 16 July, then berthed in Melbourne on 21 July, remaining in port four days. On the return trip the vessel went to Indonesia and Singapore before reaching Colombo.

The voyage to Australia must have been unsuccessful, as the ship never returned. Instead *Le Havre Abeto* remained on the seasonal pilgrim trade from Indonesia to Jeddah, being idle at other times, until 28 March 1978, when it was laid up in Jakarta.

The vessel remained idle at Jakarta for six years before being sold to shipbreakers in Bangladesh, arriving at Chittagong on 17 June 1984.

Index of Migrant Ships

Achille Lauro 115
Al Sudan 9
Amarapoora 85
Angelina Lauro 111
Anna Salen 58
Arcadia 103
Arkadia 84
Arosa Kulm 40
Arosa Star 96
Assimina 37
Asturias 68
Aurelia 105
Australia 79
Australis 137

Begona 26
Brasil 86
Bretagne 132
Britanis 141
Brittany 132

Cameronia 42
Canberra (1912) 62
Canberra (1960) 125
Castelbianco 24
Castelverde 24
Castel Bianco 24
Castel Felice 100
Castel Verde 24
Charlton Sovereign 38
Cheshire 60
Chitral 46
Chusan 131
Columbia 63
Conte Grande 123
Continental 16
Corsica 91
Cyrenia 54

Derna 37
Dominion Monarch 30
Dorsetshire 44
Dundalk Bay 53

Ellinis 133
Empire Brent 72
Esperance Bay 23

Fairsea 73
Fairsky 112
Fairstar 135
Flaminia 102
Flavia 130
Florentia 92

Galileo Galilei 128
General Ballou 10
General Black 10
General Blatchford 10
General Bundy 10
General Greely 10
General Haan 10
General Heintzelmann 10
General Hersey 10
General Howze 10
General Langfitt 10
General Muir 10
General Stewart 10
General Sturgis 10
General Taylor 10
Georgic 50
Goya 35
Groote Beer 75
Guglielmo Marconi 128
Gumhuryat Misr 116

Haven 61
Hellenic Prince 64
Himalaya 71
Hwa Lien 7

Iberia 109

Jenny 93
Johan de Witt 8
Johan van Oldenbarnevelt 77

Kanimbla 66
Komninos 28

Largs Bay 23
Le Havre Abeto 143
Liguria 91
Luciano Manara 39

Maloja 32
Marianna IV 76
Misr 9
Mohammedi 55
Monte Udala 24
Montserrat 26
Mooltan 32
Moreton Bay 23
Mozzafari 55

Napoli 33
Nea Hellas 47
Nelly 69
Neptunia 79
New Australia 83
Northern Star 127

Ocean Monarch 140

Ocean Triumph 55
Ocean Victory 55
Oceania 79
Oranje 110
Orcades 31
Oriana 119
Orion 19
Ormonde 20
Oronsay 99
Orontes 67
Orsova 104
Otranto 67
Oxfordshire 52

Paolo Toscanelli 48
Partizanka 15
Patris 121
Protea 40

Queen Frederica 117

Radnik 14
Ranchi 34
Ravello 90
Rena 43
Roma (1914) 88
Roma (1942) 97

San Giorgio 94
Sebastiano Caboto 48
Seven Seas 69
Sibajak 87
Skaubryn 95
Skaugum 29
Somersetshire 44
Sontay 81
Southern Cross 107
Strathaird 21
Stratheden 17
Strathmore 17
Strathnaver 21
Surriento 56
Svalbard 35
Sydney 97

Tasmania 58
Tidewater 16
Toscana 27

Ugolino Vivaldi 48

Volendam 6

Waterman 75
Willem Ruys 114
Wooster Victory 24

Zuiderkruis 75